Dynamic Stillness

Dynamic Stillness

PART ONE: THE PRACTICE OF TRIKA YOGA

SWAMI CHETANANANDA

edited by
Linda L. Barnes

Rudra Press
Cambridge, Massachusetts

Rudra Press
P.O. Box 1973
Cambridge, Massachusetts 02238

Cover & Text Design: Juliana Wright
Cover Photograph: Tony Arruza
Photograph of Author: Tim Reese

Manufactured in the United States of America

Library of Congress Cataloging-in-Publication Data
(Revised for volume 2)

Chetanananda, Swami.
　　Dynamic stillness.

　　　Includes bibliographical references and indexes.
　　　Contents: pt. 1. The practice of Trika yoga -- pt. 2. The fulfillment of Trika yoga.
　　　1. Kashmir Śaivism--United States--Doctrines.　2. Rudrananda, Swami, 1928-
1973--Teachings.　3. Spiritual life (Hinduism).　4. Kundalini.　I. Title.
BL1281.1542.C44　1990　　　　　　　　　　　　　　　　　90-62101
ISBN 0-915801-19-1 (pt. 1)
ISBN 0-915801-27-2 (pbk. : pt. 2)

92 93 10 9 8 7 6 5 4 3 2

Also available in hardcover
ISBN 0-915801-29-9 (hard cover: pt. 1)
ISBN 0-915801-28-0 (hard cover: pt. 2)

Acknowledgments

A project of this magnitude necessarily relies on the input of many people. Among these, I would like to acknowledge the following for their assistance in everything ranging from typing the manuscript, to reading and critiquing its various drafts, and then to designing and producing it: Together, Joan Ames, Diane Asay, Andrew Bonner, Norman Bodek, Howard Boster, Jim Brissette, Rachel Brooks, Chris Burns, Connie Dyer, Camilla England, Sarah Fahey, Tim Hickey, Gayle Joyce, Kerry Kaplan, Judy Katz, Richard Kins, Jan LaRue, Susan Lennertz, Cecilia Littleton, Bob Lurie, Joel Marver, Robin Mesch, Aurelia Navarro, Steve Ott, Nanette Redmond, Cheryl Rosen, Paul Rosen, the graphic production staff at Rudra Press, Patty Slote, Theresa Smith, Duncan Soule, Sharon Ward, Frances West, and Juliana Wright have helped make this book possible. I appreciate all their work and their support.

I am particularly grateful to Navjivan Rastogi and Carol Zaleski for their input and help, and most special thanks go to Linda Barnes, whose editorial skill and devotion to this project have made it a fine work.

Finally, special gratitude to Joan Ames and Amyas Ames for their generous support of my work.

Dedication

This book is dedicated to Dr. Rollin E. Becker, whose life work I hold in the highest regard. He has served humanity deeply by demonstrating to thousands the healing potential of "Dynamic Stillness." Thanks, Dr. Becker.

Contents

Foreword

When Swami Chetanananda suggested to me that I write this foreword, I did not anticipate the difficulty the task was going to entail — a difficulty stemming from the precise cultural context of the work itself. This appears to be a perennial dilemma whenever a person, born and brought up in one rich cultural setting, undertakes to address himself to the fundamental issues of another, equally powerful, cultural tradition. The challenge deepens when that person, instead of confining himself to the mere analysis of an alien spiritual heritage, commits himself to the regular practice of the same.

Such experiments always carry the grave risk of oversimplifying the adopted tradition and, therefore, of rendering it superficial through the mixing of cultures. On the other hand, when the value-orientations of one cultural tradition seek answers to its unresolved questions by tracing the natural extension of these questions in another tradition, there is also the real promise of the older tradition's acquiring a new meaning and ethos. It is perhaps from this perspective that the ancient Tantric text, *Mālinīvijayottaratantra*,[1] portrays the *svabhayastajñānavān* — a kind of yogin who thoroughly practices meditative knowledge — as the most promising of yogins. We shall look at the present work from this vantage point.

I met Swamiji for the first time, quite briefly, in India during 1988. More than by the infectious openness of his person, I was impressed by his deep, creative leaning towards Kashmir

Shaivism and by his wish that, based on its own merit, it acquire a status in the present commensurate with its historical role and significance. Our sharing in this desire brought me to Cambridge the following fall at the invitation of the Nityananda Institute, affording me an opportunity to know Swamiji at closer quarters. From his talks, and from our long dialogues and exchange of ideas, I was easily able to gather that here was at least one person who not only wanted to know Kashmir Shaivism, but who also strove to live it. Here was someone who was seeking to make it a co-operative, collective, and institutional effort.

This was a matter of particular gratification for me, for ever since beginning my lessons in Kashmir Shaivism I have had the increasingly deep-rooted feeling that it is not just an important Indian philosophical sect or a significant spiritual tradition; rather, it contains the seeds of a basic pattern of life and value-structure consistent with democratic ideals, homologous with a humanistic view of life, and congruent with a scientific world-view, in ways that may eventually prove seminal in our effort towards making human life richer, happier, and more meaningful. I heard the echo of my longing in the efforts of Swamiji and came to feel, over time, that we stood together in the face of this challenge.

We may sometimes feel that Swamiji's presentation does not reflect a traditional systematic formulation of some of the peripheral issues of Kashmir Shaivism; yet, his insight into the core issues underscores his grasp of the spirit of the system as a whole. This is an inevitable and inherent part of the process when we are talking about the creative evolution of a line of thought. In other words, his grasp, while not scholastic, is refined by experience — "Everything is essentially of the nature of one's own experience."[2] Thus, for Swamiji, Kashmir Shaivism is not only a living philosophy, but also the philosophy of life.

Kashmir Shaivism

Kashmir Shaivism is a comprehensive, but vague, term. It came into currency with the publication in 1913 of the book bearing the same title by J.C. Chatterji. Today, the term is frequently used to cover all those currents of thought which, in the past, went by the designation of Shaiva Monism (*Śivādvayavāda*) in the

hands of Kashmir authors, along with all subsequent developments which derive their basic thought-structure and conceptual
framework from those traditions. In the traditional parlance, the
term *Trika* may also be used in its generic sense (drawn from its
generic and specific meanings) to denote Kashmir Shaivism.

The logical structure of Kashmir Shaivism may be said to be
rooted in recognition (*pratyabhijñā*); its ontic structure, in auton-
omy (*svātantrya*); its metaphysical structure, in the synthesis of
Being and self-referential consciousness (*prakāśa-vimarśa*); its
process of spiritual practice (*sādhanā*), in the refinement of the
mental constructs (*vikalpa-saṃskāra*); its yogic framework, in the
awakening of the spiral energy (*kuṇḍalinī*); and its empirical and
epistemic transactions, in synthetic activity (*anusaṃdhāna*).

All of these processes derive their sustenance from the notion
of perfection (*pūrṇatā*). Moreover, in actual practice, whether
they pertain to cognition, creation, yoga, or aesthetic appercep-
tion, each of these represents the well-known Upanishadic idea
of emanating from, and returning to, the same source while
never losing their original, undifferentiated identity:

> *It is full, this is full, the full proceeds from the full. Even after
> subtracting the full from the full, what remains is the full.*[3]

Kashmir Shaivism, in its basic contexture, is a Tantric system. By designating it as Tantric, the intention is not to project it
as an opponent or antagonist of the mainstream Upanishadic
ideology but to focus on a particular emphasis of Indian thought
and religion. One such emphasis is evident at the level of values,
according to which nothing in life is to be rejected or looked
down upon, impregnated as everything is at all times with the
meaningfulness of its source or content.

The other emphasis discloses itself on the plane of existence,
in the intrinsic potentiality inherent in each and every entity —
that is, in the possibility of each one's flowering into infinite
forms and relationships, and contributing to the authenticity of
each instant of being. The fundamental philosophical assertion
of Kashmir Shaivism is that our existence is nothing but the
boundless energy of consciousness.

All the cultural traditions (*parampara*) of India have literally been "*Parampara*," or linear successions — one following the other — and have been transmitted without interruption through the teacher-taught lineages. Unfortunately, it has not always been possible to maintain this unobstructed flow over the past few centuries. Kashmir Shaivism is no exception to this phenomenon. Hence, it would be unfair to expect the lineage of Nityananda-Rudrananda-Chetanananda to act as a vehicle for the uninterrupted transmission of Kashmir Shaivite wisdom in that sense.

Swamiji is fully aware of this historical reality and, instead, envisions a deep affinity of content and form between the spiritual moorings of his lineage and those of Kashmir Shaivism. This awareness has a positive element to it, in that it nurtures his commitment to Kashmir Shaivism. His resolve is to carry forward the teachings of Nityananda, received through Rudi, and to refine them along the way in the light of his own reflection and experience. The present work comes as a partial realization of that resolve.

The basic inspiration of Swamiji for orienting Kashmir Shaivism towards life as we live it comes from his teacher Rudi. In this connection, one must bear in mind that the currents of religion and metaphysics in India are inter-dependant and inter-penetrating, in the sense that both seek the central meaning of life and being. This "seeking" is not for bare knowledge, but for its actual attainment in one's own life. It is the reason why knowledge is termed "attainment" (*upalabdhi*) in the Indian context.

It may sound strange to people from other traditions that, in Indian discourse, nouns and verbs expressing "movement" also mean "knowledge," and the latter, "attainment." Yet, this equation of movement = knowledge = attainment brings into sharp focus the basic thrust of Indian philosophy, especially in contrast with its Western counterpart. The fundamental orientation of Indian thought can be reckoned as experiential, perceptual, or aesthetic, in contrast with the frequently more conceptual orientation of Western thought.

To call philosophy *darsana* — vision, or perception — reflects the same mental make-up. The catalyst for this "vision" of reality is spiritual practice (*sadhana*), which operates as a bridge between knowledge and life. It purges knowledge of its sheer intellectuality and connects it with life, thereby infusing life into knowledge. The above equation is in tune with the Kashmir Shaiva position, which posits knowledge or attainment as nothing but the experiential awareness of the inner dynamism of reality. This awareness lies at the heart of what Rudi calls spiritual work, or what Swamiji, alternatively, later describes as meditation. This is so because it calls for mental preparation at the conscious level, and also because it is not independent of the variety of patterns that Life assumes.

The other fundamental aspect of Rudi's teachings is the consumption of life in its totality, with all its attendant stresses, tensions, pains, and joys. Only with this approach to life does one clear the way to absorb, digest, and transcend these very experiences. To me, it appears that Rudi echoes the following lines from Abhinavagupta:

> *Infatuation and repulsion, pleasure and pain, rise and fall, conceit and helplessness — all these (diverse) feelings that occur (to you) are not by nature different from One with the Cosmic form. Whenever suddenly you experience one of these feelings, why not at the same moment, view Awareness as identical with it and rejoice instantly filled with this realization.* [4]

Swamiji pushes this process of aligning oneself with Life even further. The connotations with which he invests the technical terms of the tradition derive their nourishment both from the tradition and from a contemporary environment in the context of Life and lived experience. His presentation of fulfillment (*siddhi*) as "meaningful, authentic living," choice (*niścaya*) as "the commitment to grow and to be happy," will (*icchā*) as "the wish to grow," God as "the vast self-awareness that goes beyond all things, and yet is the subtle essence of all things," Life as "a dynamic event" or "a dynamic ground of all things," and the purpose and expression of spiritual practice as being "continuously centered in the flow of our own creative awareness" unmistakably mark a reverential, yet creative, attitude towards Life.

At this point it may be relevant to observe that Swamiji's commitment to Life favors immanence over transcendence, and thereby proclaims the essential divinity and creativity inherent in each and every bit of existence. This commitment spells out his unflinching faith in the infinite creativity of Life. I cannot resist quoting him: "Kashmir Shaivism is the celebration of the creative power in every individual and the recognition of every person's power of free choice."

This follows from the basic assertion of unity between the microcosm and the macrocosm, an idea beautifully resonant with a statement by the physicist David Bohm, who observed, "You can overcome the problem (*i.e.*, of unifying the laws of the inner and the outer) only if you accept the premise that in some sense man is a microcosm of the universe; therefore, what man is, is a clue to the universe."[5] Kashmir Shaivism goes a step further, asserting that everything that exists is such a microcosm.

I must confess that the aesthetic undertones of the title of the work — *Dynamic Stillness* — fascinate me. In the history of Indian thought, Swamiji is perhaps anticipated by Vyasa, the celebrated glossator of the *Yogasūtras*, who conceived of two types of eternities, or realities: still-eternity and dynamic-eternity, pertaining to the primordial principles of awareness (*Puruṣa*) and causality (*Prakṛti*) respectively. Just as the Absolute (*Parama Śiva*) in Kashmir Shaivism is the synthesis of these bipolar realities — being "still" in its *Śiva* aspect and "dynamic" in its *Śakti* aspect — so is the title of the work, *Dynamic Stillness*, a fusion of these two discrete notions.

Trika Yoga

At the root of the title of this book lies its author's primary motive: the propounding of Trika Yoga, the yoga which explores *kuṇḍalinī*. Kuṇḍalinī symbolizes the energy of Life, or the divine experienced at the individuated level. Likewise, the practice of Trika Yoga carries the consciousness of this energy to such a point that it may be grasped not only as the power of the finite self but also as the fundamental power of the infinite Self lying at the base of everything. It is this creative energy that is defined as dynamic stillness. It is also depicted as the breath of Life.

The most useful component of Swamiji's analysis of Trika Yoga, to my mind, is his formulation of an argument-structure that permeates his work, extending through the different strata of illustration and argumentation. Proceeding towards the awakening of kuṇḍalinī, the movement pauses at a point, and then continues forward at a different, accelerated frequency. This process persists until such time as it opens the gateway of identification of the adept's energy with the supreme, creative power of Life.

In the present context, it may be pertinent to point out that we encounter four models of the flow of this creative energy. These are provided to explain the kineticity of reality. Vibration, or contraction-expansion, constitutes the quintessential form of movement — be it the journey into the world defined by Self-expansion, or the retreat towards the inner Self characterized by Self-contraction. At the same time, it assumes four alternative patterns: spiral, linear, cyclic, and wave-like. Among these, kuṇḍalinī designates the first, although, actually, all four models support the metaphysical scheme of the system. A more detailed treatment of the ways in which this is the case will have to engage the attention of future studies. However, one might contend that, whatever the answer it must, by definition, emanate from the idea of "perfection," or totality.

In the present work, as in the *Tantrāloka*, the treatment of Trika Yoga occurs as ancillary to the discussion of *āṇavopāya*, although the author does not explicitly address this point. The presentation of āṇavopāya, to which we shall return, constitutes the key objective of this discussion.

The non-dualistic principle which is posited as being at the heart of all existence is also the synthesis of pure being and consciousness, of awareness and freedom. Put differently, it pulsates, vibrating by virtue of its inner potential. Each time our consciousness fails to grasp it completely, we are said to be in bondage. The state prior to such bondage is called that of "complete comprehension" (*anu + graha*), while the state of bondage itself is called "non-comprehension" (*ni + graha*). These two states represent the twin divine phases of grace, or self-disclosure, (*anugraha*) and self-concealment (*nigraha, i.e., tirodhana*), respectively.

The comprehension and non-comprehension of this totality both have two dimensions, namely cosmic and individual. In the cosmic dimension, both are powers, or potencies, in their essence. The total self-disclosure of consciousness is the power of grace; the event of self-alienation is the power of concealment (also one of the five powers of consciousness).

At the individual level, both comprehension and non-comprehension express themselves in two ways — namely, as being and as intellect. At the level of being, comprehension signifies Spiritual Knowledge (*pauruṣa jñāna*), consisting in the full realization of freedom, while non-comprehension signifies Spiritual Ignorance (*pauruṣa ajñāna*), consisting in imperfect knowledge and freedom. Similarly, at the level of intellect, comprehension stands for Intellectual Knowledge (*bauddha jñāna*), consisting in the awareness of freedom, while non-comprehension stands for Intellectual Ignorance (*bauddha ajñāna*), consisting in intellectual indetermination.

The Upāyas

From the perspective of ultimate consciousness, bondage and liberation are meaningless terms, since the two are nothing but the contraction and expansion of that consciousness. However, from the perspective of individuated consciousness, bondage and liberation acquire a meaning and also a context. It is in this context that the *upāyas* — the means of liberating knowledge — are specifically devised to eliminate Intellectual Ignorance, and that *dīkṣā* (initiation) is developed to remove Spiritual or Existential Ignorance.[6]

For the removal of Intellectual Ignorance, four types of upāyas have been envisaged: *Anupāya, Śāmbhavopāya, Śāktopāya,* and *Āṇavopāya.*[7] Despite the tremendous importance assigned to them in the system as a whole, only a few brief remarks are possible here. Barring the first, which is an upāya only in a figurative sense, all the upāyas involve some sort of refinement of the logical constructs (*vikalpas*) generated by the mind.

The notion of upāyas in Kashmir Shaivism is fairly old. In the *Vijñānabhairava Tantra*[8], the upāyas — not by name, but as forms of instrumental cognition — are considered to be cognitive in nature and represent not only the awareness that goes beyond knowledge, but non-dualistic, dualistic/non-dualistic, and dualistic knowledge respectively. This formulation is designed to enable one to grasp the essential nature of knowledge. By propounding this "quartet of knowledge" in the *Tantrāloka*[9], under the direct impact of the *Vijñānabhairava*, Abhinavagupta not only lays down the steps for spiritual progression; he also performs a historical feat by lending a cognitive structure and a hierarchy to Kashmir Shaivism.

This triplicity of knowledge, as articulated in the upāyas, attracts the support of a triplicity of practice (*sādhanā*) in the *Mālinīvijayottara Tantra*. Here are advocated three types of divine immersion (*Rudraśaktisāmāveśa*)[10], which bear the same names as the upāyas. Indeed, Abhinavagupta utilizes the definitions accorded to the *śambhava*, *śakta*, and *āṇava* immersions (*samāveśā*) in the *Mālinīvijaya*, in order to highlight their direct relation to the upāyas.

What constitutes the source, or the outcome, in the *Mālinīvijaya*, emerges as the upāyas in classical Kashmir Shaivism. The tendency, seen in several places, towards portraying the upāyas as Shaiva Yoga is also rooted in the *Mālinīvijaya*, in which the Yoga is modelled on the pattern of the triple immersions.[11] The synthesis of jñāna and Yoga frequently discussed in Kashmir Shaivism stems textually from this very tantra. Since the upāyas unify the fettered soul with the Supreme Self, they constitute Yoga. Thus, the Yoga of Kashmir Shaivism is a path of spiritual unification.[12]

Several equations are resorted to in order to bring home the implications of the upāya thesis. As is evident from its name, āṇava is related to *anu* (finite being), in contrast to Śambhu (God) and *śakti* (power). Similarly, it is related to the power of action (*kriyā*), one of the three powers of the ultimate — will, knowledge, and action (*icchā*, *jñāna*, and *kriyā*) — and is one of the factors responsible for the occasioning of immersion (*samāveśa*). Among the impurities (*mala*), it is linked with the "impurity of action" (*kārmamala*). In the domain of emission (*visarga*), the aspect of divine creativity as external projection, it represents the gross emission (*sthūla visarga*), and signifies the dichotomy of mental states.

All the upāyas, however, share a common objective, which may be divided into three parts for the sake of clarity: (i) unfolding the central core of reality, (ii) eliminating ignorance, and (iii) attaining liberation during one's lifetime.[13] Moreover, these upāyas are interconnected by a relation of reciprocal support and nourishment. Out of śambhava, śakta, and āṇava, each preceding one nourishes and animates the one that follows; likewise, if we reverse their order, each succeeding one becomes the instrument of the upāya that precedes it. Even so, this is not an inviolable progression. A spiritually advanced person endowed with intuitive knowledge may easily transgress this sequence and establish him- or herself in the divine essence instantaneously.

Abhinavagupta dwells on āṇavopāya at length in the 5th and 6th chapters[14] of the *Tantrāloka*. As noted earlier, the notion of refining the logical constructs generated by the mind (*vikalpasaṃskāra*) forms the crux of the entire upāya doctrine. Āṇavopāya, as a strategy, follows in the wake of our dependence on ancillary measures to refine the mental states. (The same evolves into śāktopāya as such dependence diminishes.) Āṇava, which is also conceived of as an aggregate of different practices and methods, retains or allows scope for several methods defined by their respective proximity to, and distance from, the seminal consciousness. Āṇava is viewed as especially related to the intellect, vital breath (*prāṇa*), and physical body.[15]

Viewed from the perspective of the ordinary practitioner ardently seeking his or her spiritual elevation, however, āṇavopāya happens to be the most effective means. This is because, in the course of the spiritual regeneration of a person, the multiplicity of upāyas finds its genesis in the gradual removal of impurity.[16] Thus, each of the three instrumentalities of cognition results from divine grace, appearing as strategies at ultimate, intermediate, and empirical levels, in keeping with the spiritual suitability and degree of awareness of the aspirant for divine favor. As a whole, this is referred to as "the descent of grace" (*śaktipāta*).

Perhaps the most meaningful equation in the context of upāya is the assertion of its śakti character. The śakti character of an upāya underlines its nexus with the immanence of ultimate reality and, simultaneously, establishes the transcendent quality of the same. By resorting to śakti as the bridge, the realization that all aspects of reality possess this potential constitutes the essence of the notion of liberation within one's lifetime (*jīvanmukti*).[17] Viewed dispassionately, the conceptual framework of recognition and the practical aspect of spiritual practice (*sādhanā*) emerge as the discovery (*anusaṃdhāna*) of the substratum of that power.

The question is whether the notion of discovery, which consists of an ontological, synthetic activity, is the rationalization of śakti in the system. The synthetic activity (*anusaṃdhāna*) involved is not just the unification of two disparate points (*saṃyojana*), although this is certainly one of the characteristics of free consciousness; rather, it is something more. It is repose of the Self within the Self. It is the seeking of the Self by the Self, within the Self. It cannot be dubbed a tautology, because it both furnishes the basis of the harmony (*sāmarasya*) of reality, and defines creativity in terms of its flow. The realization that life is harmony from the point of view of its essence, and creativity from that of its function, brings perfection within everybody's reach in this lifetime.

Identity and Agency

The rationalization, or assertion, of śakti as anusaṃdhāna — ontological synthetic activity — finally emerges as a reductionist thesis, in the sense that it reduces everything to the notion of agency (*kartṛtā*). This notion of agent, or "do-er," is the nodal and fundamental concept of the system. Since the entire synthetic activity takes place within the body of the cosmic agent as its experience and also, in a derived and extended sense, in the individual agent, it hardly matters if we describe this synthetic activity as ontological or epistemic. The distinction becomes merely nominal.

This line of thinking has several far-reaching implications, the discussion of which we shall defer for some future occasion. However, it needs to be briefly mentioned that one of the major problems confronting the student of religio-philosophical cultural traditions has been the problem of identity. In the Indian context, this problem is being discussed afresh, in ways that place Kashmir Shaivism on a different track altogether from the general tenor of Indian philosophical systems.

Generally speaking, in most Indian religio-philosophical traditions the notion of identity reflects the predominance of purity over power. In Kashmir Shaivism, however, the reverse occurs, reflecting the predominance of power over purity. Granting that such reductions are prone to omit many factors from their purview, this comparison is nevertheless substantially intelligible in the immediate context of the schools of Mīmaṃsā, Advaita Vedānta, Nyāya, and so on. At the same time, by delving more deeply into Kashmir Shaivism we notice that this power is basically of the nature of agency. That is, the assertion of the śakti character of identity, by transgressing the usual notion of śakti, re-establishes it as agency (*kartṛtā*). Agency is thus a further rationalization of the thesis of power, which is lacking in most Indian systems.

At this point we come to perceive that Kashmir Shaivism moves in a different direction from that of Upanishadic philosophy. The main emphasis of the Upanishads is on the knower; here, it is on the do-er, or agent (*kartā*). No doubt the latter, too, is knower, but by virtue of being the agent of knowing-activity. This agency is *a priori*. It is divinity par excellence. It is *I*.[18] This perception is strengthened by another premise, too. This is the positing of initiation, instead of cognitive means, as the effective strategy for the removal of our existential restriction technically referred to by the system as "Spiritual Ignorance," "individuation," or *āṇava mala*.

This assertion endorses the importance of agency in Kashmir Shaivism for the simple reason that initiation eliminates the restriction on agency or doership, making it instead that without which liberation is not possible. As a natural outcome of this concerted emphasis on the role of agency, Kashmir Shaivism makes one the hero of one's life, and renders one master of one's own destiny. It vests humanity with divinity, making the focus of Kashmir Shaivism sharply different from that of other schools.

In the context of the intrinsic agency of human being, there thus remains no place or occasion for fear, doubt, or inhibition. There is no scope whatsoever for what Swamiji in his characteristic style describes as "the mantra of stupidity," that is, the fear of the unknown — "what is going to happen to me?" In the ancient texts of Kashmir Shaivism, going beyond this fear, doubt, or terror is a recurring and favorite theme.

The immediate implication of the preceding lines is to recognize the state of liberation as the state of spontaneous agency. It is the reason why liberation is held to be self-emergence or self-repose — and, even in this latter state, the flow of dynamicity of the Self remains uninterrupted. Infinite compassion and concern for the welfare of all beings — the exalted ideals of Indian thought — are the expression of the infinite activity of the Self, and not its cause. In this way, each moment of being becomes the joyous festival of Life. Says Abhinavagupta of the person who lives in this awareness:

> *Whatever word that comes out from (his) mouth is the trans-worldly* mantra. *Every frame of (his) body from which pleasure and pain proceed is the unique* mudra *(posture). The spontaneous flow of breath is the marvelous Yoga.... During the celebrations marking attainment of your abode what is not prodigious for the people of refined wisdom.*[19]

Swamiji raises important issues in the course of his thought-provoking and novel exegesis of life in the light of Kashmir Shaivism. This is neither the occasion — nor is there the need — to respond to all of them. I am grateful to him for offering me an opportunity to participate in this celebration of Life. I take this occasion to invite you all to share this joy with me.

— *Navjivan Rastogi*
Department of Sanskrit
University of Lucknow, India

Dynamic Stillness

Two Kinds *of* Intelligence

There are two kinds of intelligence: One acquired,
as a child in school memorizes facts and concepts
from books and from what a teacher says,
collecting information from the traditional sciences
as well as from the new sciences.

With such intelligence you rise in the world.
You get ranked ahead or behind others
in regard to your competence in retaining
information. You stroll with this intelligence
in and out of fields of knowledge, getting always more
marks on your preserving tablets.

There is another kind of tablet, one
already completed and preserved inside you.
A spring overflowing its springbox. A freshness
in the center of the chest. This other intelligence
does not turn yellow or stagnate. It's fluid,
and it doesn't move from outside to inside
through the conduits of plumbing-learning.

This second knowledge is a fountainhead
from within you, moving out.

— RUMI

Introduction

There is nothing but water in the holy pools.
I know, I have been swimming in them.
All the gods sculpted of wood or ivory can't say a word.
I know, I have been crying out to them.
The Sacred Books of the East are nothing but words.
I looked through their covers one day sideways.
What Kabir talks of is only what he has lived through.
If you have not lived through something, it is not true.

— KABIR

This is a book about the practice of Trika Yoga as it has come down to us through the Indian Tantric tradition of Kashmir Shaivism. In the twentieth century, a form of Trika Yoga consistent with Kashmir Shaivism has made its way to the United States through a number of teachers. One of these was my teacher, Swami Rudrananda, also known as Rudi.

Rudi was born Albert Rudolph on January 24, 1928, in Brooklyn, New York. Thus he grew up during the Depression. He was a person who, even from childhood, felt a deep conviction about his own spiritual potential. This conviction led him to deepen his on-going, intense inner work by studying with Gurdjieff in New York, with the Indonesian teacher Pak Subud, and then with the Shankaracharya of Puri.

The Shankaracharyas, who uphold the Vedantic tradition, are one of the orthodox Hindu groups in India. This particular Shankaracharya had come to the United States at the invitation of the Self-Realization Fellowship. Rudi knew people from this group and, through them, met the Shankaracharya, becoming his attendant for the duration of his stay on the East Coast. Rudi did this at a time when it was not yet popular either to go to India or study with Indian teachers. Rudi, however, travelled extensively throughout Asia to collect Oriental art and was one of the first people to import and sell the art of Tibet and Nepal in the United States.

After the Shankaracharya passed away, one of Rudi's associates took him to Ganeshpuri, in southwest India. There, he met a remarkable teacher whose name was Nityananda (respect-fully referred to as Bhagavan, or Lord). Details of Nityananda's early life are difficult to verify, but from the 1920s until his death in 1961 he was surrounded by ever-increasing numbers of disci-ples and devotees. In the late 1930s, he settled at Ganeshpuri, located in the forests near Bombay, where an active ashram, or spiritual community, gradually evolved around him.

Nityananda never explicitly identified himself with a par-ticular spiritual practice or tradition — in fact, he rarely spoke at all. The thousands of people who came to see him did so because in him they experienced the miracle of pure consciousness in human form. This, too, was Rudi's experience. He was to write, "My first meeting with the great Indian saint Bhagavan Nityananda was of such depth that it changed the course of my life." Rudi continued to study with Nityananda and, after the death of the Bhagavan, was initiated into the Saraswati monastic order by another of Nityananda's disciples, Swami Muktananda. One of the first Americans to be recognized as a swami — a master of oneself — Rudi came back to the United States where he lived and taught until his own passing in 1973.

His years of study with great teachers of several traditions impressed on him the need to separate the essence of a teaching from its cultural trappings. Established in the continual aware-ness of the Self, Rudi lived from this state, sharing it with other people in the simplest, most open way possible. As a response to the extraordinary quality of his awareness, various ashrams formed around his teaching in the United States. In addition to traveling widely to be with his students in these different loca-tions, he also continued to work at his art store every day.

I met Rudi in 1971. I had already been studying Hatha Yoga for a while when an acquaintance gave me a picture of Rudi and suggested that I go to New York City to meet him. For reasons that were not entirely clear to me at the time, I made the trip. When I walked into his store, I looked at him and felt my heart shatter into a thousand pieces. From that moment on, I never had a second's doubt about the power of the experience into which I had entered.

After his passing, as I continued to practice, read his writ-ings, and meditate on the things he had told me and discussed with me, I realized that my perspective on what he had been communicating to me was incomplete. In the last year of Rudi's life, for example, he was in the process of articulating what he spoke of as his Tantric work. This was the natural evolution of his own spiritual practice and of what he had absorbed in the company of Bhagavan Nityananda and, later, Swami Muktananda. At the same time, it was work in progress, left unfinished at the time of his death.

In my subsequent explorations of our practice, an important moment came about when I encountered Kashmir Shaivism as a written philosophy. I already understood that the meditative technique was the departure point and the underlying basis for the whole endeavor. That had been there from the beginning. But in examining the conclusions articulated by the teachers of Kashmir Shaivism, I found that they helped me to understand further what Rudi had been doing. I realized that I had discovered the heart of Kashmir Shaivism in Rudi's presence.

Rudi himself had read none of these texts. I recall that he mentioned *The Secret of the Golden Flower*, a Taoist text, but for the most part he was immersed in the process of unfolding through his inner work what he had absorbed in the company of his teachers. Yet the descriptions in the Kashmir Shaivite texts corresponded directly to what Rudi had said about his own experience, to what he had taught me, and to my experience in the ensuing years of my own practice. It was clear that both Nityananda and Rudi, through the intensity of their inner work, had been espousing the essence of this tradition, even though they had not called it by that name. All of the pieces converged.

Indeed, one of the things that dazzled me when I first encountered the *Shiva Sutras* — a foundation text of Kashmir Shaivism — was the discovery that the whole of what Rudi had been doing had been worked out by these people a thousand years earlier. Their descriptions of the experience of certain types of awareness coincided exactly with what Rudi had been saying and with what I myself was experiencing. It all had the feeling of finding the autobiography of my own practice. This was a wonderful thing.

Kashmir Shaivism and Trika Yoga have come forth from people deeply involved in spiritual practice. In my own experience, it so happened that for the first ten years of my spiritual work I, too, read none of the texts of the tradition. I was too busy practicing and exploring the results of that practice. I have, however, come to find the study of texts stimulating and suggestive. It is helpful on occasion to examine the thinking and the descriptions of people engaged in the same practice in which we are involved. But by no means is any of it a substitute for practice, which is the most important thing.

The study of any text — whether it be one of the foundation texts or this book — is useful only if it helps you to recognize the essence of what you are. If it gives your mind some steadiness in daily living, this is a good thing. If, on the other hand, it becomes another brick in the wall of your conceptual framework of life, it can be manipulated into anything at all and is of no use. Better just to practice.

Our method, in our practice, is to release tension and allow the creative energy within us to flow unobstructed. This is the orientation of Kashmir Shaivism and of Trika Yoga. The method for doing this has three parts. The first involves our work with a teacher, the second is our private meditation and study, and the third is service, or extending the flow of our creative energy. Each plays a critical part in our spiritual work.

In the process of our learning to release tension, the teacher is the means; in other words, the primary function of the teacher is to release the tensions within us, train us to do the same for ourselves, and support the flow of our creative energy as we become established in a state of increasingly refined awareness. At the same time, Kashmir Shaivism as a practice and a philosophy is trans-personal. This means that it goes beyond the interpretation given it by any individual teacher. It is not identified with any single teacher, just as it is older than any particular teacher. This is important because it is not a practice aimed at cultivating dependence. A real spiritual person needs only God, period.

The second part of our method is our private meditation and study. By "meditation," we mean the process of taking our attention within. We could also call it "centering." Rudi did not use the word "meditation" to describe this. Rather, he called it "spiritual work" because it requires a conscious effort and because it is never independent of the patterns of our ordinary life. We become quiet and centered inside. We master our senses and become established in the awareness of what is really great within us. We manifest that awareness in the world, and the world gives us various kinds of feedback as to how clearly we have gotten the message across. It is a continuous interplay of energies.

When we talk about meditation as centering, we are saying that a spiritual person is one who is seeking to establish him- or herself in that center, and to extend it. What does it mean to extend the center? It means that we learn to maintain an open and relaxed state of awareness no matter what kind of activity is manifesting before our eyes and engaging our attention. It means bringing ourselves into that deep, quiet state in which our creative energy flows, and extending that state to the situation in which we find ourselves.

This evolves into the practice of service, the third aspect of our method. We can talk all we want about degrees of awareness in meditation and about the structure of our spiritual development, but the heart of it is the issue of love and service. As we release tension and allow Self-expression to happen, we become an instrument of the Divine.

The objective of Kashmir Shaivism is to recognize our complete unity in Life. This process has nothing to do with ideology of any kind. Indeed, no ideology is of any use in the pursuit of this awareness. Rather, it is a question of practice, experience, study, reflection, and more practice. This is the nature of our spiritual work, or *sadhana*.

This work is also not a matter of replacing one world view with another. A world view may emerge through one's practice, but that is incidental. Rather, spiritual work is a living, lived-through experience that we both work at and discover. I sometimes think of it as analogous to the cultivation of vegetables. The effort is made by the farmer. We work, we plant the seed and cultivate it. We harvest it as well. But do we *grow* anything? I would say not. The seeds do that for themselves. Isn't that the essence of the event? If it were up to us to do the actual growing, we would be in a lot of trouble. It is like asking what would happen if you had to remember to breathe. What if breathing were a voluntary activity?

Spiritual work is a question, every day, of releasing tensions and being aware of the flow of energy within ourselves and our environment. We discover our potential ever more deeply as we pull away the layers of tension and misunderstanding in which we wrap ourselves. Growing of this kind is an intense effort. It is also an experience. It takes all of your reference points and dissolves them from under your feet, leaving you a deeper place to stand on.

Something of the process of this discovery is what I hope to share with you. For the person exploring spirituality and the practice of meditation for the first time, this volume will serve as an introduction and an overview. Whether you are interested in Trika Yoga in particular or come with questions about another practice, this discussion addresses issues pertinent to both. For the person who has been practicing for a while, the same material will hopefully be of help in reflecting on the nature of his or her own experience. The second volume will address the experience and concerns of the advanced student. As we pursue our spiritual work, we discover that we see the same things over and over again, but each time see them differently.

What follows is what I have learned from my teacher Rudi and from my own practice and study. Of course, Rudi was constantly evolving in his own work and constantly reworking its articulation. Thus, he never suggested that he was giving us the final word. In fact, not only was his teaching unfinished at the time of his passing, but he himself repeatedly challenged us with the promise of change.

My role has been to take Rudi's teaching and carry it on, refining it along the way on the basis of my experience and study. Everything I have attempted to articulate over the past twenty years of my own practice has been the continuity between Rudi's work and this. To share this with you is an attempt, on my part, to express my gratitude to those who have shared it with me.

The Wish *to* Grow

Friend, hope for the Guest while you are alive.
Jump into experience while you are alive!
Think . . . and think . . . while you are alive.
What you call "salvation" belongs to the time before death.

If you don't break your ropes while you're alive,
do you think ghosts will do it after?

. . . Kabir says this: When the Guest is being searched for,
it is the intensity of the longing for the Guest that does all the work.
Look at me, and you will see a slave to that intensity.

— KABIR

Lillian Silburn, a French scholar who writes passionately about her experience and understanding of Kashmir Shaivism, has said that grace is a mysterious power which transforms the very structure of our experience. She also suggests that any intense longing we experience is a first and important manifestation of this grace in our lives.

When such longing arises, however, we don't necessarily recognize what is really happening. Usually, we identify this longing with the desire for some external object — a more fulfilling job, a better house, car, or clothes, or a new and deeper relationship of some kind. We rush out to gratify one of these desires or another. There is nothing wrong with fulfilling our desires, but if this is all we do with our basic sense of longing, then we become about as smart as a dog in heat.

Few of us ever stay with our longing until we fully understand it because it is painful to do so and we are conditioned to think of pain as bad: If we feel pain, something must be wrong. There must be something missing. Then, of course, we have to get a quick fix of something. The real issue with any longing, though, is learning to sit through it, to come out on the other side, and to learn something about where the longing itself originates.

When we do, that longing sets in motion something within us which, hopefully — and necessarily, if it is to succeed — leads us to feel a strong desire to discover authenticity in our lives. This is desire in its profoundest sense. It leads us to turn away from what we begin to perceive as inauthentic experience. Then, our intuition that there must be something more to life, along with our desire to be authentic, leads us to look to the deepest part of ourselves.

As we become aware of our own desire for transformation, our biggest difficulty is that we don't necessarily know at first exactly what it is we want. Not knowing what we want, we become entangled in many things, some of which are alright but many of which represent a major waste of energy. They consume our resources, and the complications and tensions they generate eat away our creative capacity.

As we attempt to grow, the first things we learn are what we *don't* want. These are the easiest to recognize. Often, our initial experience shows us little more than this, but it is still a good thing. At least it reduces our confusion by one more degree and gives us some definite parameters within which to start to function.

The process itself boils down to deciding what is important. How long it takes us to do this is a matter of how long we can avoid acting on what we know from our own hearts to be true and valuable. Once we do decide to act, it becomes a matter of putting one foot in front of the other along the road to finding out what it means to be the best person we can possibly be. As we go along making this effort, what we *do* want becomes simple and clear.

Still, it comes down to this: In everything we do, growth is the most important thing to want. It is certainly the easiest thing to recognize as being of value or benefit. If all we are interested in doing with our lives is to have a relationship, a career, and make money, then what are our lives, anyway? If we don't have a deeper intent in our lives — if we don't see the different things we do as the little steps we take in an ongoing process of Self-realization — the pursuit of these other things will devour us and our many accomplishments become nothing but blocks that we put between us and the Self. With that, our lives turn into something that just happens to us, and all we can do in return is react.

This became clear to me when I was a senior in college. I had become involved in politics, which was then the primary vehicle people were experimenting with to bring about change. I had become disillusioned about this approach, however, and was deeply unhappy. One night I was watching a series on public television made from the novel *David Copperfield*. In this particular episode, David was walking down the beach. Suddenly he asked himself, "Will I be the hero of my own life?"

That question hit me full force, and I started to think about what it meant to me. In a sense, that is why I am where I am, doing what I'm doing now — because I decided that I did want to be the hero of my own life and that I did deeply want to grow.

I suggest to people who want to understand the longing they experience that they concentrate within themselves on what I call the wish to grow. When I use the term "wish," however, I don't mean it in the sense of prayer or entreaty for something. Rather, I have in mind an emphatic statement of intent that is neither tentative nor pleading. In a way, it becomes a statement of fact — a way of orienting our will.

The true process of asking to grow differs from prayer, which is usually some kind of conversation aimed at negotiating with God: "You do this for me and I'll do this for you," or at least, "I'll do this to prove I'm worthy of what I want you to do for me." On some level, when we pray, we are trying to strike a deal. This kind of prayer aims at *using* God instead of *knowing* God and at giving as a means of getting. It also addresses God as if God were separate from us. If only on a subtle level, it directs our attention outside of ourselves, instead of taking it within.

This is what it means to have the wish to grow: It is reaching within ourselves and focusing our whole attention, our whole mind, indeed *ourselves*, on our own life force — on what we call the kundalini energy, or the shakti. We learn to bring our attention to a stillpoint, to become one-pointed in the wish to grow. In the process, our mind becomes completely still, completely clear.

The wish to grow is a strategy for taking our attention beyond our present condition and beyond our immediate experience of time and space — not to some future time, but just *beyond*. Having this wish arouses the life force — the kundalini energy — within us. As it rises up and coalesces, it brings about every kind of change within us. We have engaged the fundamental power of Life Itself, and *it* reveals to us its own course. This is what allows real change to happen within us — change that comes through us and manifests in our total environment.

I said earlier that the wish to grow is a statement of intent. There is an important difference between the feeling, "I guess I want to grow," and the feeling that "I deeply wish to grow, no matter what." With the first, we are likely to be all over the place. But to express our determination by saying "I deeply wish to grow," generates an entirely different feeling. The essence of this effort lies in our ability to focus our attention in our hearts without becoming tense or contracted.

Asking to grow is not the only thing that we can do. Often, I simply repeat Rudi's name. The point is not to get caught on the specific words of the wish. Whatever words you use, it is not something that you think but rather something that emanates from your heart. Practice it, and you will understand the difference.

Among other things, it should give you a visceral connection to a deeper part of you in a way that will mobilize the deepest energy you can connect to inside. Simply by doing it and doing it, by asking and asking, repeating and repeating — by feeling this wish penetrate more and more deeply into you — you will connect to that immediate yet transcendent power of Life Itself. If you do it regularly over time, you will become established in that state.

In the process, your body will run hot and cold and your emotions will wiggle and jiggle all over the place. Basically, these fluctuations don't matter. You will be presented with ten thousand reasons to stop, while forty thousand distractions will come forward to attract your attention. Somehow, you have to get through them. The outcome of doing so is that you learn to focus your mind and heart in a one-pointed way. You begin to experience a simple, clear state, in which there are no thoughts and certainly no other agendas at all.

On one level, we focus on this idea of growing and the energy of growing. More importantly, we learn that becoming one-pointed and beginning to experience the clarity that exists within one-pointedness are the real reasons for doing this exercise. We practice it to become aware of and familiar with that one-pointed state. We develop an appetite for it — even a taste or a feel for this clarity that exists underneath the thoughts, the desires, and the pull and tug of everyday, ordinary life. For this to be possible, the basic understanding we have to have is that our actual growth is a direct function of our own inner commitment and of our conscious effort toward that end.

Growing has everything to do with what we want and the depth to which we want it. Rudi must have pointed out a thousand times that passage in the Bible which says, "Ask and you shall receive." This is true because it is our deep longing to grow that mobilizes both our own life force and the energies around us toward what we desire.

To ask with this intensity requires discipline. If we don't have a real commitment to it, the first time we get into a situation in which we are over our heads, we won't have the patience or the resolve to swim our way out of it. Instead, we will simply sink. It is our conscious wish to grow which makes the difference.

We find a deep awareness of this in the Indian tradition of *bhakti*, or devotion to God. There is a whole tradition of bhakti saints in India in the area where Bhagavan Nityananda and Swami Muktananda lived. Rudi often visited it and I have also gone there several times. In this area, you often hear stories about the saints from past centuries. Their life stories are remembrances of the extraordinary longing felt by people to know the divine. These stories are filled with the poems and poetic ways in which the bhakti saints sang and expressed this intense longing.

What we see, in each case, is that these people sustained their longing over a long period of time. It was not like here in America, where we tend to long for something until we get to the nearest mall. It is not like that. With this particular longing, we have to want it and want it and want it — and be prepared to work at it.

Basically, it goes like this. If the Absolute is infinitely free, then every one of its manifestations — all of its limbs, as it were, and all of manifest reality, including ourselves — is also free. We could say that the Absolute has a profound respect for Its own freedom, whatever the level on which it occurs. Indeed, so great is the respect for that freedom that we ourselves choose whether or not to turn in the direction of spiritual growth. We have to ask for it or it won't happen. Nobody is going to show up at our door and say, "You must do this, you must do that. You must meditate two hours a day." The fact of the matter is, we *don't* have to. If we want to grow, we must ask and work at it. Then we get it.

This is true in every area of our lives. It is only what we truly work for that we attain. Again, it is only what we sow that we reap. (This may be conventional wisdom, but that doesn't make it any less true.) It is also what makes it so important that we learn to go beyond the information provided by our minds and our emotions. When we have only this information as the frame of reference for our existence, then our capacity to sow anything special or interesting, and certainly our capacity to sow anything with longevity, is limited. Only when we cultivate something special within ourselves can we give something special and expect that something special will come back.

We don't have to cut off anything from our lives in order to pursue our own growth. All we have to do is be deeply serious about wanting to grow. Our wish itself mobilizes the depth of the force of Life to renew itself once more. In that renewal, we are uplifted, and whatever can't sustain itself in the more rarified atmosphere of new growth and refinement simply falls away. Furthermore, it does so in a fine way most of the time. This is why there is never any reason to reject anything or anybody.

Wanting to grow doesn't happen accidentally. It is an open-ended event that will be expressed differently by each person. It is also the one way to respond to our longings that will never disappoint us. We don't need to wish for money; we don't need to wish for success; indeed, we don't need to wish for anything else. Those things are easy enough to get if we work for them. The real point is to understand ourselves as growing people and to stay with that.

As we grow in everything we do, our understanding of growing will also become more refined and what are not opportunities for growing will become clear to us. We will find that we are no longer stymied by forms because growing has to do with substance and we will see with increasing clarity what to participate in and what to avoid. We come to have a sense of what the fineness within us looks like and can then work to actualize it, refining our expression of it along the way.

In the process, we will bump into parts of ourselves and of others which will feel like dilemmas. We will face choices, and have none of them seem all that good. Life, being a dynamic event, doesn't necessarily give us what we think we want. Through all of it, however, if we maintain our focus on wanting to grow we become able to take in every difficulty so that it turns into a part of our strength. It is only when we close ourselves to it that it becomes a part of our shell and our prison. Whenever we try to avoid anguish we get kicked twice — once by the anguish and once by the avoidance.

Asking to grow reverses all the polarities we ordinarily experience, since growing involves transcending all duality. It brings together all the distinct voices within us and directs them toward one purpose — to grow as a human being. When we can do that, we go beyond the limitation implicit in every other desire. Then, each activity in which we engage becomes an opportunity to have contact with, and a deeper participation in, the creative flow within us. What expands, after all, is our understanding of "I," which gradually submerges all sense of "other." In other words, what grows is our recognition of the universal *I*.

If you are going to ask for anything, ask to grow. This has an immediacy and a transcendence that centers you right now — at least in your intention — to extend your awareness and become centered and open. Ask to be the best person you can possibly be. Ask for honesty, integrity, and discrimination, because these are all a part of growing. Attain those things, and you will be a great person. Attain them, and your life will manifest the clear reality of grace.

The Stream *of* Experience

Then Uddālaka Āruṇi said to Śvetaketu, his son:
... "Place this salt in the water. In the morning come unto me."
Then he did so.
Then he said to him: "That salt you placed in the water
last evening — please bring it hither."
Then he grasped for it, but did not find it,
as it was completely dissolved.
"Please take a sip of it from this end," said he. "How is it?"
"Salt."
"Take a sip from the middle," said he. "How is it?"
"Salt."
"Set it aside. Then come unto me."
He did so, saying, "It is always the same."
Then he said to him: "Verily, indeed, my dear, you do not
perceive Being here. [Yet] verily, indeed, it is here. That
which is the finest essence — this the whole world has that
as its soul. That is Reality. That is Ātman [the Self].
That art thou, Śvetaketu."

— CHĀNDOGYA UPANISHAD

~~~~~~

We Are Not
What We Think We Are

"WHO AM I?"

Any Indian spiritual tradition begins, in its proto-history, with the simple question, "Who am I?" The people who asked this question tried out one answer after another. "Am I my body?" they asked. "Is it my sense of being 'I' that defines me? Am I my finite ego, my mind, or my different psychological states? Or can it be that I am the result of my personal history?" Yet, as deeply as they looked into each of these possibilities, over and over again they came to the conclusion that the essence of what they were was none of them. "*Neti, neti,*" they said. "Not thus! Not so."

The early philosophers and practitioners of Kashmir Shaivism raised this question and concluded that there are two primary aspects not only to what we are, but to all of reality. The first of these is awareness, which they also called consciousness. The second is the conscious energy of Life, which is also a vital impulse. So they said, "We are, in our very essence, both pure awareness and conscious energy."

Seeking the boundaries of awareness and of the conscious energy of Life, they found none. In other words, there are no limits to the awareness and the conscious energy that is Life Itself. Moreover, these two things are not separate. They are two ways of talking about the same thing, which is both one and infinite. Kashmir Shaivism calls this infinite vitality God.

How is it possible, though, to say on the one hand that *we* are conscious energy and, on the other, that this same conscious energy is God? In various religious traditions, we encounter the idea that God and human beings are separate and that human beings are somehow flawed — or at least inherently limited. One version of this suggests that if we play by the rules, God will take care of us; another, that unless we accept a savior, we are excluded from the circle of salvation and from being able to know God.

From the perspective of Kashmir Shaivism, these notions are problematic because they assume that we can, in some way, be separate from God in the first place. Even the idea that the soul is in the image of God does not go far enough. It still says that God and the soul are distinct.

I would suggest, rather, that divinity itself lies at the core of all existence, including our own. Indeed, its principle manifestation is our individualized self-awareness. This is why it is called the Self.

Having determined the essence of all reality to be pure awareness and conscious energy, the early practitioners of Kashmir Shaivism then asked, "What is the connection between this and the material reality that we experience? By what process did we come to be?"

They had, as I have said, determined that the universe in its essence is infinite, pure awareness. This aspect of it they called "Shiva." But they also determined that the universe is the process by which this pure awareness expresses itself. The Infinite *must* express itself, they said, or it would not be vital. It is like a singer who must sing — otherwise he or she is not a singer. They gave the name "Shakti" to this vitally active, self-expressive, and self-aware energy of the divine.

How does this Self-expression come about? The highest consciousness, they said, is an inconceivably fine vibration. It is like this: Think of how your own mind operates. First your awareness extends itself toward some object and, through your senses, absorbs data about that object. Then it draws back, reflects on the data it has collected, and synthesizes a response. The ongoing extension and withdrawal, together, constitute a rapid pulsation, or vibration. This is the nature of all consciousness, whether we are talking about the level of the infinitely fine, or the corresponding level of the individual mind.

We operate as the center of our own awareness and its pulsation. But at the level of the infinite, this pulsation is a medium with an infinite number of centers. Infinite pulsations arise from each of these centers and interact with each other. In other words, the infinite interacts with itself. As it does so, parts of it slow down and contract. They become dense to the point of condensation and crystallization, thereby giving rise to the whole dynamic event of manifest reality. If this sounds too abstract, take as an analogy certain scientific descriptions of the formation of the universe, according to which gasses have interacted, contracted, and formed matter.

The implication is that nothing at all is excluded in any way, shape, or form from the infinite. There is nothing that has not come forth from that pure, vital awareness — even something we experience as completely dense, like a rock. I use this example because ordinarily we assume that a rock is not mobile and that it has no awareness. At least, such is our perception from the perspective of our personal lives. If, however, we looked at it from a broader point of view, we could hardly make such a statement.

Both we and the rock have a vibration. We vibrate at a much higher frequency than does the rock, but if we were to step out into space and observe from an extended time and space, we would see that we are simply two different pulses. The rock also responds to its environment, even if over an extremely long period of time. Is this not one of the characteristics of a conscious thing? The point is that the vibration of infinite consciousness is universal and absolute whether it expresses itself as us or as a rock. We are all parts of its Self-expression.

We operate on three levels simultaneously: the level of the infinite, the level of individualized consciousness, and the level of the personal. Each of these has its own frequency, its own chemistry, and its own possibilities. Each one operates according to a different logic.

Most of the time, we are primarily aware of the personal level of our awareness. As spiritual people, however — ones who are asking the question, "Who am I?" — we are trying at all times to cultivate and sustain our living awareness of the infinite, even in the midst of our experience of the personal.

We come forth, like trees rising up from the ground, as individualized expressions of infinite Life. From these individualized expressions emerge everything we identify as the personal, including our own personalities. We are like the leaves on a tree or, similarly, like waves rising from the ocean and becoming individualized swells of water. Each swell reaches a crest and locks for a moment — then it is gone. This pause is like the personal dimension of our experience.

Only on this personal level do distinct features begin to emerge. These features include our bodies, our minds, and our emotions. They include the sphere of action that we ordinarily describe as our experience, whether we mean something physical or something mental and emotional. They include everything we call our personalities. Yet, where do our personalities come from? They are a contraction of the infinite.

So why are we not aware of this every day? In a way, we are. When we experience that vague sense of longing that I discussed earlier, it is the infinite within us attempting to make itself known. You might think that something as big as the infinite should be able to attract our attention pretty quickly. This, however, is not how it happens. Instead, we get distracted by all the ways that it expresses itself at the level of personality — by all of our desires, thoughts, and feelings. In a word, we get distracted by all of our tensions.

In talking about the infinite, I used the words "vibration" and "pulsation." I could just as easily have said "energy" — and, in this case, "the creative energy of Life Itself." If everything is the pulsation of the infinite, everything we are and do is also energy. There is nothing that is not. Whether we talk about extending our arms, feeling the movement of a dance or a game, or working intently at anything, it is all the creative energy of the divine manifesting itself.

As the energy of Life crystallizes into patterns, at no time is its potential ever destroyed. At any point, that energy can be released to take on some other form because energy is the potential to do work — to flow. For example, in the case of electricity, it is the flow of electrons through a wire that heats the wire, causing it to vibrate at a frequency higher than before and give off light and heat. The electrons themselves are not destroyed but only released, to be drawn into some other pattern until they are released again.

Tensions — what we ordinarily think of as problems — and creative energy are basically the same thing but in different states. Tension is creative energy that has contracted into a pattern. When we release that pattern, we free the energy to do what *it* wills. We release tension and allow it to flow as creative energy. This is our great challenge, because only to the degree that we learn to do so do we come to know directly the essence of who and what we are.

In fact, for my teacher Rudi, absorbing, digesting, and transcending our own tensions constituted *the* fundamental question. He said that life must be consumed whole, with all its tension, sorrow, and pain as well as with all its joy. Only when we can do this can we come to understand the vastness of our human potential.

Rudi was talking about the necessity of consuming our tensions and growing from them because they consume us if we do not. He observed that much of what we react to is nothing but our own tension. It is not really what this one did or what that one failed to do; it is only the tension within *us*. By making the simple conscious effort every day to rise above this tension, we find something truly beautiful and incredible in ourselves.

As long as there is tension in a particular event, we know that we haven't gotten to the heart of the matter. Only when we get beyond tension or, as they say in the business world, when we get to the bottom line, do we know it. In our relationship to everything, when we get to that bottom line we find a profound sense of quiet — a profound silence. In that silence, all tension becomes nil, just as all difference and distinction disappear.

Certain definite benefits come to us as a result of learning to do this. First of all, we find that we are able to engage in our lives with a greater sense of balance, more aware of and more sensitive to what goes on around us. This results in more harmonious and fulfilling relationships with others. Having a clearer understanding of our abilities, values, and motives, we are able to work more productively and generate better quality.

A by-product of this is that we tend to have not only healthier physical lives but also more vital mental and emotional lives with a greater capacity for intellectual activity. We discover a frame of reference that allows us not to become confused or distressed by the intensity of the activity going on at any level of our experience.

Rudi would say that once this flow of energy increases, it continues to increase. Flow goes to flow. As it extends itself, and as we come to appreciate its true nature, we not only increase our own capacity; we come to understand ourselves as nothing but creative energy, and that creative energy as nothing but what I call "dynamic stillness." In the process, we have gone from matter to energy, and then to pure consciousness. We recognize that we are not strangers in a strange land. We are not distinct entities separated from one another by time and space, separated from God and in need of overcoming the separation. We are expressions of the divine.

The point is that we cannot let the world be our limitation. We have to begin to live from the unimaginable potential that exists inside us. It is only when we transcend the tensions within us that we can live from that potential. Only then do we find that we have a life so full of consciousness, so vast and deep, that it shatters the vessel of our human bodies and minds, and even the vessel of our human hearts. In that shattering, the chains that bind us to the endless merry-go-round of worldly experience are broken. Then we become free human beings, established in the full awareness of who and what we are.

THE INDIVIDUAL

...My soul, where does this breathing arise?
How does this beating heart exist?
Bird of the soul, speak in your own words
and I will understand.
The heart replied: I was in the work place
the day this house of water and clay was fired.
I was already flying from that created house
even while the house was being created.
When I could no longer resist, I was dragged down,
and my features were molded from a lump.

— RUMI

When Moses met God in the flames of the burning bush, he asked what name he should use for God when speaking to the people. God said to Moses, "I Am that I Am." Kashmir Shaivism would fully accept this as the expression of God but would also say, "I Am *All* that There Is."

God is the vast Self-awareness, or consciousness, that is the subtle essence of all things. The whole universe is an expression of the vitality of this consciousness, a subtle pulsation that interacts with itself. Through various stages of increasing contraction and density, this pure, undifferentiated awareness expresses itself as individual conscious events. It is here that the sense of "I" begins. Each "I," like a spiral current in the energy of Life, becomes conscious of itself, or self-aware. It comes to perceives itself as separate and distinct from the surrounding atmosphere and becomes aware of other "I's" around it. Here begins our sense of ego.

This "I" emerges as a kind of fundamental gravity around which the energy of Life coalesces as our bodies. With all its constituent energies, the "I" moves in time and space and gathers matter into an orbit around it, somewhat as does the sun with the planets. As this condensation continues, the body follows its own pattern of growth, expansion, and disintegration — a pulsation of energy arising, existing, and subsiding.

When we talk about "I," there are different facets to what we mean. These facets express themselves as our behavioral patterns and as the different interactions that we establish and sustain in the world. Each of these patterns of behavior has a psychic, intellectual, emotional, and physical component, that is, a certain life of its own with an independent vibration. Even though, together, these patterns articulate what we are, we don't fully control them; indeed, a lot of the time we are barely aware of them.

Again, think of the sun and the planets. Each of them has an independent life with a pattern and a vibration all its own. Its individual identity as a distinct component of the solar system has a powerful reality. Nevertheless, each one remains part of the unified whole. In our own case, every constituent part that constellates around what we call the fundamental "I" is, in essence, an expression and an extension of the force of Life underlying it.

Usually, we are most aware of the independent pattern and vibration. We think that we are conscious because we have bodies and minds. We also think that when our bodies die, we die. But if consciousness is the fundamental ground and essence of everything, then it is because of consciousness that our bodies and minds *are*. Consciousness is the root; our bodies, minds, and emotions are the branches.

These grosser dimensions are usually what we identify as life, and as the basic components of what we are. In a way, this is so. They do have a certain vitality. But what they are is only a rough replication of this extreme fineness — a dense version of that infinitely refined pulsation. As the facets of our sense of "I," they give us our boundaries and edges, but they do not really tell us what is truly alive about us.

At the level of our immediate experience, the first distinction we make is between what is "I" and what is "not-I." We thereby establish our sense of ourselves in contrast to everything around us. When I say "experience," I mean anything we perceive as an object. It is anything we can see or relate to, whether through a telescope to the other side of the universe or through a microscope to the elements of the cellular biology that we are. All of these things constitute experience. Our body is an experience; our thoughts and feelings are experiences too. Even what we identify as "I" is an experience.

For example, on a gross level we experience our thoughts and our feelings. We say, "I think this," or "I thought that;" "I feel my foot," or "I have this feeling." We make a distinction between what is "I" and what is "my foot," what is "I" and what is "my feeling." We do this in such a way that even "I" and "my thoughts," or "I" and "my mind" are not the same thing. "My feelings" and "my thoughts" become part of that object of experience, "me."

What characterizes any experience is the fundamental distinction between the subject and the object — there is someone who has the experience and something or someone that is the object of the experience. Of course, such distinctions immediately turn into mud when we say something like, "My feelings are hurt." If *my feelings* are hurt, then how come *I* am experiencing all the pain? For that matter, we even make a distinction between "I" and the pain. This is a curious thing.

We generally remain unaware that the subtle pulsation of Life expresses itself as all experience, that is, that all experience emerges from, and within the context of, this one fundamental ground. Instead, we get caught up in trying to know these individual experiences in all their contracted forms. We give them great importance as we try to define just what this "I" is. So, when we ask, "Who am I?" we come up with some aspect of our experience. We miss the point that both this "I" and all of our experiences are variations on the same thing.

It is something like this: When we look out over the waves on the ocean, there is clearly a certain uniqueness to each one of the hundreds that we see. However, when we identify or even become too fascinated with that uniqueness, we are likely not to see the ocean as a whole.

Your notion of "I" — this individualized expression — and my notion of "I" are, on a fundamental level, no different. In fact, if we step back from our own individuality for a moment and take a wider view, we will see that every human being refers to "I." When we make that reference, we all talk essentially about the same thing — consciousness individualized.

To focus on trying to understand what makes us different, unique, and therefore special, is to get caught up in the waves and tossed around by every squall we run into. It is, moreover, to lose sight of what is truly special about us. Indeed, I would say that what, in the beginning, fascinates us as our uniqueness is, in the middle, our separateness and, in the end, our mortality.

By talking about everything as vibration, though, we go beyond what we usually think of as our boundaries. We no longer see ourselves as isolated individuals. For the purposes of our movement in the world and in our everyday lives, of course, we can have such discussions, but the only way to do so effectively is to be grounded in our awareness that everything is one thing. Only then do we have the real possibility of absorbing all distinctions and developing some legitimate discrimination.

Everything we experience is nothing but the vital energy of Life giving rise to appearances. When we understand that every appearance is not as it seems, then it becomes more difficult to be deluded by what we see, feel, or even think. It is easier to have insight into the real nature of the circumstances that present themselves before us, to go beyond delusion and, consequently, to avoid anxiety, frustration, disappointment, and the whole complex of feelings that arise as expressions of our polarization with the world and with ourselves.

I encourage you to explore the limitlessness of the consciousness that you are, free of the limited patterns that emerge within the personalized field of our experience. This is what allows you to go beyond the confines of your individualized consciousness. To know the essence of what we call "I" — indeed, to know the essence of all your experiences — is to go deeper than these experiences themselves. It is to go within yourself and to know the ground from which these experiences grow, the ocean upon which they are merely the passing waves. It is to know that what we *are* is all that there is.

THE BIOLOGICAL IMPERATIVES

What is the body? That shadow of a shadow
of your love, that somehow contains
the entire universe.

A man sleeps heavily,
though something blazes in him like the sun,
like a magnificent fringe sewn up under the hem.

— RUMI

One evening, I watched a program on television about creatures of the sea, the first of which was a jellyfish. The program pointed out that a jellyfish is not a single organism but rather a colony of single-celled organisms, each of which has adapted to fulfill a particular function within the colony as a whole. At the same time, each one also remains a singe-celled animal.

If we pursue the idea that cells organize and interact with each other, adapting to each other's needs and organizing themselves to support a common purpose, what we end up with are simple animals. As the cells go on in this process, we have more and more complex organisms until finally we come to the organism that we call a human being. Yet, this does not change the fact that we ourselves are an elaborate colony of cells.

We look at our bodies and, since we see something contained by unbroken skin that looks like one thing, we say, "Well, this is what I am." Much of our attention is then taken up by our experiences of the body and its processes. It gets born, it grows up, it ages. It engages in activity and it rests. It gets sick and it feels healthy. It generates children and feels the pain of loss. It is always with us. We get up, we look at it every morning in the mirror, we hit it, we feel it, it complains to us if we don't treat it right. Consequently, we think we have something that we can call "my body" — "me." In fact, however, it is not. This is not *you* that you are sitting in, but just a group of cells.

Moreover, there is nothing truly solid about the body, however much we may be attached to it and however fiercely we may hold on to it. Today, it is not composed of the same cells that made it up even as recently as yesterday. Rather, it is a composite of individual living organisms that are constantly changing. We are, in other words, a highly temporary event.

Furthermore, what our egos and minds identify as "me" is not only this colony of cells but also a separate colony of resident bacteria. These four hundred billion bacteria have nothing to do with our cellular makeup. Rather, as residents in our bodies, they live in symbiotic relationship with the cells and are essential to their welfare. If we killed all the bacteria within us, we would die. In addition, all of the microbes and cells are constantly exchanging body fluids not only with each other but also with the atmosphere around them, so that on a material level there is a continuous, dynamic interchange. We are each really a community, existing in complete dependence upon both our internal and external environments.

We tend to look at this body and everything we associate with it and find the whole event so significant that we should go out and try to get as much fame and glory for it as we can. We'll get some diplomas to hang on it, along with a couple of women or men to keep it company. (You'll notice that we tend to define success and a meaningful life in terms of some purpose that ultimately relates to the body).

This is a somewhat skewed perspective of our own importance. As far as Earth is concerned we ourselves are something of an infestation. For that matter, bacteria have colonized virtually every environmental niche, from deep-sea thermal vents to Antarctic ice, and function much like a great super-organism. That makes us — or at least our bodies — just one of the many sub-environments inhabited by these colonies. As far as the solar system is concerned, we are of little more importance than the muck under a rock on the floor of the sea.

It is an amazing thing to discover that our bodies are not what we thought they were and that our lives, therefore, are not about what we imagined. This is no excuse to become indifferent, but it does tend to revise our take on our own importance.

Likewise, we tend to operate with a skewed understanding of what informs many of our activities. Without being all that conscious of doing so, we become involved in the biological imperatives that motivate us as colonies of cells — namely, the imperatives to eat and reproduce. We identify with these inner forces, even though they do not and cannot satisfy the fundamental sense of longing that we feel. We engage in the activities our biology calls us to carry out — when it surges, we move. When biology talks, people listen. E. F. Hormone. We constantly act out these imperatives, entangled in our idea of ourselves not as luminous beings but as biological events.

Because of this, a certain dull frequency of awareness overcomes us. As we move our attention from sense object to sense object and from goal to goal — as we struggle for one thing and another — we become highly contracted individuals. As this contraction progresses, we become more and more condensed, more and more occupied by tensions of one kind or another.

This contraction takes place when we identify with objectives related to our physical world. The process of focusing on anything outside ourselves arises within the context of the biological imperatives. This is true whether it is a condition to which we are exposed or a desire we are attempting to fulfill. By their nature, these imperatives orient us to look outside ourselves to meet the needs which they impose. Within this contracted awareness, bound by this horizon of our misunderstanding, we suffer.

In saying this, I want to make clear what I do *not* mean. There is a reductionist line of scientific thought called socio-biology in which the proponents say, essentially, "What is all of this about consciousness, humanity, and love? We are just groups of cells that plug into one another and communicate messages to each other like 'Let's eat' or 'Let's reproduce.'"

What I have said may, at first, sound the same, but it is not. We cannot be reduced to biological functions any more than we can be reduced to a set of psychological states, a social background, a group of personality traits, or any other conditioned reality. There is infinitely more to us than that. The biological imperatives may drive the functions of all the cells, but the cells themselves come from some place deeper, as does the energy that composes them. We talk about the biological imperatives and about what we are on a mental and emotional level precisely so that we can cease to identify with these aspects of our lives. Only by doing so can we begin to get at the true nature of that energy from which the whole event that we are arises.

If what I'm saying seems simplistic, then I've been successful, because it *is* relatively simplistic. Rudi used to say, "Life is profound only in its simplicity." He found it remarkable that people managed to miss this, and that they could keep everything so complicated. What we are physically, biologically, and even psychologically, has little to do with the true nature of the source behind the whole creative process. The cells are not the final expression of Life. At a deeper level within this whole event, a pure, vital energy pulsates. It is the reality of this deeper level that puts our discussion beyond the narrow constraints of reductionism.

When we understand the real nature of the energy that composes both our bodies and all the chemicals that underlie our minds and emotions, we enter a level of understanding that goes beyond biology. This is important because as long as we have bodies, biology will be present, accompanied by all the issues that biology brings with it — the need for food, the desire for companionship, the yearning for sexual experiences and families, and so on. There is simply a tide that manifests in us, drawing us to some things and repelling us from others. It is like an electricity or magnetism that causes us to embrace certain ideas and reject others, according to whether they promote or frustrate the fulfillment of the imperatives.

I should make it clear that there is nothing wrong with the biological imperatives at all. Our systems are made up of chemicals and chemical responses, and this chemistry is a natural part of life. We don't deny any of it. For that matter, it is of no use to do so. Indeed, it is not even particularly healthy to deny any of it, so long as we maintain the big picture.

The basic chemistry itself is not a bad thing, but it is not in its proper place when it dominates us. An old saying has it that,

"There is never enough of that which does not satisfy." Since the fulfillment of these biological imperatives does not inherently satisfy us, there is never enough. Thus, they give rise to an endless journey. When we get lost in them, the feelings of self-doubt and self-rejection arising in that state, along with a tendency to project it onto others as doubt and rejection, are the first steps down a steep hill. The first step may be small, but the second drops four hundred feet. The problem is that we usually don't watch to see where the road is going.

The whole point of spiritual work is to begin to understand that we are not what we appear to be. As we understand this more and more, we begin to find within ourselves a real and deep connection to the source of all Life. As we understand the ephemeral nature of our physical existence, we become able to attend to something more essential within and about ourselves.

How do we do this? First, by having priorities. This is what yoga is all about — having priorities and having a focus. We decide that one thing is the most important, and that we will keep it at the forefront of our awareness while assigning other things a position of lesser importance.

This is exactly what a person who is oriented toward the biological imperatives says. The difference is that such a person makes relationships and objects his or her priority and places these things at the forefront of his or her awareness. But this is to ignore the inevitably temporary nature of these things. Consequently, a person who makes such objects a primary pursuit in life is focused on transitory circumstances. The irony is that these things require repair and replacement on a regular basis because they are always breaking down. Then we are back on the old treadmill again, with the biological imperatives in full swing.

The alternative is to choose, as our priority, the wish to grow. If we took about eighty-five percent of the energy we now expend on being concerned with variations on the need to eat and reproduce, and redirected that energy to this deeper pursuit of growing, we would release qualities within ourselves that would alleviate much of what we experience as need. When we can do that, we find a new sense of wholeness because our physical needs assume their proper place within our lives.

I don't mean that we try to push the hormones out of the picture. This, in fact, is not possible. What I do mean is that by directing our attention to something deeper, we let the sun shine in a little bit more every day. Gradually, it burns off the fog and we don't have to do anything specific to get rid of anything. The warmth and light that enter then dissipate the dense atmosphere which the hormones generate. This is what I mean when I say that we become free of our bodies. At that point, they are simply there.

Releasing our biological tensions is both challenging and difficult. It goes contrary to the natural tendency of our bodies and minds. Thus, there is a need for us to be steady and vigilant in training our awareness. This vigilance is what makes a disciplined spiritual practice not only extremely helpful but actually necessary. Ultimately, it establishes us in the experience of always being aware of that which enjoys all of Life.

This is a process that continuously turns us back into ourselves. Over and over again it directs our attention to the vitality and the transcendent power that is the source of our biology. It causes us to seek and to know the essence of our lives in a deeper way. With this understanding and awareness, we begin to penetrate the biological cloud. We learn to allow our biological urges and impulses to go on, but not to identify with them in any way. We then find that we are simply observing more and more of the whole process without being attached to the limits it imposes.

When we experience that deeper part of us, the limits that we usually experience begin to dissolve, and the dynamics of the process itself become increasingly clear to us. Then, because we are increasingly aware of participating in this fundamental vitality, we begin to let go of our efforts to build up and reinforce the dikes we've always raised to resist the flow of Life Itself within us.

In so doing, we become established in an awareness that goes beyond both bodily consciousness and the pulsation of our minds and emotions. It is a state of dynamic stillness. At that point, we look at this biological event and its emotional, intellectual content in its purest form, and see that we are nothing but conscious energy, a manifestation of the creative power implicit in the highest state.

THE EGO

My ego is stubborn, often drunk, impolite.
My loving: Finely sensitive, impatient, confused.
Please take messages from one to the other,
reply and counter-reply.

— RUMI

What we recognize as our ego is that mechanism in the colony of cells which perceives us as a single entity, independent of other entities. It is the self-monitoring capacity within us — the part responsible for recognizing and dealing with imbalances in the system and with challenges to its integrity. It is also part of the stupidest aspect of our existence.

I say this because the ego is utterly reactionary. When faced with a difficult situation, it immediately thinks and thinks and thinks. It figures out one angle after another and is constantly trying to calculate how to get one thing or another. "What if this happens?" "What if that happens?" "If this happens, I'll do that; if that happens, I'll do this." The ego is always like this. For all its effort, however, every question it ever asks is nothing but a variation on what I call the mantra of stupidity: "What's going to happen to *me*?"

Different desires arise in us, such as, "I want that" or "This one belongs to me." All of them have to do with the image we create of ourselves. In time, as all the things we desire naturally go their own way, we ask ourselves, "What happened over there? That was mine and now it's gone. I lost it, it left me, I was rejected, I blew it." Or we might say, "I never had it in the first place" or, "I'm a big shot because I *do* have this or that and besides, I was just elected president of my Moose Lodge."

Whenever we respond to our lives in this way we allow ourselves to become reduced to a trivial level. We try to conceptualize the nature of our experience. We struggle to fit it into some kind of framework because we haven't the composure to live with the alternative — the profound uncertainty that Life really is. There is real pain and anguish in relating to this uncertainty. Rather than facing it, accepting it, opening to it, and allowing the uncertainty to begin to teach us about itself, we close our hearts and minds to it.

We don't recognize that our resistance to this uncertainty causes us to erect boundaries around ourselves. These boundaries encapsulate us in tension. They prevent any higher, finer vibration or joyous experience from penetrating and uplifting us. As we build up an identity — an ego — to protect us from this uncertainty, the ego itself becomes more and more of a prison. The more we are in pain in this prison, the faster, higher, and bigger we build the walls.

In the mechanism that we are, the ego is simply a given part, just as it is a part of everybody else. It functions to help us structure our experience. Every dynamic event has such a structure, and this is not a problem. Only when we get stuck in the structure set up by the ego do we also get caught in the boundaries it erects. This happens when we take the ego to be the limit of who we are. It happens when we don't see that there is something so much vaster about us that the ego can only appear dense and stupid by comparison.

The ego cannot help in our pursuit of growing. As a reactionary event, the ego itself doesn't grow, just as the mind and emotions don't grow. Indeed, when it comes to spiritual growth, all of these do little except get in the way. Our identification with any of them is nothing but a reaction to a reaction to a reaction.

Our wish to grow, to be authentic, has to translate into action. This is what sustains a unity between our will and its expression. Yet in becoming action, our intention always passes through the filter of the ego. In the process, our intention gets refracted, becoming both diffuse and complicated. This, in turn, gives rise to many shadows and distorted perceptions. This filter comes into play particularly as our minds work to maintain a sense of consistency in their perceptions. They are always trying to tell us that we are just as we think we are. We are not.

The organization of images, concepts, and ideas that compose our ego is a fraud we unknowingly perpetrate upon ourselves. The notions by which we evaluate ourselves have no force in any kind of profound reality. What *does* have force is the power of Life Itself. When we can still our minds and tone down all the distinctions that we arrive at by comparing ourselves to others — or even to our own past performance — we begin to experience just why all these distinctions are beside the point.

Any spiritual practice — indeed, any quest for truth — requires that we let go of all superficialities instead of building up an identity and then defending it. This idea makes many people uncomfortable. We may find it frightening just to imagine it, or at least extremely disorienting. This is understandable. After all, if we weren't too thrilled about who we thought we were before — and, most likely, that discontent is what originally sent us into the whole building program — then who wants to go back there? And isn't that what it means to let go of all that composes our identity?

Not exactly. This process of letting go includes the identity we weren't happy about in the first place as well. Secondly, "letting go" doesn't leave us a human vacuum. Rather, it means becoming aware of the much deeper part of ourselves, quickly, simply, and naturally. It means becoming aware of the Life deep inside whatever prison we have made.

What is alive in that prison, and always has been, is the energy of Life Itself. Simply to turn our attention to that takes us into a dimension different from the one we were in when we started the building program. Once we see this, all of that other construction work dissolves and we are left with the most vital, authentic part of who we are.

This involves paying attention to the quality of our effort all the time. In the process, we discover at least two things: first, that making a quality effort is hard, and second, that doing it humbles all of us. When we are really honest with ourselves, we recognize that, on the level of experience, much of what passes for work and effort in the world is made up of incompetence, inefficiency, and laziness. Moreover, we understand that, as personalities, all of us play out some of it. Once we have seen this, it becomes difficult to be as proud and cocky about the person we present to the world. This is one way to begin to go beyond the ego.

We also come to see that this is not where our true experience of success lies. What real success any of us has in our lives comes from a mysterious and subtle place that is difficult to name. We come to know this by being careful in our effort and attentive to doing a good job all the time. When we truly do this, it is also hard to become egotistical.

We make the effort to pay attention to these details within ourselves, to watch our energy and how it manifests in every relationship, and to keep ourselves focused on the subtle balance we hope to establish in each of these relationships. Out of this effort, our intention to grow begins to flow freely into action. This process is what slowly teaches us about our own nature and about the nature of Life. It is, to a great extent, what liberates us from fear, tension, and need and transforms us into a fountain of well-being.

Instead of being frightening, this is a wonderful and joyous process. It is like taking a deep breath on a clear, brisk morning and simply feeling alive. To feel that Life flowing in and around us plucks us right out of our prison and takes us as close to heaven as we can possibly get. We understand that no destruction of the ego is necessary, that no rejection of the ego is required — but that the ego is also not the most important part of what we are. Then we find, over time, that our ego assumes its appropriate place and that we no longer have to struggle with it.

By becoming aware of the multiplicity of processes which compose what we call "I," we begin to see things from a perspective that makes the ego look extraordinarily superficial. We see that the ego and the identity we all try to create for ourselves are both like finding a pile of rabbit pellets in our backyard. Something has been there and left a residue of its presence, but this residue is fundamentally irrelevant. The best we can say for it is that, in a way, it is nice because we know it will make our grass grow greener. But that is about as meaningful as the whole ego event finally is.

Desire And Purpose

LIMITATIONS

Chang Wu-tzu said, "What's more, you're too hasty in your own appraisal . . . I'm going to say some reckless words and I want you to listen to them recklessly. . . . Ordinary men strain and struggle; the sage is stupid and blockish. He takes part in ten thousand ages and achieves simplicity in oneness. For him, all the ten thousand things are what they are, and thus they enfold each other.
"How do I know that loving life is not a delusion? How do I know that in hating death I am not like a man who, having left home in his youth, has forgotten the way back? . . .
How do I know that the dead do not wonder why they ever longed for life?"

— CHUANG TZU

One of the activities of the mind is to categorize our experiences. We decide that they are good or bad, that they will help us or limit us. We judge them as problems or as solutions. This always strikes me as a little shortsighted. Why do I say this? Because as far as matters of the world are concerned it has been my observation that every solution ends up being equivalent to what we ordinarily think of as a new problem.

47

This holds true of every condition, every life style — indeed, of every experience — in which we find ourselves. We can think, "I'm married and I want to be single," or "I'm single and I want to be married," or "I'm a Boston person and I want to be a world traveler," or "I have to travel all the time and I wish I could stay in one place." Whatever condition we identify as a limitation, we discover that the opposite condition contains just as many difficulties. If we let ourselves take any of these apparent limitations seriously, pretty soon we start to think they are real. Then we start to worship them. Next we erect a temple around them and, in the end, we are buried in them.

The *Malinivijayottaravarttikam*, a text composed by the Kashmir Shaivite master Abhinavagupta, discusses "what is to be eschewed," or avoided. On one level, Abhinavagupta is referring to desire, attachment, fear, anger, lust, greed, and laziness. He points out that, through the process of various yogic practices, we begin to recognize and manage these.

What is really to be avoided, however, is any sense of ourselves as inherently limited — any sense of our lives as intrinsically finite in terms of time and space, resource and opportunity, value and worth, or simply in terms of its horizon. When we stop thinking and feeling in these terms, the stage is set for a more open awareness of the nature of Life to unfold. That open awareness is also one of the things discussed in the text.

At the same time, it is important that we be aware of the constraints that do operate in our lives, so that we don't rush heedlessly and headlong into some ill-conceived endeavor, telling ourselves that we are transcending them or wiping them out. In Greek mythology, the story of young Icarus who attempts to fly toward the sun and falls to his death is a demonstration of this — a person heedless of both his own capacities and the limits to the support mechanism around him. This is the activity of a fool, of someone who is bound to fail. Immature people are often reckless like this and may come to a violent end. There is no point to approaching life in this way.

The issue is to penetrate and understand the nature of limits, which we can also describe as part of the structure of our lives. It is like this: At the same time that our physiological structure — for example our skeleton — limits us, it also serves us. Similarly, our existence in this world both limits us and serves us. On the one hand, we exist as a contracted form of the highest reality; on the other, it is because of our existence in this world that we have the opportunity to understand ourselves and to come into direct contact with the very essence of all that is.

Only people who carefully continue to unlock the secrets of their limits are able to ascend to the heights. We have to do this thoughtfully, with discipline and great care. We may feel that we simply cannot get beyond the barriers of self-protection we have put up. This may even be true right now. However, bit by bit, our inner work will take us beyond these barriers.

It doesn't happen in the way we might think. Most people wrongly imagine that, to go beyond a barrier, they have to tackle it head-on. This is not so. Indeed, we don't have to focus on the barrier at all. We do, however, have to attend to where we are going. In martial arts, people sometimes like to prove how skillful they are by breaking things. Visually, this is impressive. We may tend to think of going through boundaries as being like this. We put up a stack of boards and figure that we will chop through them. Then, we fix our entire concentration on the boards. What we find when we strike them, though, is that we break our hand.

People who are skilled at breaking boards, bricks, or anything else project their energy through to the other side. They are not imagining the boards as such, but are thinking instead that the boards don't exist as an obstacle: "What I want is for my hand to go *there*." Then the boards break because the energy is much stronger. This is true for working through our barriers, too.

There is no need to try to change or eliminate whatever walls of resistance or blocks of self-protection we have put up. Instead, we keep working to attain and maintain the highest degree of self-awareness possible for us to live from at any given moment. No matter what our power of concentration may be, each and every moment we reach for an even deeper state of openness. If we can do that, then every kind of block will dissolve over time. We will look back and say: "What blocks? They must have been in my imagination." Then, what difficulty can there be?

When we stop trying to do the impossible — that is, reinforcing boundaries and limitations, or recklessly ignoring them — when we learn to feel, experience, and understand the flow of the energy within us, we also allow the limitlessness we are to come to the forefront of our awareness. Then, the ways in which the energy appears to be individualized and distinct no longer hold our attention. We no longer identify with any of that but with the pulsation at the heart of all things.

Think of it this way: The same creativity that has given rise to the whole universe has also given rise to you and is within you. The resource that is the source of all abundance and all that is, is within you. Instead of condemning yourself for anything or being unhappy with yourself in any way, you can begin to work each day to discover this creative power within you. Then you will also discover that every limitation you have assumed about yourself is false.

When the energy emerges, it is beautiful. As it coalesces it holds our attention. As it reaches a crescendo in a still point it is profound, and as it releases and rapidly returns to its most primitive, pure state it is dazzling. The aim of spiritual work and the expression of spiritual understanding is for us to be continuously centered in the flow of our own creative awareness. Being centered in this awareness represents our presence within the Presence that is divine. It renders irrelevant every question of limitation.

PSYCHOLOGICAL STATES

Hui Tzu said to Chuang Tzu, "Can a man really be
without feelings?"
    Chuang Tzu: "Yes."
    Hui Tzu: "But a man who has no feelings — how
can you call him a man?"
    Chuang Tzu: "The Way gave him a face; Heaven
gave him a form — why can't you call him a man?"
    Hui Tzu: "But if you've already called him a man,
how can he be without feelings?"
    Chuang Tzu: "That's not what I mean by feelings.
When I talk about having no feelings, I mean that a
man doesn't allow good or bad to get in and do him harm.
He just lets things be the way they are and doesn't
try to help life along."

— CHUANG TZU

Two fundamental principles distinguish spirituality from everything having to do with self-help. The first of these, as I said earlier, is that we are much more than this body. When I say "this body" I do not mean just the physical body, but everything involving the manifest world. We are so much more than this, in fact, that the ancient sages of India would say we are *not* this body at all.

The world, after all, is nothing but an accidental by-product of the great elegance and joy of the infinite. We keep thinking that something about it must be important, but compared to the full wonder of the infinite, it is not. Some things about the world are entertaining and pleasant and some of them may even be meaningful to us individually, but none of them is important. This is so because all of it — you and I, and everything in the middle — will move on. The only issue is which end will lead. Will we go out head first or feet first?

From this perspective, nothing that we accomplish in the world is particularly important. This may come as a piece of bad news if we are invested in our various projects and relationships or if we are preoccupied with success. On the other hand, it may come as a relief. After all, what if our lives were no longer defined by these things? What would we be free to invest ourselves in then?

Nothing that is truly spiritual exists to help us accomplish anything in the world. Being released from bondage, pain, and suffering naturally brings us into a state of deep happiness — which makes the world a more enjoyable place to live in while we are here. It does not, however, make any of it more important.

The second principle that distinguishes spirituality from everything else naturally flows from the first, and that is that all psychological states are false. This may seem to contradict our experience of these different states, all of which, in the moment, may feel both powerful and real. If we step back, however, we can see that they pass across the horizon of our awareness like clouds across the sky. Not one of them is permanent. We may find their shapes, patterns, and movement fascinating but that doesn't change the fact that they are merely the condensation of something far more refined.

This holds true of every one of the psychological states that engages our attention. All the concepts, constructs, ideas, and thoughts that emerge in our minds are transient and, by definition, limited. This is why I say that all psychological states are false.

There are curtains and there are curtains. Sometimes, we walk around talking about how beautiful the curtains are instead of opening them up and looking out the window or actually going outside. Psychological states are like such curtains. They are the draperies by which we become distracted, forgetting that we might simply look past them. But does this ever make them the real view?

Most people don't like themselves very much. Either we become psychological slashers attacking ourselves or we set out to prove to everyone (including ourselves) that we are not as bad as we think. Both programs are ways of beating ourselves to pieces. Yet, if we want to restore a person to psychological health or find a deeper state of health ourselves, then chasing after one issue or another will not resolve anything. It is like the old Arabic saying about five fingers and five fleas. Trying to figure out a problem is like putting five fingers on five fleas. Every time you move a finger to get one flea, another flea gets away from you. You might pin down four only to find that to get the fifth one you have to let three of the others go.

Often, we define personal progress in terms of the problems we solve. We say, "I want to be this or that kind of person. I want to change this or that about myself." We might change two of these things and feel terribly proud of ourselves. Then we discover, when we try to change the third thing, that it doesn't happen so easily. We get frustrated and, in the process, let the first two slide. At that point, we are right back where we started. This is not useful.

Thinking that we have problems and that there are solutions to these problems is also not useful. The creative energy which is the essence of our lives and of all manifestation has no problems at all. The Self has no problem. Since the Self is essentially what we are, we, too, have no real problem. Yet, whenever we get caught up in one psychological state or another, we want to figure out what it means. We don't see that if we start out with something limited, we have little hope of getting it to add up to anything expansive or intelligent. It's like my daddy used to tell me, "Boy, if you ask a stupid question, you'll get a stupid answer."

Some people feel there is a lot to be learned from the pain and trauma they have experienced. To me, this is like asking whether we can learn a lot from chasing our tails. If they ever develop an Olympic gold medal in tail-chasing, we may be well trained for it. But in most of our explorations of trauma we are simply dissecting ourselves into little pieces. We shred our integrity in pursuing the meaning we believe the trauma holds for us. Ultimately most trauma has no meaning at all. The only thing to be learned from it is that it is readily dissolvable.

Indeed, trauma is a natural part of our lives. Any healthy, living thing takes trauma and structures it into its own expression, just as our systems do with any nourishment. Our real concern, therefore, must be not for going through the trauma and picking it apart — indeed, that always strikes me as a little bit like picking through our morning constitutional to see what lessons we can learn about ourselves from the dinner we had last night. Better just to pull the chain and get on with the next thing.

When we become fascinated with what we perceive to be the complexity of our different psychological states, we should realize that we have taken a wrong turn into a form of self-deception. When we pick up on some complex idea that catches our attention, we set off in pursuit, only to find, as we follow it, that it moves from complexity to ultimate density. Complexity naturally leads to crystallization and contraction — indeed, to a kind of a black hole. Only when things are simple are they clear and the real brilliance of Life revealed. Only then do we appreciate the self-regenerating quality of that brilliance.

But what about, ... but what about, ... but what about...? Well, what about it? When things start to get complicated, it is better to relax, be simple, and see what happens next.

The creative energy of Life cuts both ways. This means that its nature is both expansive and contractive. We may think that we have not experienced this directly but, in fact, it constitutes one of the things we struggle with every day. I say this because in us, these contractions express themselves as tensions. We give each of them a different name, whether it be anger, fear, desire, or pain, and we look for ways to avoid them.

What if we were to say, instead, that *all* tension is only something for us to rise above? A person whose awareness is really centered recognizes the value of both pleasure and pain. When we are there in the middle, we see that truth contains both the highest pleasure as well as the greatest pain. Here is the paradox:

Truth is at once something extraordinary and joyous and something intensely painful. How do we wrap our minds around that? We cannot build walls to separate the discussion of pleasure from the discussion of pain because they are two sides of the same coin.

It is like trying to make an absolute separation between male and female. It is difficult. We cannot have day without night, there is no good without evil, and there is no justice without injustice. When one arises, its opposite automatically arises as well. This means that we have to be careful not to lock ourselves into one side of a situation or another, not recognizing that, underlying it all, there is only one essential thing and that in that unity, all opposites support each other.

Whenever we hear ourselves saying "either/or," we can be reasonably sure we are on the wrong track. We are framing our thoughts in such a way that we can only end up with some kind of alienation. Reality is never either/or; it is always both. When we see beyond the dichotomies and the dualities to the fundamental essence of our own Self — to our own, innate sense of well-being — we begin to have the capacity to extend our awareness of that well-being beyond the various psychological states. Then, increasingly, we allow this awareness to become the lens through which we view all things, instead of fogging it with the distractions of duality — the idea that there are many things instead of only One.

Often, when we are caught up in a particular frame of mind, we experience it as something that takes us over, as something about which we have no real choice. However, when we talk about releasing tensions and allowing the creative energy to flow, we are also talking about expanding our free power of choice. Implicit in the term "creative energy" is the free power of choice because power and choice are two additional ways of expressing the same thing.

Why is this issue of choice important in the discussion of psychological states? A sutra in the text *Pratyabhijnahridayam* states that the Self "By the power of her own will (alone), unfolds the universe upon her own screen (*i.e.* in herself as the basis of the universe)."[1] One analogy to this is the way waves move through a medium. Waves in the ocean move through water; sound waves move through space. Light waves, however, move through the vacuum of deep space in which there *is* no medium. They do this by projecting a magnetic field which then becomes the field through which they move. In other words, the light wave first projects itself, and then manifests itself on its own screen.

In our own case, we project our lives onto a screen of our own making. We have the freedom to choose what our lives will be and are responsible for what we choose. This doesn't mean that we are able to do so without pressures or constraints. Consider the example of a tree. Every tree is an expression of two things: the articulation of the creative power of the seed and the limitations of the environment in which it springs up. A tree has a remarkable capacity to grow, but its form expresses the constraints of its place in time and space. Nevertheless, each tree strives continually to take advantage of every opportunity within its environment.

Similarly, in our own case, social and economic factors certainly affect the range across which our choices can express themselves. They never, however, alter our fundamental freedom to choose. Everything in our lives organizes itself around us according to the vibration, or the frequency, that we are. No matter what the feeling — anger, sadness, sexual desire, joy, or longing — every feeling is nothing but a frequency, an energy with a particular vibration.

We have the absolute power to choose the vibration that we are and will be. In this way, we choose our lives — not because we choose all the details, but because we choose the frequencies upon which we will broadcast. We attract whatever resonates with these frequencies and, from there, everything else follows in a continuum. Just as the individualized comes forth from the divine and the personal comes forth from the individualized, so our personal lives come forth from us. In this way, the energy continually unfolds itself.

If we consume ourselves in thinking about problems, we will set up within ourselves vibrations that end up justifying our initial concerns. This is so because we attract to ourselves whatever concerns us and whatever we fear. Whatever vibrations we allow to fill us are what we magnetize to flow within our environment. Instead of recognizing this, however, we usually say, "Ahhh, I was right all along. I knew this was going to happen."

Yet the world is not thrust upon us. We unfold from within ourselves whatever our experience will be. When we understand this, we begin to recognize that all psychological states are only manifestations of the frequency upon which we are broadcasting the creative energy of our lives. We can choose at any point to go beyond our personal histories. To think otherwise is to buy into the constraints and spend our energy on them.

In our experience of the world, our self-awareness is the power that enables us to recognize the places we have already been so that we don't have to travel the same roads again. It is what keeps us from making the same mistakes over and over again. Our lack of self-awareness, on the other hand, is what causes us to step in every possible pile of fear, anxiety, self-denial, and desire lying there on the sidewalk.

We step in these piles when we fail to see that all psychological states have their foundation in desire and in a sense of purpose: We want something we don't have, or we want to protect what we do have. I would contend, however, that we are as close to eternity in this very moment as we will ever be. This being so, then what discussion can we have about wanting or protecting anything? Likewise, what discussion of gain and loss is possible? How can there be more or less of anything?

Authentic happiness is within us at all times, unaffected by any of our experiences. It is within us, simply and purely. This means that all our feelings of lack and inadequacy — the roots of the different psychological states — are simply a part of our ego. The ideas and feelings we sustain that tell us we are lacking in something, or that we are not good enough, are all expressions of our resistance to the work it takes to cultivate that self-awareness.

It is a little like strengthening our muscles. Everybody *has* muscles, but the real question is whether we will choose to do the work it takes to develop them, or whether we are going to sit around groaning about how weak we are. The fact is that we tend to moan and groan about what is missing in our lives when, in fact, nothing is. The moaning and groaning is just our strategy to avoid the work, and we all get into it.

The work, however, is utterly simple. It involves nothing more than determining to be authentically happy, no matter what happens in our lives. No matter what. This determination then requires us to think, speak, and act in ways that promote this happiness within us, enable us to extend our participation in this state, and allow others to enter into it.

We usually feel as though there are many things we want. Our desire for these things obscures our awareness of the biggest thing we can hope to attain, which is also the simplest experience from which everything else flows. Being filled with strong desires for one thing or another, how can we be aware of anything else within us? We have no room to be filled with anything new.

It is a law of the universe that whatever is empty becomes full. If we are filled with and consumed by any psychological state, we cannot grow because growing involves first being empty and then being filled with something different. When we empty ourselves of our tensions and worries, we allow something different to fill us. For that matter, we don't even worry about what fills us, we just concern ourselves with being empty.

Of course, emptiness and uncertainty are somewhat the same thing, and this will tend to make us nervous until we recognize that uncertainty means every possibility remains open. It means we stand at the edge of our freedom to choose among many potential outcomes. It brings us back to the fact that each and every one of us is essentially free. We can do whatever we want.

At the same time, every action has its natural consequences. As we do whatever we want, certain lines of behavior will unfold more choices for us and promote our essential freedom while other choices will confine that freedom, causing our world to condense and collapse around us. After a while, we are either living in the awareness of our freedom or are trapped in an existence that has become a prison. This is not because we started out with any particular advantages or disadvantages. It is not because our mothers abused us, or our fathers were drunks, or any other such reason. It is only because we choose the form we give to our freedom.

Once we choose to cultivate the highest creative capacity within ourselves and do so with an interest in the balance between ourselves and the lives that our lives touch, we gain insight into both the nature of balance and the limits of our flexibility and freedom. Our deepening insight, in turn, allows us more choices, promoting diversity and creativity in our lives. We recognize that doing whatever we want indiscriminately only denies us the opportunity for growing. This is natural.

We also recognize that when we have value for our energy and for our lives, we invest ourselves well in the opportunities that endlessly present themselves to us. It doesn't matter whether we were born into a wealthy family or a poor one — people born high can fall, and people born low can rise. It does have everything to do with how we use our creative energy.

Only when we cultivate the conscious energy and power of self-awareness do we make choices that promote our own happiness and the happiness of those around us. By extending our own access to that state of happiness and promoting it as an atmosphere within and around us, we enable an inner mechanism to begin to function openly, naturally, and completely all of the time. This, too, is a natural process.

When we stop everything else and simply become centered inside, our lives can release their creative power — an energy which has been present in us all along. That power will guide us, teach us, and reveal to us both its own nature and the structure of self-expression appropriate to our existence. We don't have to struggle over it; it simply shows itself.

That is why the philosophers of India called this power the Self. It is in us and yet it is also, ultimately, beyond anything we can identify as our finite selves. It has nothing to do with our personalities or our egos, our bodies or our minds. At the same time, it is intimately a part of us. The experience of it propels us to an awareness that goes beyond our bodies, minds, and emotions. It goes beyond every psychological state and has everything to do with the creative power that is our own essence. In this we learn to trust.

Someone asked me once whether I thought anything at all was important. I said, "Yes, love is important. Nothing else, just love." I say this because anything else will be the basis for some difficulty in our lives. The fact of the matter is that the creative energy of Life Itself within us has only potentiality and is always available. As I said earlier, it has no inherent problem — the Self has no problem. Consequently, neither do we.

We can either complain about how hard our lives are and tell one person after another how upset we are, or we can sit down and open ourselves to changing the vibration within us. When we can do the latter, we magnetize an entirely different experience within and around us. We allow our lives to become transformed. We have to make a definite effort to do so, but it is nevertheless a simple thing. With this understanding, everything within and around us can change and we discover that every human being is essentially unlimited.

In a simple way, our work in this life is to open ourselves, to feel the creative flow within us and, from that state, to digest the substance of all experience. In so doing, we rise to a level where we have transcended every kind of psychological conditioning. We recognize the complete temporariness of all psychological states. We reside instead in our awareness of the potential inherent in Life Itself within us, and of its constant availability.

By taking our attention inside and directing our awareness to that within us which is more than our bodies and our minds, we experience a profound joy. Abhinavagupta describes it as being different from the joy we feel in union with a lover. He says that it is more subtle than that. It is not like the joy of any worldly experience, but more like the joy we experience when we lay down a heavy burden. Then the mind rests within the Self.

The point is to find well-being within ourselves — to be at peace within ourselves and to share that peace with everyone. Repeatedly, we will face challenges to that peace, yet if we can think, speak, and act from that state, we will express it clearly, even in the face of great difficulty. It is in doing this that our understanding becomes strong and powerful.

Our lives will never go where we think they ought to. Fortunately, if we allow it, they will go in a direction much better than anything we could ever have imagined for ourselves. This is why it is a good thing to be as quiet as we can and look to the creative power within us that is the source of both our distress and our relief. When we let that creative power work in us, it is the same thing as saying, "Thy will be done." It will be, anyway, so we might as well relax.

PERSONAL HISTORY

When you look in a mirror,
you see yourself, not the state of the mirror.
The fluteplayer puts breath into a flute,
and who makes the music? Not the flute.
The Fluteplayer!

. . . When you eventually see
through the veils to how things really are,
you will keep saying again
and again,
  "This is certainly not like
we thought it was!"

— RUMI

I have a keen interest in history and enjoy reading about it. The two kinds I find particularly intriguing, though, are military and religious history. One reason I like them is that you can pretty well follow the strand of one along through the other, because they are often closely related.

The most fascinating historical discussion I have encountered recently was a study of the Bible and history.[2] What caught my attention was the author's claim that there seems to be no archaeological evidence supporting the notion that six hundred thousand Jews exited from Egypt and wandered in the Sinai desert. While the author makes no definitive claims that the Exodus never happened, he does raise interesting questions about the nature of the evidence upon which the historical accounts are based.

In keeping with the same discussion, the author also points out that Christmas originated as the festival of Sol Invictus, a principal god of the Roman legions, rather than being the celebration of the actual birth of Jesus. The emperor Constantine proclaimed that day as the birthday of Jesus to placate the army and maintain their support for his efforts to establish Christianity as the dominant religion in his empire. Thus, the historical Jesus was merged with the sun god.

Various historians have concluded that the only parts of the four Gospels in the New Testament that can be attributed to Jesus with real certainty are the Parables and some of the Sayings. The other parts of the Gospels seem to consist of stories pulled together by different early Christian writers as literary documents with theological tendencies, in some cases aimed to respond to the concerns of specific communities.[3]

What interests me about these discussions is that any religious tradition can have, at the core of what it celebrates, events that possibly never happened at all, or at least not as the tradition has come to portray them. I find it quite wonderful to see how the world knits itself together — how literally millions of people base their lives and their entire existences on doctrine, dogma, and history that may never actually have taken place as we are taught they did.

This doesn't mean that these stories haven't been important to people over the centuries. It doesn't falsify the experiences people have had in relation to them. Since such issues do permeate the entire history of civilization, however, it does bring us to a profound recognition of the questionable reliability of historical accounts.

History, for the most part, is a fiction fabricated by people over time to maintain a sense of continuity which, itself, may also be a fiction. When we read it, we come to recognize that much of it is a mix of bias and speculation. Personally, I find it interesting to try to sense the flow of it, to get a feel for what kinds of developments dominate the account, and to see what pieces don't fit the picture.

These days, in our search to know who we are, great emphasis is placed on exploring our past. We are encouraged to seek the roots of our misfortune and unhappiness in that past. We learn to look for the ways in which these roots may express themselves in the limitations of our relationships with others, in the limitations of others themselves, and even in what we think of as our own limitations.

Yet, as I compare our personal histories with history as a whole, it seems to me that much of this personal history is equally fictitious. We decide — in hindsight — what spin to put on the experiences we have had. We decide what the flavor of one experience or another might really have been and in what way the experiences that compose our lives are linked together.

When we look at all of this carefully, however, our interpretation often has little to do with actual fact — if, indeed, there is such a thing. More often, our account reflects the perspective of some stage in our maturing, and possibly a lack of maturity. The "facts" themselves remain obscure. The dramatic events we identify as turning points in our lives — the ones we blame for having made us the sad creatures that we are — never happened as we think they did.

We weave the fabric of our history into an artistic creation that explains and justifies our sense of a present we experience as limited. Instead of learning to live happily with the ephemeral nature of our own existence, we buy into the propaganda our egos promote concerning the importance of our lives — and much of our account *is* actually our personal propaganda. There is nothing wrong with this, but we might also want to acknowledge that our version of our lives falls short of the real thing. As long as we buy into the stories we tell ourselves and everybody else, we prevent ourselves from seeing the limited nature of the program we are operating on.

As long as we hold on to these fictitious versions of how things were, we can anticipate little real change in our lives. By "change," I mean that we will not grow. We may modify our exterior — this week dressed one way, that week dressed another — but every week and every day we will remain charlatans and rogues, people hiding from and deceiving ourselves. After all, we never deceive anyone but ourselves; everybody else manages to see us quite clearly.

From the point of view of growing, our personal history is beside the point — it is, in fact, an obstruction. To grow in a real way is to drop our identification with this history and appreciate, instead, the dynamic, creative power at work in all of our history. We need not judge whether one part or another is good or bad. There is no possibility of our ever making complete sense of any of it and no point in trying to evaluate it one way or the other — "I did this good thing," or "I did that bad thing." "This was a turning point, but that was a waste." "I am a genius," or "I am terrible." Such thinking is the mill that keeps us going up and down, around and around, a prisoner in the stream of experience.

There is also nothing in history itself — no substance and no information — that can guide us to the experience of our complete fulfillment. When we turn to it looking for this, it becomes a justification for the betrayal of our own creative potential. If we are serious about growing — if we intend to learn to manage change well and discover our real potential as people, then it becomes necessary for us to go beyond this history.

In India, people who are serious about doing spiritual work eventually leave their families and their homes. They travel, staying in no one place for more than three days. They do this because, in seeking out the divine, they are also trying to articulate the importance of transcending their personal identities and histories.

This is not to say that it is either possible or necessary for us to leave our homes and go wandering; it *is* to say that we might want to take another look at the meaning we assign to our past. There is no need for us to deny our experiences or run away from them but, if we care about growing, we must come to have a deeply open mind toward all experience. This alone will allow us to absorb as nourishment the various things that happen to us. From this we grow.

Think about someone like Rudi, who came from extremely difficult circumstances. Had he been willing to circumscribe his horizons according to the opportunities provided by his background, he would never have become the extraordinary person he did. However, his powerful commitment to his own growth nullified every effect of his personal history. It need be no different for any of us.

When I say to people that we can let go of our history, one question they sometimes ask is, "But what about the lessons of history? Can't we learn anything from these?" I would say, "Yes, and no." In one sense, hopefully we get to a point where we see the accident coming down the road and, because we have lived through that wreck before, move out of the way. This is known as rising above the tensions in our lives and is a progressive use of our experience.

At the same time, we can also fool ourselves into thinking we understand a situation merely because it resembles a previous one. For example, Rudi once received a letter that was somewhat weird, and he burned it. Several weeks later *I* received a weird letter, so I also burned it, just as Rudi had done. I was proud of myself and told Rudi about it. This was one of the few times in my association with him where he became genuinely angry with me. "You dumb-ass," he said, "if I wanted my students to act like me, I would go to the zoo and get a bunch of monkeys. I could train *them* to behave exactly like me."

I never forgot this incident. It taught me that when we imitate someone else's example without being completely open to the nature of a particular moment, we are likely to mishandle the whole thing. Whenever we try to confine the present within the resolutions of the past, we overlook the uniqueness and the potential inherent in the present.

This is not to say we cannot be inspired by the spirit of great people but, when we think about imitating their example, we have to be extremely careful about what we mean. Never should we use it as an excuse for not opening our hearts to whatever we face. With regard to a teacher, a real student does not imitate the form of the teacher or his or her behavior. This is stupidity. A real student knows and lives in the state of the teacher.

Likewise, we can misjudge an event if something painful we have experienced in the past bears a resemblance to it. This can cause us to respond not to the person or situation in front of us, but to the memory we project onto it. We then close ourselves off from a potentially wonderful experience. The point is that when our hearts are truly open, *they* will tell us all we need to know about any situation in which we find ourselves.

One of my concerns about our dependence on our personal history involves those relationships in which we have some kind of ongoing exchange. Such exchange is almost always obstructed by the history of the relationship, expressed in our need to keep score. Have you noticed how relationships can be totally destroyed by this need for *quid pro quo*? What is really an opportunity for love and nourishment can rapidly deteriorate into a morass of tensions and confusion because we allow the history of the relationship — even if it happened only five minutes before — to undermine the potential for its development.

I suspect that you may be saying to yourself, "How simple-minded that is. He can't possibly know what a hell my life was, growing up. How am I supposed to forget what my mother did to me, or what my father didn't do for me? I am the product of that background." We have all had the experience of being upset and of going to the personal history library to check out a book or two to entertain ourselves. We look through the volumes on psychological states and on relationships. If neither of these does it for us, we turn to ancient history: Then it's time for the volumes on parents and other close relations.

I am saying, though, that at every moment we create our own lives. At no time are we defined by any past choice if we now choose to do something differently. When we simply drop our disappointment, anger, bitterness, and grief, we free the creative energy we have tied up in these tensions over the years. If we can do that, then change becomes a fabulous adventure.

If we don't take it personally, Life is also a fabulous adventure. However, if we insist on personalizing it, Life basically becomes a seventy-year tour of the Bastille. While I think that everybody ought to see the Bastille once for ten minutes, after that, we have done it already! What is it but an empty prison, the relic of another fiction.

There is no real way to keep score. We simply cannot know. A person's life is a whole textile, a whole fabric. Which knot is good and which one is not, which thread is strong and which is not — who can say? They all weave together. Often, the things we thought were mistakes were not and the ones we thought were good also were not. Over and over again, we see that our lives — the actual flow of our experiences — run counter to our intuition.

If we insist on keeping scores and accounts, we cannot but lose. In the process, we deny ourselves the possibility of the truly extraordinary lives that are trying to come forth from within us. Yet, if we can manage our disappointments carefully, we allow ourselves to see that maybe we had the wrong idea about something in the first place. The need to blame or abuse ourselves slips away. We have no further need to say things like, "Here I am repeating the same pattern of failure again — a pattern undoubtedly visited upon me by my father or mother because *they* had parents who were unloving, and so felt the uncontrollable urge to brutalize me — and that is why *I* am such a mess and so terrible to everyone else."

This is not to say that either we or the people we have known have not experienced difficult times; it *is* to say that we can release every one of them. There are neither good nor bad people in our past — there are only people like us, struggling (sometimes inappropriately) to know what it is to be good people and to experience their highest potential. We release them and dismiss our fictions from our awareness with love — we simply send them packing. We can see the whole thing as a wonderful drama or perhaps a poem, if we wish; we can think of it as a picture to take down and put in the closet.

Release those people you feel have done you harm and those whom you feel that you have harmed, and experience in this release the possibility for infinite growth and reorganization.

Only when we consume life with all its tensions and joys can we dissolve the tensions, transcend the particular circumstances, and discover the infinite nature of our individual consciousness. This requires effort. Yet, is it not true that an effort we undertake for someone we love, or a long journey we make to visit a real friend, represent no difficulty at all? Rather, the whole event is a joyous occasion. So it is when we discover the essence of our own existence. It is a joyous occasion from start to finish.

Think of it this way: When you are fully open to love, how much are you thinking about the past? When we love, we simply love. The depth of our love takes us beyond the tensions, the dilemmas, the difficulties, and the disappointments that usually crowd their way into our attention. Then, instead of getting lost in our tensions or imposing them on everyone around us, we find that everything we say and do is flavored with our love.

This has nothing to do with our history. Nor is it a theoretical statement about ethical behavior. Rather, it is a description of how we experience the world as we come to know the Self. As we recognize the fundamental love that we are, we become able to absorb the nourishment and the real exchange that exist in every relationship, and we allow these to expand the breath of Life within our own life. This is the wonderful release.

Tensions And Creative Energy

THE CURE FOR THE PAIN IS IN THE PAIN

We are the mirror as well as the face in it.
We are tasting the taste this minute
of eternity. We are the pain
and what cures pain, both. We are
the sweet, cold water and the jar that pours.

— RUMI

The world is not a happy place and people, in general, are not a happy group of beings. Life is so full of change and heartbreak that the only extraordinary thing about it is our surprise every time these things happen. I suppose we are surprised because we work so hard to avoid them and to protect our egos in the process. We would prefer to think that anything but a heartbreak is happening, for example, because the worst moment in a heartbreak comes when we see the amount of time we have spent covering up and justifying something we have known for a long time. If nothing else, it is embarrassing to look back and see how much we resisted change.

Some people, when change overtakes them, look for a way to kill the pain that goes along with it. Why do people drink? To make themselves numb. It escapes them that not only does drinking numb them to pain; it also makes them numb to joy. Furthermore, it kills them. The same is true of cigarettes and drugs. When such things become our strategy for addressing change and pain, what begins as a way of dulling our perception of specific situations gradually takes over our capacity for clear vision in all areas of our lives.

Of course, we can always read our painful experiences as confirmations of what we already suspected — that there really *is* something wrong with us. Then, when painful things come up we close down our minds, our guts, and everything else inside. That's how many of us construct our lives. We go along, trying to figure out how to fix what we're quietly sure is wrong but without ever wanting to expose ourselves too much, because the exposure could be too unbearable.

On the other hand, when we allow ourselves to be dominated by the pressure of the pain, we are unable to see even one foot in front of us to know where we are really going. This is what makes us run around in circles as though we had one foot nailed to the floor. Then what happens? We get tired and sit down. Our foot may still be nailed to the floor, but at least we are not running around in circles any more. And we think that's dealing with the pain.

Whenever we struggle with pain, we are expressing our wish that it would just go away. Since life is inherently painful, however, the pain is here to stay. Furthermore, this is not a bad thing. The life that seasonally rushes into plants also breaks them open and transforms them. In our case, that pain — that surge of life — is what purifies and refines us. It will destroy all our self-imposed notions of limitation if we can be calm in the face of it. Only if we let it make us crazy does it strengthen our sense of limitation. This is why even wishing for the pain to stop is a trap.

It is not easy to say to someone in pain that inside the pain there resides something joyful, but you yourself know that pain and joy are never far apart. Thus, is it not possible that pain and joy are two sides of the same coin, and that what we experience depends on our response to change? Hidden in joy there is always a little pain, just as hidden in pain there is always a little joy. The two things are commingled.

There is a tree out in the corner of our yard that I have admired for a long time. Looking at it, you can see the pain it must have endured and still endures in just *being*. It is gnarled and turned and twisted, and its guts are all eaten out — it is over a hundred years old — yet somehow the life in it prevails.

Every time we grow, we split our skins — and we are growing all the time, or we would not be alive. How can that always be pleasant? It is not. Discomfort in life is just a part of the package. Nor is this a new insight. Some twenty-five hundred years ago, the Buddha described the Four Noble Truths in his spiritual manifesto. The first Noble Truth is that Life is suffering — *dukkha*, or pain.

The whole point of spirituality, and what has kept spiritual traditions in the forefront of all human endeavor throughout history, has been the opportunity it gives a person to experience and live from something deeper within oneself. It is the opportunity to relate to Life as more than just our bodies slugging it out in the trenches of the workplace everyday; more than two people or a hundred people living together. It is the chance to grow.

There is something within each of us that is beyond life and death as we understand these — something beyond our existence here and now. That something is the Self. It is accessible to each of us and we can experience it directly. As we learn to live from it, we find that slowly it rearranges our whole mind and how we think about everything.

To be in touch with the Self frees us. It does not give us the answers, but it does arouse within us the strength to go through the pain, to grow from all experience, and to understand, finally, what pain is. In this way, we find an inner stability so that, no matter what changes occur in our lives, we are also aware of an underlying continuity. This is not necessarily a continuity of form but rather one of substance, of spirit, that allows us to build upon each level of the experiences that we undergo.

As our capacity for tuning into and feeling our inner Self expands, each level of experience becomes more meaningful to us as a stepping stone to greater and greater refinement. Because of our connection to and participation in the broadest perspective of Life Itself, we are not deterred by our own or any other pain. We are freed from a reactionary existence — free to explore our re-creative capacity and free to know our infinite potential for renewal.

Pain is your best friend. It is infinitely more honest with you than pleasure. Despite what you might think, the painful experiences you have had benefit you far more than the pleasurable ones, even though most of us spend our lives trying to duck and hide from them. But when you can center yourself and be open to look pain dead in the eye then you have transcended the limits of your ego and this humanity. It is then that you enter into the possibility of becoming a great being.

The truly great people in this world know pain well and have no issue with it. They know that all pain is an opportunity to love both more widely and more deeply. Rudi used to say that pain is God's love. It is the creative power of Life Itself expanding us from within. Of course it hurts! That is inevitable. Moreover, as long as we think of ourselves in terms of our bodies, our minds, and our emotions, pain is going to be the limit of our ability to grow. But once we understand ourselves as nothing less than creative energy, what can truly hurt us?

No one has a storybook life. Only in storybooks are there storybook lives. For that matter, I don't know what a normal life is. I would go as far as to say that there is no such thing, and hallelujah! A normal life has got to be as ordinary as mud. What we really want is a wonderful life. That, however, requires a capacity to absorb heartbreak, to eat the pain we run up against, and to build upon our life experience by cultivating stability of mind and good judgment. Mostly, this takes work, and mostly, it will be a *lot* of work — and it's even more work after that. Nevertheless, it is a work that brings us a wealth within ourselves that most people can't begin to imagine.

There are two ways to go through life. We can work hard, endure a lot of pain, and die miserable, or we can work hard, endure a lot of pain, and be free. The choice is ours. We can shatter under the heartbreak, or we can examine it carefully and try to understand it for what it is.

Instead of shattering — and there are infinite reasons for shattering — we can simply rise above the pain. Through our wish to grow and our commitment to doing so, through practicing our awareness of our breathing, through taking our attention within ourselves, through the cultivation of good judgment, and through our work with a teacher, we learn to rise above it. Then, it does not limit us in the slightest.

Everybody's life is hard. We can look at many of the painful experiences we have had and see that, to some extent, we have been in pain for a number of years. We may have had a parent die; perhaps someone we loved deserted us. All of this is undeniably tough, and there is no way to avoid it. Life *is* a continuous heartbreak. This is nobody's fault; it is just the way things are. It becomes a bad thing only when we allow the pain to crystallize inside us and turn into something other than love.

To rise above our suffering is real detachment. Detachment does not mean being removed from a situation; it means accepting what is there and not denying or suppressing anything, including our own feelings. Instead, we consciously and with full awareness face every circumstance that presents itself. This is the ultimate position of strength. Indeed, there is no greater strength in the whole universe than detachment. A person who can undertake it has the opportunity to live from the sweetness that is at the very core of our being.

To be detached is to see things as they are, not as we might wish they were. It rests in accepting the reality of pain — not in resisting it, not in trying to get an angle on it, not in trying to finesse it, but in just accepting it and allowing it to burn through us. To do this *and* choose to be happy, even as the pain passes through us — this is what changes us deeply and opens us completely.

Paradoxically, this is also what frees us from the pain and releases our deepest creativity and understanding. One of my favorite poets, the Sufi teacher Rumi, writes:

> ... *Stretch your arms and take hold of the cloth of your clothes*
> *with both hands. The cure for pain is in the pain.*
> *Good and bad are mixed. If you don't have both,*
> *you don't belong with us.*

When we accept our pain, it can nourish us. When we fight it, it only becomes another brick in the wall that isolates us from ourselves.

Nothing, at our core, is ever damaged by anything that happens to us. Only the surface gets scarred. If we live on the surface, of course, we live with all the scars. So, better to go deep inside. Being detached and being able to enter directly into our pain are one and the same thing. Both are ways of accepting the presence of pain in our lives. When we deal with it directly, we face the fact that it is *not* comfortable, and we take responsibility for it. For a few moments, for a few hours, or even for a few days, weeks, or years, our discomfort might increase. What is sometimes hard to see is that, compared with the deeper benefits we experience, it is no discomfort at all.

When we open ourselves to pain — when we stop resisting it and just accept it — we learn to live beyond it. It is a little bit like trying to tame a thirty-eight foot python. This takes a lot of work, but it can be done. Shall I tell you the secret? In the first place, there may be no way to avoid getting wrapped up in the python's coils. So, when it has us bound and is starting to squeeze, the best thing to do is relax completely and play dead. Then, it lets us go. Likewise, in the face of pressure and pain, if we can stop struggling with our fear, doubt, insecurity, and any other form the pain may take, we will feel something more deeply within us starting to work. Slowly, we realize that we can choose to be happy.

Before you decide that this sounds too corny to be real, consider giving it a try. Starting with that decision to be happy, regardless of what is going on, we see that everything around us begins to look different. As it begins to *look* different, gradually it *becomes* different. Because we have allowed the light to come forth from within us and dispel the darkness, we can then see the reality of the situation. We can see its future and its past.

We accept our pain with our whole heart. We don't express it or resist it; we do surrender to it. The inner fire that we feel when we do so is the power of love at work within us, transforming our tensions and resistance into pure consciousness. Surrendering to this process takes us above all difficulty and beyond all blame. It allows the event to show us the direction we must take in order to put our life together. Then, somehow it happens.

To me, this is always an amazing thing. Again and again I see people who have been beaten down and broken, yet who experience profound transformation as a result. This is the true power of love — a power which unfolds Itself as endless renewal and regeneration. When we learn to live our lives according to the direction of this love, we understand what it means to grow; we discover that this love is who we are.

STILLING THE MIND

*The human mind is not capable of grasping the universe.
We are like a little child entering a huge library. The walls
are covered to the ceiling with books in many different
tongues. The child knows that someone must have written
these books. It does not know who or how. It does not
understand the languages in which they are written. But the
child notes a definite plan in the arrangement of the books —
a mysterious order which it does not comprehend but only
dimly suspects.[4]*

— ALBERT EINSTEIN

Some of the most modern learning techniques have been
designed to take advantage of the pattern recognition capabilities
of the mind. The idea is to extend these capabilities both to correct known patterns and to create more comprehensive ones. In
this whole process, though, the mind itself can go only so far.
Even at their best, the patterns and models the mind constructs
are inherently limited. Any one of them necessarily selects certain aspects of reality and passes over the rest, making them only
partial representations of the whole.

The constant jumping around of the mind draws us away
from our relationship to our deepest inner Self. This is why Rudi
used to say that the mind is the slayer of the soul — it is the root
of our basic misunderstanding. Moreover, the nature of the mind
never changes. We can refine it to a certain point, but beyond that
we are still talking about a cloud of swirling gas that prevents us
from seeing reality as it is. Only when the mind is quiet does reality become apparent.

When I say "reality," I am talking about Life as the dynamic
ground of all events. When we learn to quiet our minds, suddenly
the nature of this reality dawns on us and we say, "Oh, of course!"
This is why quieting the mind is the essence of spiritual growth.

In the *Dhammapada*, an early Buddhist scripture, the Buddha is quoted as saying, "A person on a battlefield who conquers an army of a thousand is a great person, but a person who conquers himself is greater still." He is talking about the struggle to conquer the mind. In early Hindu texts, the mind is compared to the horses that pull a chariot. If the horses are not disciplined and guided, they run wildly in all directions.

It is as if the mind had two poles — one in the left ear, the other in the right — with all kinds of impulses going back and forth between them all the time. Disciplining the mind means freeing ourselves from all this static. "Disciplining the mind" is not the same thing, however, as what is sometimes referred to as "controlling the mind." For example, trying to control our thoughts makes little sense. It is somewhat like trying to control the waves on the surface of the ocean. First of all, it is not possible and, second, it is not necessary. Keeping the mind quiet does not mean that the wheels in there stop turning. It does mean that we keep out of the grip of the cogs as they engage.

Disciplining the mind involves becoming aware of all the pathways down which we allow it to travel. Discrimination, a willingness to question, and some value for our time eliminate the need to go down too many different dead-ends. We find that there are many places we choose not to go simply because we no longer have the time or can see on the front side that the experience itself is not valuable.

It can take us a while to develop this discipline. In the beginning, we often experience the sudden sense that we need something or someone, and we feel moved to go out and get the one or the other. Sometimes when we do this we meet with a certain easy flow and think, "Oh, I must have found what I was looking for!" This is not necessarily true. The things we flow with easily are often reflections of what we already are, not of what we might become.

As we train ourselves to recognize this, there should come a time when we can hear our mind starting to rev up again, and say to ourselves, "Wait just a minute. This is a road I've travelled before, and I *know* there's a brick wall at the end of it. If I have to go at all, at least let me go slowly." We begin to have a degree of self-awareness that allows us not to fall into the patterns of reaction to which we are accustomed.

This process is different from what is referred to as "controlling the mind." If you learn to direct your attention — which is also energy — in appropriate ways, there is no issue of mind control, of stopping your thoughts, or of anything else like that. Rather, what you are doing is learning to see underneath the thoughts to the vitality which is the source of their existence. If you can see and experience the energy that generates the thoughts, then the thoughts themselves become only so much static.

No mental state is either the source or the cause of anything else. It is only an effect of something deeper. Every mental state arises in the mind, which arises from something else, which in turn arises from something else. This means that if our attention becomes utterly one-pointed — intensely focused on *anything* — ultimately, our awareness traces its way back to that something else which is the source of it all.

Not surprisingly, some points of focus represent a more direct way to understanding this source. Being one-pointed on cynicism or fear, for example, may not be fundamentally different from being one-pointed on love. Both can provide an intense focus. I would suggest, however, that a focus on cynicism or fear will put us through a lot more hoops before we come to understand what underlies either of them, and that a focus on love will get us there faster. Still, the main thing is to be one-pointed. In that one-pointedness, our mind becomes still and, eventually, the finitude of our cynicism, our fear, or whatever else we have chosen as a focus will become clear.

I cannot deny that I have opinions concerning what constitutes an effective approach. I have tried to do a certain kind of serious work in my own life, and my perspective derives from this work. I have found that certain points of focus are more effective than others.

At the same time, I also recognize that no judgments are appropriate in this regard. It is like this: If we talk about building a house together, I will probably tell you that it is simpler to use two-by-fours than rubber rods. I will say it is better to have a drawing on the front side than to make up the plans as we go along. This is my judgment, based on my own experience. At the same time, if someone feels the need to learn by testing these other options, that is fine, too.

It is true that I would much prefer to see you choose to focus your attention on love rather than on cynicism, fear, or anger. But if, for some reason a person can't be one-pointed on love — can't cultivate and work on trust, or deepen and build a commitment — then it is better to take the thing with which one *is* comfortable and be one-pointed about that. If what you can be one-pointed about is cynicism, then be one-pointedly cynical with full energy and concentration. The specific focus is not the issue. It can just as easily be parenthood, painting, sculpture, or music. Ultimately, it is the *practice* of being one-pointed that brings us to an understanding of what it means to grow and of what it means to quiet the mind.

If the function of the mind is to recognize patterns, then only when we quiet it do we allow it to do this most efficiently. In other words, the mind is not *only* an obstacle. Like everything, it cuts both ways. It is either a support or a resistance, just as all forces in nature are one or the other. But when we don't cultivate our intuition that there might be something more to everything than life and death in L.A., the mind is a deep resistance.

My own experience is that this quieting of the mind best takes place through meditation. By focusing on our breathing, by beginning to be aware of the subtle but extraordinarily powerful flow of energy within us, and by becoming aware of the nature of that energy, it is possible to still the mind and to understand that all of the noise going on in there is irrelevant. It becomes possible to develop the discrimination to know what is useful to pursue and what is not.

Basically, one of the characteristics of any misdirected focus — any obsession — is that the mind goes on endlessly without stopping, like a broken record stuck at the same place. Meditation occurs when we stop listening to the broken record and begin to pay attention to the electricity that allows the whole event to happen. In fact, both the record and the phonograph are expressions of that electricity.

When we look at the fundamental current that powers and allows the event to take place, the focus of our attention begins to shift to a deeper place within us, a place of vital stillness free of tension. It is also freed from identification with external judgments. It doesn't think, "I'm good, I'm bad — I'm stupid, I'm smart — I'm ugly, I'm beautiful — I'm rich, I'm poor." Instead, it thinks, "I *am*."

If we train ourselves to feel the energy of Life Itself within us, our analytical capability disengages for a time and stops being a problem as such. It is a problem only when that aspect of the mind dominates our awareness and we become impressed by its ability to do so. We get A's in school for being able to perform analytically, and our culture pays well for it. (Notice how people have only to tell us once or twice that we have a wonderful analytical mind, and suddenly we are trying to analyze everything from our first duty in the morning to our last duty at night.)

We are not trying to get rid of these analytical abilities, but only to put them into proper perspective — to find our balance within a broader frame of reference. Disengaging from our dependence on our analytical capability — or any other talent to which we are attached — is simply part of what we do to refine our awareness. We quiet the mind to give us greater skill in articulating our experience of what we can call pure beauty, truth, spirit, Presence, the highest Self, and even love. There are thousands of names we can call it and it is always present.

Unless we learn to expand our horizons beyond our minds, we remain handicapped, even crippled. By becoming aware of the mind's constantly changing nature, however, we can also become more circumspect about the thoughts that manifest in it. We can begin to step back from them instead of identifying with every one that springs up. The same is true of our feelings. We become able to question them and to develop a deeper sense of discrimination. The fulcrum point is this: Be quiet and don't worry.

There is an old story about a man who goes into the mountains to ask an aged *rishi*, or seer, "Will you tell me the secret of Life?" "Yes," the rishi says, "I will tell you the secret. It will bring you complete happiness and countless magical powers." Then he tells him the secret. But as the man is about to go, the rishi says, "Oh, by the way — whatever you do, when you start to meditate on the secret I've given you, be sure not to think about monkeys." Of course, that was all the man could think about for the next fifteen years. Only after he had learned to go beyond *that* was he able to think about the secret of Life unhindered. The point of the parable is to quiet the mind. Then, the secret of Life will explain itself to you.

What we strive for is to simplify ourselves. When we can do that just by being quiet, then whatever we are relating to automatically becomes simpler too. When we are caught up in complexity, we get absorbed by complexity. This is why, in every situation where we find ourselves over our heads, we have to go inside and become still.

When we recognize the wealth hidden in our souls, we no longer live in the poverty of our minds. Something changes in the process of moving from the shack to the mansion. Also, something stays the same. The difficulty of being human is the mind. The challenge of being human is also the mind. The effort of our spiritual work — our sadhana — is to still the mind. A person who stills the mind looks into the eyes of God.

~~~~~~

Allowing The Creative
Energy To Flow

*It is through the wisdom imparted by the Guru that one sees
the underlying unity in the infinite multiformity of
phenomena constituting the manifested universe . . . .
Until there is a meeting with the Guru, the see-er sees
the universe as the other; thereafter, the distinction
between the self and the other disappears.*

— JNĀNESHWAR

The Teacher

WHY A TEACHER?

A teacher is a person who has become established in the infinite nature of his or her individual awareness. He or she is one who demonstrates continuously, and in every connection, the great creative power that resides within that infinity. At the same time, an effective teacher is also a great student — one who is supremely and intensely committed to extending his or her contact with, and capacity for access to, this creative energy of Life. This is a person who has merged his or her awareness in the inner Self — indeed, "contact with" *means* merging one's individual awareness into the infinite Self. The life of such a person articulates and expresses this merging.

Thus, we can say that the teacher embodies the highest reality, which is both our own means and our own objective. It is the deep contact with such a teacher that nourishes us, releases the tensions within us, teaches us to still our minds, and allows our creative energy to flow. It enables us to recognize and experience the infinite nature of our individual consciousness, and to abide in the fullness therein.

It is like this: Whoever we associate with evokes in us a certain feeling, a certain vibration. The interaction generates a mindset — an attitude, a feeling, and a manner of expressing ourselves. The same holds true of our interchange with a teacher: The teacher draws from us an increasingly refined awareness of who we are — that is, of our highest Self. The process of drawing this from us strips away the boundaries and barriers that exist within us as part of our limitation and our misunderstanding.

How does a teacher do this? From the power of his or her own commitment to grow and to know God. The teacher serves God by releasing first his or her own tensions and then those of others, and by allowing the creative energy of Life to flow in all its freedom. Established in the understanding that everything is energy, and not limited by misunderstandings about his or her own finiteness, the teacher is able to reach into the student and dissolve the obstructions and blocks in the system. Doing so awakens a flow within the student.

This flow is nothing that the teacher adds or introduces. Rather, it is present in us all the time. The teacher merely clears out whatever is choking the stream, allowing it to run freely again. In doing this, the teacher arouses an awareness that is not possible to encompass with the mind, since the mind operates to define and defend boundaries. A teacher, on the other hand, dissolves these boundaries. Of course, the mind replaces them over and over again but the teacher cheats — every time he or she takes down a wall, the teacher also picks up a few extra bricks from the neighboring wall and carries them away at the same time.

This means that the whole fortress gets progressively smaller until finally, one day, we look around to rebuild and there are no more bricks. The walls are gone. Thus, it turns out to be a good thing that our minds cannot figure out all that fast what is going on: What they figure out, they only try all the harder to defend and resist.

This is why I have found a teacher to be necessary if we really want to grow. Until we are trained to do our inner work and dissolve our tensions ourselves, we tend to get stuck in one ditch or another, making for a fairly difficult ride. By dissolving our tensions while training us to do this for ourselves, a teacher allows us to have a more direct and sustained access to the energy of Life. The more we have contact with this, the more *it* becomes the immediate resource that enables us to do our inner work.

The teacher awakens this within us by sharing the fruits of his or her own experience. Through all the levels of our involvement with him or her, we literally ingest, absorb, and make this experience part of ourselves. When we can do this fully, we have the capacity to share the same experience with others.

This is what underlies any discussion of a teaching lineage. We are talking about a living essence that has been shared from teacher to student and from teacher to student over the years. This direct transmission is what makes the lineage vital. The personality of a given teacher simply reflects the vitality of the living lineage — that living energy field which is neither visible nor materialized, but remains tangible and palpable nevertheless.

The purpose of the teaching is to arouse within us the capacity to learn on a profound level. The teacher accepts us into his or her company, gives us love, deep friendship and nourishment, and arouses in us our true humanity — the capacity to love, to create, and to serve whatever situation we find ourselves in. Finally, through the transmission of his or her own essence, the teacher arouses within us the highest creative power, which is the possibility of knowing God.

This process of transmission is called *shaktipat*, a term sometimes translated as "the descent, or the emergence, of grace." It is also called "transmission of the teaching," that teaching being the direct experience of the highest state of consciousness. Abhinavagupta called it "the hand of Shiva."

What is shaktipat? It is the love that we experience in the teacher. Initially, we may not be aware of this love, even when we are in its presence. That is alright. If we had to be fully cognizant of it in the beginning, all of us would flunk. When I met Rudi I was aware that something pretty extraordinary was going on, and I knew how important it was to me, but that was all.

Prolonged contact with this love over time is the basis of our transformation. It is not something we can put a finger on precisely, but we are going to feel it strongly from time to time. Sometimes, it is gentle and warm; at other times, we feel as though we were a rabbit in the jaws of a mountain lion. In either case, we feel it, we know what is, and we know that it is changing us.

I distinguish between ordinary teachers and great teachers based on their mastery of shaktipat, just as I would distinguish between getting turned on and falling in love. There are a lot of pretty people and a lot of turn-ons in the world; still, when we find the real thing, we recognize it. Whether we have the courage to embrace it is another issue altogether, but we definitely recognize it. Qualitatively and quantitatively it is a different experience.

Unless there is someone in whom we can witness and experience this difference — someone who can arouse our interest, inform us, and support us as we develop the connections between our understanding and this experience and between our need and its fulfillment — no significant change is likely to happen. The teacher is indispensable in this process because what *does* the teaching is not the words but the contact. The teacher-student relationship is thus the foundation and the process that keep the student in contact with the energy.

This process, which can happen within us quickly, takes our minds years to grasp. This is so because our egos strive for a constant pattern of identity and resist change. It is really the spiritual communion — the merging of hearts and minds between student and teacher — which gives rise to an experience of a unity that transcends time, space, and all the ordinary limitations of structure that exist within relationships. By this I mean the limitations of motive and desire, of expectation and purpose.

Without the presence of a teacher, this experience does not happen. It is our direct interaction with the teacher that allows us to emerge with a deeper awareness of the possibilities that exist for us as students. It is then up to us to develop these possibilities and to come back again for nourishment, clarification, reinforcement, and an extension of the fundamental experience. Then the interaction as a whole becomes the message that is being conveyed.

In some traditions, the teacher might be conceived of as the objective or the goal of the search. He or she is the sun to whom everyone looks for light. The problem with this perspective, as I see it, is that anyone who stares at the sun too long goes blind. In the Kashmir Shaivite tradition, though, things get a little more down to earth. The teacher is the ground upon which we walk or stand. This is the soil from which we spring, and to which we ultimately return.

KNOWING A REAL TEACHER

People often think the physical teacher is the guru,
yet one does not become a guru by wearing orange robes
and wooden sandals or by using prayer-beads.
Preaching about the highest truth but giving the disciples
only stones is not the behavior of a guru.
Only he who lives by his teaching is the true guru.
Before teaching others, he must complete
his own spiritual practices and
attain Self-realization.
Only then can he prove the truth.

— NITYANANDA

As Life takes on form and structure, it becomes increasingly dense and contracted, like an iceberg in the ocean. The original, unbounded nature of each structure is veiled from itself as it identifies with its apparent limitations and not with the infinite from which it has emerged. So it is with us. Like so many icebergs, we go through our lives never aware that we are really the individualized expressions of infinite consciousness.

This infinite consciousness is also infinite freedom. This must be so because being infinite in its highest state, it is beyond all boundaries and limitations. Even when it takes on form and structure, its essential nature remains infinitely free. Moreover, it has an inherent impulse toward Self-liberation — that is, to become aware, even in its individualized form, of its own infinite nature.

Life has organized Itself in a way that creates a movement within us toward Self-liberation. One feature of this movement is that it attracts a qualified teacher to support its unfoldment. This is simply part of its process. So, one sign that it is occurring is the appearance and presence of a teacher.

I am reminded of a Tibetan Buddhist teacher of long ago who described such an opportunity as "a unique occasion arising at the right juncture." He meant that a person who is ready finds a teacher who is able. The essential departure point, in the context of our effort to clarify our relationship to our inner source and to truth itself, is the occasion of our finding an able teacher.

Recently, I was with a group of people who don't have any particular spiritual practice. They were raising different questions and one of them asked, "How do you *know* a real teacher?"

This is a difficult thing to put into words. No real teacher is going to whip out his or her union card and flash it on you — "Here is my Guru and Spiritual Preceptors Union affiliation card." Most of them who *do* whip it out on you don't know that much in the first place. Nevertheless, there are some things to look for.

Knowing a teacher is more of a feeling than a set of concepts and definitions. Someone handed me a book on quality the other day entitled *I Know It When I See It*. This title implies that even though we may not be able to explain precisely what quality is, we do recognize it. Similarly, it is difficult to articulate what a true teacher is but only someone very unaware will not know it when he or she encounters one.

It is a feeling. It is the experience of something special and pure, embodied in a particular person. This is different from the feeling you get when you see a beautiful man or woman walking down the street. The latter experience might change your mind or your biology; the experience of a teacher will change your life.

There is no anticipating how this experience will come about for you. Until a few years ago, our ashram was located in a town in southern Indiana. While we were there, I became friendly with a Free Methodist minister. In Indiana, Free Methodists are usually conservative, and this particular minister was somewhere between conservative and evangelical. Still, he and I found that we had an immediate rapport. He appreciated much of the social service work we did in his community, and so he asked me to come and speak to his congregation.

I went to the church and gave a talk on the Tantric tradition to his parishioners. I think it left many of them scratching their heads, wondering what I was talking about. They did ask a lot of questions, though, most of them related to one suspicion or another — all the fears that people usually come up with when they encounter an American practicing an Indian spiritual tradition.

Toward the end of the program, an old man stood up in the back of the room and thundered, "Young man, when you were in your hour of need, why didn't you get down on your knees and pray to Jesus to show you the true God?"

"But sir," I said, "I was born in Kentucky and grew up in Indiana. Until I left Indiana at the age of twenty-one, I had not been out of three states. Everyone in my family was a devout Catholic, and I went to church every day as a child. I didn't know the least bit about Indian anything. When I became aware that I needed a spiritual teacher, I *did* get down on my knees, I *did* pray to Jesus who was the only spiritual being I had ever known, and Jesus took me to Rudi. That is why I am doing what I'm doing."

It is true that I knew, in a profound way, that I needed a teacher and that I deeply wanted to find one. For a period of time, I prayed intensely to encounter such a person. Within six weeks I was in New York City, sitting in Rudi's store.

Our meeting was like a Boy-Meets-Guru fairy-tale. I took one look at him and melted. My knees turned to jelly, I became dizzy, and my heart broke open. I am not ordinarily an emotional person, and in my youth I had been in more fights than you have probably seen football games, but the tears flowed from my eyes. I couldn't help myself — I was that grateful. I felt an extraordinary beauty and love shoot into me and shatter me. Even so, I was not afraid. It took me all of five seconds to know that this was what I had lived for, and I knew what to do. I never had any doubts about it, not even for a second. Thus, there was nothing to get in the way of my dissolving into that love and becoming one with it.

The first meeting with a teacher does not necessarily happen like this, and you should not measure your experience against mine. I paid a lot for the opportunity to be at that point. What is more, not everybody had the same experience of Rudi. Some people met him, said "Hi," and walked away. It may have taken them a year or so to puzzle it over and say, "Why didn't I stay there?" and then come back.

Finding a teacher happens in all kinds of ways. The one aspect that remains consistent about it, though, is that some part of us recognizes it as a special event. If we do recognize it, whether in a simple or a big way, it compels us to return to it over and over again. Sometimes it shouts at us, sometimes it whispers but, however it happens, it is hard not to pay attention to it once we have been touched. Then we ourselves have to determine just what it means to us to be given the real and rare opportunity to grow.

There are two terms in India: One is *acharya*, the other is *guru*. There is an important distinction between the two. Acharya means "teacher" in the sense of "instructor," while guru refers to the teacher as "dispeller of darkness" or "giver of the light." When we interact with a guru, we are participating in a shared learning experience of a different order.

Such a teacher sets up a particular vibration or energy field. It is up to us, as students, to open, to connect to that energy field within ourselves, and to find our own balance point within it. We may distinguish between teacher and student in this process but, in a way, this is a false distinction. Rather, we are both participating in an event in which one person is simply more experienced than the other.

Furthermore, this event must be initiated by the student. Only then does the teacher respond. A teacher cannot do what he or she has not been asked to do, or go where he or she has not been invited. These are the rules.

I talk about finding a teacher in contrast to taking on a doctrine or dogma. How do they differ? Doctrine and dogma only add more concrete to the walls within which we already suffer. These walls may initially have had something to do with our becoming certain about things that once confused us; they may also have had to do with feeling that we had discovered some kind of answer. A real teacher, however, is not going to fill our minds with concrete, nor will he or she give us *the* answer. In fact, if we are looking for that kind of answer we are in the wrong place. Any person who is dogmatic about anything and who claims to have the answers is not a real teacher.

Growing has nothing to do with getting answers to anything because authentic growing takes us beyond the need for answers. Moreover, it is not a teacher's job to give anyone the answers because whatever we truly need to know is always inside us. We find this for ourselves through our inner search. By the depth of our love for and devotion to this search, we will discover the truth from within ourselves — that is, the truth about what we are and about what Life is.

A true teacher is free from doubts but has the understanding and the tools to respond to any question that really requires a response. At the same time, great teachers uplift us beyond dogma, fanaticism, and rigidity. They bring flexibility, kindness, and compassion into our lives. They don't fill our heads with credos or our hearts with guilt.

Instead, they fill our heads with light and our hearts with joy. They are not concerned with talking about ideology, codes of conduct, or anything flowery but rather with talking about what works. And what works for human beings is love. Ultimately, the relationship with a teacher is the opportunity to cultivate a dynamic connection with, even a living immersion in, that love.

Furthermore, a teacher is someone who, in almost every instance, has been the student of a real guru. As a student, he or she has spent years carefully studying and ardently practicing the techniques and methods transmitted by the guru and cultivating to a one-pointed focus an understanding of the highest power that dwells within. Generally speaking, if such a person comes from a lineage and represents a tradition, then we can be relatively certain that he or she has been trained and is not making things up along the way.

Furthermore, if such a person has been empowered to teach by a guru, then there is some inner substance that has been recognized by his or her predecessors and peers. This is helpful. It has to be so — after all, would we want a doctor to perform heart surgery on us who had only read the book or seen the movie? Or would we want somebody who had actually performed such an operation many times and was recognized as competent by his or her own teacher and peers?

Only on rare occasions does somebody come along who is so gifted as to be born nearly complete. When I say this, I am thinking of Nityananda, who appears not to have had a teacher. If, at some point in his youth, he did encounter someone whose presence, in a moment, established him in full awareness of the Self, he never spoke of it. It is also entirely possible, though, that he met someone whose awareness was so powerful that it ignited and consumed Nityananda's own awareness like cotton in a flame.

It is certain that the very nature of his presence and the events that happened around him gave witness to his complete immersion in the divine creative energy of Life Itself. This is the state of the teacher or, we could say, that state which the teacher embodies. This state is a mysterious thing because it is both immanent and transcendent. It is both immediately present to us while, at the same time, it transcends everything we can conceive of in the realm of our senses and perceptions, our concepts and our ideas.

The teacher should also have a profound understanding of the texts of his or her tradition. This is not the same as having read them and knowing their contents. The difference is that a real teacher has the capacity to transmit — and I think "transmit" is the operative word here — the understanding of the tradition inherent in those books. The teacher must be able to do this not only verbally but, more importantly, in the one-on-one contact with his or her students.

Ultimately, our work with a teacher is a living experience which transcends anything that can be conveyed in written teachings. A real teacher doesn't give ideas or concepts as the teaching. Indeed, a real teacher is one who doesn't even need words to teach, but whose very being is the transmission of something extraordinary. This transmission is the living relationship between a teacher and a student. It is what allows for the cultivation of stability in the mind and for a complete openness which begins to emerge from within us. It culminates in our becoming established in the ongoing awareness of the energy of Life Itself.

Another thing to look for is this: Anybody who insists on defining him- or herself as a teacher is a fool. I myself share my experience with people, and I suppose they have to call me something. Maybe "teacher" is as good a term as any. But if *I* begin to identify and to think of myself as such, then I am certainly a fool. Likewise, if I think that I am trying to teach anybody anything, the very process of my trying complicates the whole interaction. It means that someone else has to learn what I think he or she should. This is useless.

In general, this is the problem with thinking of oneself as a teacher. First of all, you have to have a subject. Then you have to have an object — both in the student and in what you are teaching. This unavoidably promotes the notion of duality. If a teacher buys into that, then he or she has to get caught up in liking the people who learn what is being "taught," and in feeling some contempt for those people who don't — either that, or get upset over not being a better teacher. None of this is helpful.

A teacher simply shares, person to person, without trying to "teach" anyone anything. Hopefully, people will learn something, but that learning takes place based on their own effort and their own inner work. It is true that there is a certain stage at which instruction takes place. In spiritual terms, however, that instruction is also called "transmission" because it is more subtle than anything verbal. Furthermore, functioning in the background of this interchange is a unity — a oneness that implicitly allows for and promotes the freedom of both the teacher and the student to learn and express themselves as is appropriate to their particular dynamic.

In this regard, any teacher really worth his or her salt should be able to transmit to you, even if not immediately, the experience of meditation. He or she should be able to give you the tangible experience of this creative power and make it easier for you to go back to it on your own.

In every case, a living teacher is more important than a connection we may have with a teacher who has passed on. This is so even when we talk about Nityananda. For example, I myself never met him in person. Nor, during the many times I went to India, did I go there looking for that kind of contact with him. Even though I had a number of powerful experiences at his shrine, I never thought of these in the same way as I did about my relationship with Rudi.

I would say that we have to have a living relationship with a living event in order to facilitate the unfoldment of Life — not an imaginary relationship with some illusionary event. Such an illusion may make us comfortable, but it takes us nowhere. It is also important that, in some way, we have one-on-one access to this teacher, if we are to connect with and absorb the tremendous reservoir of creative experience represented there. Otherwise, we cannot really benefit from it.

People occasionally ask me whether or not I think it is possible to have several teachers to help in this process. My response is, "Not really." First of all, the style of each teacher is very different, making it difficult to balance several at once. More important, a teacher is a doorway. True, there is a personality involved, but this personality is essentially irrelevant and immaterial to what we, as spiritual people, are trying to know. To some extent, we have to get through the personality to get through the doorway, but the doorway itself is really our connection to the energy of Life Itself within us.

How many doors can we go through at the same time? If we try to go through two at once we only bump into the wall between them. It is hard enough to love and to cultivate a deep sense of respect for one person. If we can do it with just one, then we should be able to do it with everybody in the whole world. But to try to do it with two, three, four or however many is not so real.

I have suggested that recognizing a true teacher has to do with feeling something. There is a kind of immediate chemistry. This, however, brings up a second point — namely that there are also many people who have extraordinary energy or charisma without necessarily being true teachers. How do we know the difference?

I would say that all great teachers come from God. I say this because for me, "God" and "Life" mean the same thing. It is Life Itself that has power. Various people demonstrate various degrees of that power in different areas. Some tend to be dominant and, in a particular set of circumstances, come across as being powerful and persuasive. They are easily able to magnetize other people to follow them. Yet, they may not be able to help their followers grow spiritually. The real bottom–line test is this: In any spiritual group or situation, an inauthentic teacher takes the energy from a student and focuses that energy on him- or herself, while a real teacher gives the energy to the student.

On the one hand, anyone who is real should both nourish us and free us from every sort of superstition because superstitions and weird beliefs are only hooks to capture people's minds. They prey on our fears and uncertainties instead of building within us the strength and the equanimity to live in the heart of uncertainty. On the other hand, a real teacher respects all the various forms of the creative expression of Life, no matter how different these may be from his or her own.

Someone who is not a real teacher has a problem with this. Such a person, instead of taking the philosophical statement "I am That" to mean "I have to *serve* That," thinks, "*That* is mine." From there it is only a short step to thinking, "So, whatever I decide to do is irreproachable and, since I'm the one doing it, it must implicitly be in the interest of the highest well-being of whomever I'm relating to. Just my presence in the room is a service."

It comes down to this: You don't want to study with someone who is going to sit there and tell you how great he or she is. Rather, you want to meet somebody who can show you how great *you* are. That is why you go to a teacher. You want to learn where that greatness is, how to connect to it, and how to live from it every day. Any teacher who is busy telling you how great he or she is will not be able to show you that. This is not so difficult to detect. If you find that a person is always talking about "Me, me, me, me, me," then you should be careful.

The point of coming to a teacher or of having a guru is to bring you to a point where you can feel and live from the guru within yourself. Any teacher who is insecure or threatened by the possibility that you will become independent is someone who has not yet really matured. You can appreciate such a person and simply move on.

In a person's life, there is probably nothing to be treasured more than the connection with a real teacher. The ultimate thing about such a relationship is that it should free you and not make you attached to the teacher. A person who is already free does not need anybody to be attached to him or her. Nevertheless, with a true teacher, the relationship endures and continues to sustain and support you as you grow. Furthermore, the relationship should become increasingly meaningful over time.

Think of a teacher and a teaching as a well from which you drink. Even though the water comes from a particular point in the earth, it has no identity. It comes from a place much deeper than the individual well. Furthermore, when the water merges with what you are, of itself it goes to where it is needed. Once you take it in, you cannot distinguish between the two of you anymore. This is a real teacher: a well sharing its substance and its content freely, without asking anything in return.

NOT PERSONALITY, BUT CONTACT

Knowledge of the Self is the gift that he disseminates.[5]

— SHIVA SUTRAS

Many people have experienced great disappointment in teachers over the last ten or fifteen years. This does not make having a teacher any less essential to a person's spiritual work. It does, however, suggest the need to examine the criteria and expectations with which we go to a teacher. If there is a gap between what we expect and what we find, does this mean that the teacher is not authentic, or is it perhaps because some of our expectations are unrealistic?

These are not new questions. Indeed, they occurred to the thinkers of Kashmir Shaivism who, over time, tried to determine what characterizes a true teacher. They identified five signs: unswerving devotion to God; mastery of all the mantras; capability in the world; a spontaneous understanding of all the scriptures and literature; and, above all, the capacity to transmit the essence of the highest teaching to others.

The significance of these criteria lies both in what *is* said and what is *not* said. For example, they don't say that the teacher has to be a good guy. They don't say that the teacher has to be honest or forthright. They don't say that the teacher has to be a vegetarian or celibate, or even a particularly religious person in any orthodox way. In other words, none of these criteria has anything to do with a teacher's personality.

I bring this up because being a teacher is not contingent upon meeting certain external conditions. It does not pivot on some particular behavioral manifestation. Teachers come about in as many ways as they do because there are so many minds and so many diverse personalities involved. There is no special form of behavior that the teacher has to adopt in order to *be* a teacher. As our experience of this deepens and as we understand more and more about love, slowly we learn that love is unlimited by any form. It is simply something that reaches into us and uplifts us.

This is one reason why the relationship with a teacher can be difficult. A teacher is always an individual and, on one level, never loses the form of that individuality. For example, Nityananda was extremely difficult for students. Yet, even as his behavior was in one sense eccentric, in another sense, he was a sharp person with a powerful capacity for discrimination. He was no spaced-out hippy.

For the most part, Nityananda lived a solitary life. Even when still fairly young, he was a great fountain of spirituality. He started to gain prominence in South India in the early nineteen twenties when he was in his late twenties. After wandering for many years, he moved north in the late nineteen forties and settled outside Bombay, where he then stayed most of the time.

According to one story about him, one day Nityananda was taking a walk when he passed a woman on the road. He walked up to her, took hold of both her breasts, and squeezed them hard. India, in this regard, is not that different from our culture. If a tall, solid, almost naked man walked up to a woman and did that, she would have a rather strong reaction. Nevertheless, Nityananda did it. A big local man did try to restrain him, but it soon became clear that Nityananda did not consider himself to be doing anything wrong.

As it turned out, the woman had lost two children because something was wrong with her milk. Nityananda, in his simple way, asked her about this, and she said, yes, this was so. Then he said "From now on you will be fine" — which, it turned out, she was. Then, everyone let him go and he walked away.

By our common standards, what he did was not the behavior of a scrupulously polite, impeccably behaved person. Nityananda, however, had little concern for such things. He didn't have a mind at all for the niceties of human interaction. Yet, can we say that he failed to act from love or that he failed to facilitate a transformation in someone else's life?

Having a teacher is not the same thing as having a friendship or even a relationship with another person. Rudi was my teacher, yet even though of the people who were present when he passed away I probably knew him best, I cannot say that I knew him at all. It was not necessary. Indeed, the more I think about it, the less I know because everything about my experience with him was surprising and yet, somehow not surprising at all.

Long ago I gave up trying to discover words that would, in some real way, describe Rudi or my experience of him. Whatever words I use end up being something of a disservice both to Rudi and to the person with whom I am speaking because they fail to convey the full flavor of the experience. It is not possible, for example, to characterize an encounter with a person who lives in a different dimension as simply "a meeting." This may be the conventional term, and we may use it, but the truth is that we cannot really talk about it this way. All I can tell you is that when I first saw Rudi, I realized immediately that I was in the presence of somebody extraordinarily special. That specialness is the event I have spent the twenty years since then trying to know and absorb.

For that matter, walking through Rudi's door — whether he was immediately present or not — was always and every time like walking into a different universe. The quality of the spirit and joy permeating the experience, as well as of the work being done, was remarkable. At the same time, there was never any getting to know Rudi and never the need to do so, because Rudi's own purpose had nothing to do with anybody's getting to know him. Indeed, he could not have cared less about that.

He *was* concerned with conveying both the understanding and the actual means by which people could discover the quality of specialness underlying every experience. He felt that they could not only discover that quality but could also develop their understanding of how to be in touch with it within themselves and extend it throughout the entire field of their individual experience.

One of my fondest memories of Rudi is from an evening when he walked up the stairs to his house and went immediately into the meditation room to start teaching class. Just before beginning to teach, he pulled up the front of his shirt and wiped some mustard off his mouth. We had just been to the Second Avenue Deli where he had eaten two hotdogs with sauerkraut. This went against everything I had ever read about spiritual teachers. Who ever heard of a spiritual teacher eating hotdogs with sauerkraut and mustard?

For that matter, Rudi didn't conform to many other norms either. He recognized, for example, that there are people in the world who draw their nourishment from other people by fighting. His own mother was like this.

Once, she was in the hospital, near death. Rudi came in and surveyed the situation. He was quite concerned about her, so he said loudly, "Look at you! You haven't been to work in a month, and all you do is lie around this hospital, costing me money. You're just bumming around. It's disgusting and I'm sick of it. Look at this doctor bill! And nobody's done the tax return at the store..," and so on and so on. He started off slowly and built to a crescendo. Within half an hour, he had her sitting up in bed, shouting back at him. Two days later she had recovered and returned to the store. Rudi used to tell this story to illustrate that not everybody is the same in terms of the mechanisms through which they draw nourishment.

There is an appropriateness to all forms in different moments in time — even to shouting. Of course, if anyone else had walked into the room when Rudi was doing this I am sure he would have been denounced in the newspapers — "SWAMI BRUTALIZES MOTHER!!" or "TEACHER TAKES RUBBER HOSE TO MOM IN HOSPITAL BED." Something like that. Yet, such an account would have had nothing to do with the essence of the event.

This is why it is important to be careful about our judgments concerning the different styles adopted by a teacher. When we see something unexpected happen, instead of judging the event we should ask ourselves what might really be going on. What is the true appropriateness of the whole expression?

I tell these stories to encourage you to understand that the teacher is a living, vital energy that is both dynamic and continuously changing. We look for some kind of consistency, and often we don't find it — certainly not in the exterior, formal sense. We have certain expectations about how teachers should behave, which they simply will not fulfill because they live beyond stereotypes.

The point is that we are not with a teacher to become experts on personality. Everybody has one, of course, and teachers are no exception. Still, this is not the place to get stuck. Sometimes people who came to see Rudi would go away saying, "He's fat — how can a spiritual person be fat?" Or, "He speaks with a Brooklyn accent — how can anybody from Brooklyn be spiritual?" Such questions can go on endlessly. The real issue is that either we find something there for us or we don't. If we encounter a teacher with whom we don't feel a connection, we simply move on. We don't waste time examining something that has no value for us. There is no need to criticize. We go on to something that does have value for us and study *that*.

Our time in this world is limited and represents a precious opportunity to gain an understanding of the nature of all form and function. In this regard, the wonderful thing about close association with a teacher is that we will see both the humanity and the divinity of the person. We will understand the limits in the one and the profound absence of limitation in the other.

This is much better than living with other people and only seeing the limits of our own humanity reflected in them every day. At the same time, every teacher in the universe takes a crap every morning, the same as everyone else. When we discover that a teacher has a body and is a real human being, that shouldn't knock us down. There is still perfection there — a perfection that encompasses and is essentially no different from our own.

In our relationship with a spiritual teacher, what we really hope to understand is the perfection that extends from the simplest, finest, purest manifestation of Life all the way to the densest and most complex level. Then we can see that, from our own physicality and the whole material world to the highest state of the divine, there is but one creative power continuously pulsating. When we understand that, our awareness of Life and the logic from which we live are transformed. Then we become free people — free to face great pain and live in tremendous joy, no matter what happens to us.

When I talk about our connection with a teacher, I am not suggesting that we crawl inside the body of the teacher or that the teacher crawl inside ours. Rather, I am talking about a connection that has nothing to do with space and time or with questions of near and far. I lived in the house of my teacher for six months and was so grateful to be there that whenever I looked at him tears would run from my eyes. I think Rudi got so sick of seeing this that he finally said "Go back to Indiana," which was over eight hundred miles away.

For the next two years, until he passed away, I would return every month or so and say, "Please let me come back." I never got away with it — he always sent me back to do my work in Indiana. Still, I tried. Maybe that was not as noble of me as I would have liked. I suppose I could have been more stoic and just sat there in Indiana — but no, I begged and pleaded. I even tried to cheat. It didn't work. He was always too fast for me.

When he sent me back to Indiana, I could have sat there and thought, "Oh, doesn't he like me? Here I am in Indiana, cut off from everybody. Woe is me." But where do such questions lead us? Only into the further conviction of duality. It is when we get caught up in misunderstanding the whole time-space continuum — in thinking that there are two things here, and not one — that we entangle ourselves in the business of, "He loves me, he loves me not. What's wrong with me? Why doesn't he like me? Why can't I see him?" The truth is that every one of these questions is beside the point.

There is, of course, no substitute for being together with the teacher, but Life doesn't always allow that. So, it is not utterly necessary. It *is* necessary, though, for us to understand that the connection we have is unlimited and to develop our ability to tune into and participate in it no matter what else we are doing. What happens then is truly amazing. We find that it becomes possible to be with the teacher, no matter where we are.

This point requires careful understanding. In a real way, the energy field that becomes our field of awakening — our own field of complete happiness — is simply an extension of the field which is our teacher. At that level of connection, there is no distinction between us because this energy field is the essence of what we ourselves are, just as it is the essence of the teacher. It simply exists, although we forget to be aware of it. Thus, wherever we are, if we can sit down and simply attune ourselves to that field, we find we are not separate at all from the teacher. Communion with the teacher does not require that we always be in their physical presence to sustain it.

This is a good thing to understand and try to practice. If we have real devotion, we always have the opportunity to tune into that field. It is an infinity, not limited by time and space. We only have to remember to connect to it. When we do this within ourselves, *that* connection becomes the support of our spiritual practice and of our activities in the world.

Then we discover that our contact with the teacher is not a question of distance. Neither do going and coming have any real meaning. Indeed, we can go and come all we need and want to. Such a relationship is not intended to box us in in any way, and we don't have to sit there every day to merge with the spirit of that teaching. All of this can be done without always being in the company of the teacher, as long as we are truly committed to growing. It is totally up to us.

It is our contact with the teacher that allows us to recognize the highest reality, which is at work within us all the time. In this process, it is not that someone or something from outside ourselves comes and touches us but that Life, from within, expands. We find that this contact with the teacher dissolves the lumps in our throats, the knots in our chests, and the rocks in the pits of our stomachs. It pulls down the dams inside us and allows the vast creative reservoir of Life Itself to become tangibly present to us as the fundamental wellspring of our existence.

From that great resource, we face all the challenges of life without feeling wasted or abused. We live in a continuous state of grace, as gracious and graceful people, moving through the sometimes brutal experiences of our everyday existence. The expansion of happiness, love, and vitality that takes place within and around us through the direct contact with the teacher is not just our contact with another soul. Rather, it is Life Itself, as it floods through us and revitalizes our lives.

THE TEACHER AS WORK

If, O Lord, there be in my heart
A place for you that is free
Of inner and outer obstacles —
What else then would be needed?

— UTPALADEVA

A spiritual teacher comes into our lives to help us recognize our independence. To that end, the teacher nourishes us, loves us, instructs us, and sometimes gets tough with us. The connection can manifest in many ways. Usually we don't have too much trouble with being nourished, loved, or even instructed; we do tend to get stuck, though, when a teacher starts to get tough. We start remembering all the newspaper and magazine articles we have read about gurus, we think about every aspect of the teacher's personality that ever bothered us, and we come up with a catalogue of reasons why it is impossible for us to be wrong about anything.

At the same time, if we are really honest with ourselves, we also usually have to admit that we have, at some point in our lives, had an experience where being given a hard time by someone turned out to be extremely important and a good thing. Sometimes, we actually need this kind of feedback. In any case, it always represents an important challenge.

Suppose we find ourselves in a situation with a teacher who, we feel, is giving us an especially hard time. How do we discern whether it is an abuse or an opportunity for growth? I would put it this way: *Any* time we get to spend in the company of a real teacher is a tremendous opportunity for growth. Every aspect of the relationship is intended to bring us to the point where we are able to appreciate ourselves as entities, see our lives clearly as they unfold, and have nothing but respect for Life as a whole.

Indeed, as we go forward in our relationship with a teacher, we will inevitably experience some occasion or other of being given a hard time. (Of course, we are not the only ones. Just try putting on the orange skirt a swami has to wear, walk down Main Street, and you will see what a hard time is in mere minutes.) The challenge for us as students is how to respond to these hard times, because they are a lot of work. I would suggest, however, that when we have a real connection with a teacher — when there is an extraordinary interchange by which we feel ourselves to be deeply nourished — being given a hard time is no hard time at all.

Why is this? A person who has the ability to transmit that energy also has the ability to understand the difference between care and abuse. If such a person is taking a hard stand, we can be certain that he or she is doing it for a thoughtful reason. This, at least, has been my experience.

The most important thing is not that we understand, in the moment, exactly why this person is being hard on us or, for that matter, that we let ourselves be confused or seduced by the softness that such a person might also demonstrate. Rather, the important thing to understand is that we are in the situation to be open and learn — to observe, internalize, and be nourished by every form the learning takes, and to grow from the whole experience. Then, gentleness and hardness simply become different expressions of the same love.

Moreover, when I say, "nourished," I do not mean what gets promoted a lot these days as a "nurturing environment," in which nobody ever takes a strong stand with anybody. Such an environment is neither my primary interest nor major concern. If you think that Rudi cultivated a nurturing environment, then I haven't described him clearly enough. Rudi was wonderful, he was generous, and he was loving — but he was also fierce.

A teacher who sets up a "nurturing environment" only attracts everyone in the world who wants to be nurtured. The people who really want to work don't come — they go someplace else. A teacher who sets up an environment where work is happening attracts people who want to work. Then it is the people who don't want to work who don't come. We have to be careful not to be misled by appearances. What appears to be a "nurturing environment" may, in fact, only be nurturing our

tensions by indulging them, while what seems to be a tough environment may actually be supporting us as we learn to release
these tensions and go beyond them.

I'll tell you another story. Over a period of years I spent a lot
of time in India going around to meet devotees and disciples of
Nityananda in order to put together a book from their many
stories. One story that impressed me went like this.

It seems that Nityananda was an extremely gruff person
who, as we have already seen, was not particularly concerned
with social conventions. For example, he never really went out
of his way to be nice to anyone in the more customary ways.
People report that only in the last year or so of his life did he show
kindness or reach out to them with some gentleness. Most of the
time, he was just plain tough and difficult.

In the early 1950s, a ten-year-old boy, whose name was
Shetty, heard about Nityananda and wanted to meet him. Being
too young to go by himself, he went to his uncle and asked him to
take him. This uncle was a gambler. He was a fairly unreformed
character and, most of the time, gambling was all he really
wanted to do. So he said to Shetty, "I don't want to go, I have bets
to place." But the boy persisted and finally talked him into it, so
together they went out to the temple.

When they got there, they came to a large dirt area and saw
Nityananda sitting against the side of the temple. A semicircle of
people was standing in front of him, while other people were
coming forward with fruit, flowers, and coconuts and putting
them before him. Indeed, during his lifetime, thousands of
people came to him in this way, bringing tons of fruits and flowers. Nityananda rarely responded in the slightest to any of them,
so they would stack these things up in piles, which he would also
ignore. He simply remained in his still and silent state.

Shetty and his uncle saw everyone standing around Nityananda, enthralled by the grace and sweetness of his presence.
The gambler uncle, who had no real interest in any of this,
started thinking to himself. All of a sudden, Nityananda looked
over at him and shouted, "You bloody son of a bitch, how dare
you? You bastard, you come to see me like this, you rotten...!"
Seizing a coconut from the ground by his feet, he winged it at the

uncle and hit him square on the thigh. Then he picked up a second coconut and did it again. During this time, he continued cursing at the man — and Nityananda, when he got wound up, could curse with the best of them.

In any case, the man got struck by two coconuts. He limped back to Bombay that night and, the next day, went to the races where he bet on the number two horse and won the equivalent in rupees of around one hundred thousand dollars. It turns out that what he had been thinking to himself — and the reason why Nityananda had shouted at him — was, "If only he'd give me a number to bet on. That's what I would really like." So, Nityananda imprinted the number on his body. Nityananda was rather nice about it, too — he could have gone for a head shot.

The best way to think about what happened between this man and Nityananda is that Nityananda simply gave him a number and made him pay for it on the front side, although not too much. After all, the man had not been particularly concerned with anything spiritual before he went to see him and, although he had great reverence for Nityananda whenever he spoke of him, I don't believe he ever went back. The point is that Nityananda was often abrupt like this. There are more stories of his picking up a stick and whacking somebody than there are of his reaching out a hand or in any way embracing a person.

Yet, even in this total abruptness, Nityananda gave people what they asked for and what they wanted. Sometimes, a fierce appearance can cover a generous act. It is difficult to recogize this, however, if we are established in the mode of always asking, "What's going to happen to me?" When we live a defensive life and are busy trying to justify our assumptions about it, we find it difficult to be open and allow the presence of a new breeze or energy to enrich us. We are too busy defending ourselves against change.

It doesn't really matter whether or not the teacher is tough with us. What *does* matter is how we take it. This trains us to face our lives with balance and equanimity. Life, after all, is going to hit us a lot. If the strokes we receive cause us to freeze up and become internally crystallized with one tension or another, then we are nothing but stuck. The real issue is not what seem like blows or abuse; it is maintaining the connection we feel. If we have examined the situation with some care and, from our own experience, feel that we are with a real teacher, we will also recognize that this is someone committed to the highest state as it manifests in all its forms — including us.

It simply doesn't matter whether we experience such a person as difficult or easy. Nothing is always easy or always difficult; no experience is always hard or always gentle. The point is that, whatever form it takes, we have to have a consistent response of openness and the ability to flow within ourselves each and every moment, no matter how difficult the pressure may be. Furthermore, the hardness we experience in a teacher may, in fact, be a test. The teacher may be difficult with us just to see how much we have learned.

I would say, frankly, that it is a good thing to have a teacher who sometimes gives us a hard time. We can look at this in many different ways, but the bottom line is that any real teacher who gives us a hard time does so in order to prepare us to deal with the realities of life. So it is better, I think, to have somebody who is capable of being tough with us, when necessary.

Nor does a real teacher ever do this to entangle us in his or her life. We are not here ever to be tangled up in anybody else's life. The point of having a teacher is to become independent — not to exchange our entanglements in one thing for an entanglement in the teacher.

Any teacher worth his or her salt is going to require that we recognize our own independence, that we encourage the independence of others, and that we also appreciate the interdependence we all share. Fully recognizing these things brings us to a profound appreciation and respect for Life Itself. Not only do we see that thread of Life in everyone; we see the fabric of Life Itself extending in every direction as only one thing. This is called realizing God.

It must be so since, as I have said, the real teacher is not the personality but the energy field that has the capacity to arouse and draw out of us the deepest and finest aspect of what we are. That energy field, like a magnet, attracts that within us which is like it, and draws it to the forefront of our own awareness.

If our relationship with the teacher is a truly honest situation, we will find, as we go more and more deeply into it, that it expands at the same time as the constraints of our personality fall away. Through the contact with the teacher our barriers dissolve, and there is only freedom mingled in freedom — Life being poured into Life. This becomes the love from which we live our lives.

This love goes beyond the relationship between the teacher and the student to encompass everything. It is infinite space, complete time, and total acceptance. When we understand this, then wherever we go and whatever we do, we live in that common spirit. Indeed, we *are* that spirit. In that expansion, we come to have great value and respect for every aspect of our lives that has uplifted us, and everything we once experienced as difficult becomes a way to our upliftment.

BEING A GREAT STUDENT

Do not draw near to God
presuming he is kind:
Can he be kind who broke you on the rack?
Can he be kind who makes you weep and laugh?

But if you slave for him
without alarm and fright,
he will abandon himself
for your sake,
the Lord of the Meeting Rivers.

— BASAVANNA

You may think that the main issue in the teacher–student relationship is the quality of the teacher. Having talked about the teacher in a number of ways, I am now going to tell you one hundred percent differently. The real issue is not the quality of the teacher; rather, it is the quality of student that *we* are. A great student can never be limited by any teacher. It is even possible to receive from teachers things they have no idea that they have. It all depends upon the extent to which we are dedicated to this search within ourselves. If we are truly dedicated, it is not necessary to have found a perfect teacher.

I'll tell you a story that a Zen priest told to me. A few years ago, a certain American was living as a monk in a Buddhist monastery in Thailand. After a time, he went to the head monk and said, "You know, I don't think this is such a high practice."

The teacher said, "Oh?"

"No," said the American, "and, for that matter, I don't think *you* are a very good teacher, either." The teacher looked at him and said, "That is fortunate for you, isn't it?"

The American said, "What do you mean?"

The teacher replied, "If this were such a good teaching or I were such a great teacher, you would still be looking for the Buddha outside yourself."

The spiritual literature of the Tantric tradition in Hinduism and Buddhism articulates over and over again that it is the depth and purity of our own devotion, extended over time, that cause to coalesce within us the strength and creative power which are the source, the cause, and the effect — the alpha and the omega — of our Self-realization. It is the spirit of devotion to our own learning which, in the long run, carries the day. No teacher — indeed, nobody at all — can do this for us. We have to want to do it for ourselves, we have to be willing to work at it, and we have to bust our guts in the process.

As students, we cannot sit around and wait until the perfect teacher happens along before we begin our inner work. Rather, we simply have to get on with it now. The real issue here is *us* and always will be us. There is no issue about this son-of-a-so-and-so, or that whomever, or that other wonderful person. In fact, it is never the *other*; it is always us. What do *we* want? What are *we* going to do about it? Where do *we* stand? What is our own relationship to our highest Self? As Rudi continuously stressed, *we* are responsible for getting it, not the teacher.

What does it take to be a good student? I would say four things: devotion, the willingness to work hard, honesty, and love. The first and most important of these is our devotion to the quest for truth and our persistence in it. This is what enables us to connect to, sustain, and support the unfolding of the energy necessary to allow awakenings within us to take place.

Because I was fortunate, knew what I wanted, and recognized, when I met Rudi, that I had found what I'd been looking for, I also knew what I had to do. So, I just did it. I didn't go through nine hundred thousand circles of doubt. There was never any "What about this? What about that?" I just did my work.

At the same time, it is possible to sit with a great teacher for a million years without showing any effect. Toward the end of his life, Nityananda used to sit at the temple while ten thousand people a day passed before him. On big holidays, a hundred thousand people would come. But of all those people, only a few really took in what his presence was all about. Only a few integrated it into their own lives so thoroughly that it made their lives a creative demonstration of what they had experienced. In other words, although many people benefitted from the contact with him, few became like him. Rudi was one of those who did.

In our own work we can have the greatest teacher in the world, but if we are not devoted to growing, we will never experience the fullness of the event. We will undoubtedly benefit — many people will tell you about the wonderful things they experienced in the presence of Nityananda or Muktananda, and I bump into people everywhere who tell me about what Rudi did to change their lives — but there is a lot more to it than that. So, the first quality that defines a great student is devotion to growing.

A teacher trains us to participate directly in the differentiated world — and, at the same time, to turn around, look at the whole universe, and begin to appreciate the simple unity that exists between us and everything that is. That is what having a teacher is all about. It is not about dressing or talking like the teacher. It is not about thinking like the teacher, having the same concepts, liking the same food, or anything of the sort. It is simply about participating from our heart to that heart, which is the heart of Life.

Moreover, it is about our ability to take this experience, build on it from within ourselves, and translate it into a living demonstration of the power of Life. Then, whether we are near or far away, our actions will demonstrate the presence of that one Teacher, our eyes will see nothing but that Teacher, our lips will speak nothing but the words of that Teacher — that Teacher which is the essence of your life and mine, and in which we are all one.

This requires a lot of work. We have to be devoted to accomplishing it and can't let any disappointments get in our way. It is the quality of our devotion that brings us to the point where we can face every disappointment and go beyond it, recognizing that all disappointment is also misunderstanding. After all, if there is only one Self, in whom or what can we be disappointed? We may not yet know through our own experience that there is only one Self; still, our devotion will help us understand this better over time.

Everything that happens is a positive thing if we allow it to be. Every experience is what we make of it. Every difficult circumstance provides either support or resistance. We decide whether this energy will nourish and uplift us in the context of our search or become an obstacle to our further pursuit. That is how it works — which means that no experience is intrinsically positive or negative. It just is. To develop the capacity to take every experience and every energy, and turn it into support — this is the devotion that we have to cultivate.

After devotion, the second important thing is the willingness to work hard and to practice constantly. The feeling, the energy, the understanding, the techniques — in other words, the tools we get along the way as we make our search — are what we must master. We must know what to do with them. Even to understand the significance of a simple breathing exercise takes time. We have to have not merely the capacity to work but the willingness — even the hunger — to do so.

As I have already said, Rudi was a difficult person and a tough one. More to the point, he used to make me work a lot. Three or four of us lived in his house with him. We got up early in the morning and worked all day long. Only when the last grain of rice was cleaned out of the sink did we sit down in his presence for a while before he would get up and go upstairs to bed. He didn't derive any personal benefit from our work — usually, we were working on the buildings in which people at the ashram lived. The point was to bring out in us the capacity to persist at hard work. If you didn't want to work at carpentry, you did the dishes; if you weren't willing to do dishes, you were out the door.

After I moved to Indiana and Rudi would come to visit us, I used to stay up sometimes two or three days and nights at a time doing nothing but sitting and working to prepare myself, before, during, and after my contact with him, to make that contact as pure and intense as possible. I did this so that the power of that force wouldn't throw my mind and emotions around and deflect my attention.

Dealing with such energies is a powerful situation that takes a lot of hard work. The degree to which we manifest this effort is, in a way, a statement about how devoted we are to the whole endeavor. It also points to the fact that, at this stage in our practice, our relationship with the teacher does represent a great deal of work and effort.

The third thing that I would say is important for a student to cultivate is honesty. Within the context of our devotion, we have to have the ability to be honest, especially with ourselves. The awakening of the energy from inside us changes how we feel in many different ways. For example, the need we feel to grow, along with the support we have gotten from the teacher in channeling this need, lead us to want to devote ourselves to making a further effort. Thus, devotion and hard work focus our attention, and this is a good thing.

As we learn to focus our minds, we come to have a kind of confidence — a sense of new certainty and power. In the process, though, we may start to believe a lot of things about the whole business of spiritual work and about ourselves that are not necessarily true. We may get caught up in how we would like to feel, or how we ought to feel, or how we think guruji wants us to feel.

This is useless. We have to think about how we *do* feel. Then, we have to take another step and examine these feelings in the light of our ideal, our devotion, and our effort, and come to some deeper conclusions about them. We don't deny, suppress, or reject any of them, but we do have to have the ability to see beyond the limits of everything that constitutes our personality. We have to look at all the disappointments we experience and the struggles that arise within us, and understand them from a different perspective.

We also have to have the ability to recognize the discrepency between our stated objectives and our actual performance. That is, we have to cut through our propaganda about ourselves and look at where we fall short of our intentions. If we can't learn to do this, then we will never be able to bring our performance into alignment with what we wish it to be.

We have to be devoted to cultivating both our awareness of truth from within ourselves and its articulation in our everyday lives. Otherwise, as we advance in our spiritual work, the ego and the tendencies of our differentiated biological existence obscure our ability to see the truth. We become fanatics — people with our heads set in concrete instead of having brains. From there, we develop an ideology, never understanding that no ideology in the universe is big enough to hold the truth. If we live from ideology — whatever it may be — how can we be honest?

Only when we have the capacity to be honest with ourselves will we ever be able to be honest with anybody else and come to understand what love is. How, after all, can we tell anyone else the truth if we will not face it ourselves? And if there is not that fundamental honesty between us, what kind of foundation have we built for real love? Only when we understand this do we also come to understand that connection between human beings which is more profound and important than any differences in understanding, direction, or ideals.

There is a paradox here. If we cannot recognize our differences, we will never be able to transcend them to live in our similarities. These differences are real. At the same time, they are not limiting. They are what allow Life Itself to demonstrate its beauty and its endlessly creative capacity. If there were no differences, then this unity would have no power at all. It would be nothing but a void, a vacuum. Instead, because of the many differences between us, the vitality and the power of Life Itself find full expression.

All this brings us back around to the point that it is not the teacher upon whom the whole thing rests, but us. It rests upon our devotion, our willingness to work, and our capacity to be honest with ourselves. If we cannot be honest with ourselves, we will never develop the refined sensitivity it takes to be aware of the linkage points in the energy — those points where the energy goes from complex to simple, from simple to simpler, and from simplest, to one.

There will always be differences of personality between a teacher and his or her students. There will be differences of taste and interests, and disagreements about forms of expression. Still, these things are essentially superficial. Once we allow them to become important, we have turned on the time clock and set a limit to the relationship. After that, it is just a matter of waiting for the bell to ring and the thing to be over. However, once our experience leads us to recognize a person as a true teacher with whom we can learn, we accept the person. Having done so, the choice and what we make of it are our responsibility.

This means that the relationship begins within us. In our seeking and in our finding, as well as in every aspect of our liberation, we are responsible. This responsibility requires a tremendous amount of work and real effort. At the same time, it is not a burden. On the contrary, it is a joyous occasion and one to be undertaken joyfully every day by the person who chooses to make it part of his or her life. Furthermore, to say that it is our responsibility actually represents a certain confidence in ourselves — a way of saying, "We *can* do it," and that, in fact, it is all there for us to do. This is the attitude that even a new student should cultivate.

Understand that with a teacher, as in life, what we sow is what we reap. The difference is that, with a teacher, we reap it faster because he or she provides us with a mirror of our own state. This means that we must think carefully about what we bring to a teacher, because what we bring is what we will get back. If we bring fear, we will get something to be afraid of. If we bring greed, we may be cheated. (What this really means is that we may cheat ourselves.) If we bring love, we might just be freed.

Most of the time, Rudi was every bit as sweet as his pictures show him to be. I sometimes used to think of him as being like a great grizzly bear — warm and cuddly, but to be approached with great care. If you came to him with love, he responded with love. Most of the time, even if you didn't come with love he met you with love anyway. However, if you came to him with some heaviness, you often got heaviness back.

The point, of course, was to get you to change your understanding and your mode. It was not to make you drop your concern, forget about your doubt, or ignore whatever issue you had. He wanted you, instead, to learn to express these things not with drama, heaviness, anxiety, or tension but with love, openness, and honesty.

What matters in this is our ability to take whatever we receive from a teacher, internalize it, and grow from it. What matters is our ability to articulate our understanding of the teaching and continuously refine it. If we cultivate our inner purity and depth and our capacity for surrender and service, we need not be concerned about whether or not we have found a true teacher. No inferior teacher will be able to capture and hold us. Furthermore, the limitations of whatever teacher we relate to will not become *our* limitations.

This purity and depth are what bring us to the point where we see through the illusion of this physical life to the unlimited power of Life Itself upon which all appearance rests. They bring us to the point where we become established in that deeper state. The work of cultivating them requires the fourth quality of the great student, which is love.

Such love is hard work. It requires that we know our own minds and put leashes on them; that we listen to our own mouths and sometimes put muzzles on them. Moreover, it requires that we do the right thing at the right time, especially when we don't want to. It requires that we see the big picture and go beyond our own, immediate concerns. Yet, if we take up our practice with the support of a teacher, we come to understand such love. In the process, we become truly fine people, free from the kind of pain and suffering, desires and disappointments, that most people undergo.

I myself have been fortunate to share the company of people who have cultivated enormous love within themselves. My association with them has taught me a lot about this greater capacity to love and, hopefully, has given me some sense of how to practice it in my own life. That is how it happens. It is not a set of guidelines that can be taught. From such experience, without any particular expectation, we become filled with enthusiasm about life. Without any particular need, we become appreciative of everything there is. Without any particular attachment, we are able to perceive the beauty in all things.

That is big. I would say that it's worth working for.

Meditation

MEDITATION

The mystery does not get clearer by repeating the question,
nor is it bought with going to amazing places.

Until you've kept your eyes
and your wanting still for fifty years,
you don't begin to cross over from confusion.

— RUMI

Recently, it seems that meditation has become fashionable as a stress-management technique. While it is true that learning to meditate will help us deal with stress and be more relaxed, this is a superficial utilization of a powerful tool — a tool that can put us in touch with the unlimited potential and the universal power that exist within us. The more we explore that power carefully and well, the more it unfolds and extends itself throughout the entire field of our lives and the more we come to know it as the essence of who and what we are. The person who uses meditation only as a tool for relaxation will never understand this.

Neither our sense of "I," nor this body, nor anything else about us is anything other than a reflection of the creative energy which is present in all things at all times. This recognition and the ability to live from it is what underlies all our spiritual work and effort to grow. It is the true aim of meditation. As individuals, we can interact, we can talk with each other and have conversations, and we can enter into various forms of exchange. In meditation, however, when we fold our legs, close our eyes, and go deeply into ourselves, the awareness we experience in the best moments has nothing to do with who we are as people who act, talk, and carry on with other people. At those moments, we return to our identity as the highest consciousness.

Sitting to practice meditation is an important and special period in our day and, as we pursue it more deeply, we recognize it to be the very life of our Life. We could say that, through meditation, we mine the deepest treasure of our existence. It is the time when we withdraw our attention from our ordinary sense of purpose and begin to examine — indeed, come to terms with — the source from which the motivation for all our experience and action springs.

Many people tend to think that it is the act of sitting which brings about these things; however, it only looks that way. It is not sitting itself that effects any result but rather our focus on asking to grow, our extending ourselves in order to grow, and our participating in that energy field — these are what arouse the force that gives rise to change.

Think of it this way. If our minds are constantly wavering and have little capacity for concentration, how can our desire to grow come to fruition? In a garden full of weeds, how can the tomato plant bear fruit? If the mind is filled with thousands of desires and wishes, how can any one of these become powerful or strong? All we end up with are thousands of microscopic radishes instead of a well-defined crop. The intensity of our desire to grow is what does the work. It arouses our creative energy and this, when it is unwavering, has the capacity to manifest its own fullness.

When we become devoted to our longing to grow, *then* it is meditation which sustains our connection to that spirit within us. Our meditation arouses that re-creative power, allowing us to experience from within ourselves its ongoing renewal and to cultivate the experience of Life Itself, every day.

When we sit down to do our inner work, we are not going somewhere other than where and what we are. This is so because in infinity, there is nowhere to go but home — namely, here — and only one time to be there — namely, now. Moreover, if it is all here right now, we have only one real choice: to love it. This subtle surrender — this acceptance of ourselves as we really are — is like saying, "Alright, I've been put together in this way right now, and I hope I can discover what it's all about."

The wish to grow, which we practice as a core part of our meditation, is not an escapist impulse. Rather, it leads us to see deeply into the reality of what we are and to recognize something extraordinary within ourselves. Because we invite it to grow, this most extraordinary part of us can expand, break through our tensions, and begin to manifest as the special Life within our lives — the Self within our selves — with a power and direction of its own. This Life within us is an inspiration which we can only serve.

We are participants in a profoundly simple, beautiful, and harmonious event called the Self. The more we appreciate that the Self is truly universal, the more we understand that what we experience as intimate and personal is also happening on a vast and infinite scale. This understanding brings us to see that this unity also works through us, giving rise to everything in and about us.

It gives us access not merely to our deepest creative potential but to something even deeper than that — to a kind of magic which is neither mysterious nor complicated at all. We find that there is something refreshing and amazing — indeed, something completely joyful — in how this demontrates itself in our lives. For that matter, it *is* Life, and because we connect to it and live from it, our whole experience is transformed into something joyful.

Our spirit is alive all the time. Meditation is simply the time we take everyday to get to know and relate to this inner Self. It is what happens as we cultivate our awareness of that Self. It is our vehicle for being in touch with our source and our strength — for being in touch with the power of Life Itself. As you think about this, ask yourself what it would be like to realize that your own creative resource was infinite in nature.

Meditation, as I have been talking about it, is a state of awareness. It also involves the techniques by which we center the mind so that we can enter into that awareness. The techniques of meditation train us to focus deeply within ourselves in order to feel both an ever deeper vitality and creative flow, and the simple joy and sense of total well-being that emerge from the experience of that flow.

What I give you to practice, in this regard, is both terribly simple and terribly complex. Right now, I am thinking about how terribly simple it is. The whole method — indeed, the entire practice — has only one aim: to penetrate and go beyond our tensions so that we can begin to connect to the simple, pure joy that is our very essence. Indeed, the techniques I give you are only as complicated as we are: When we are complicated, so are they. When we are simple, they become simple. They mirror our inner state. Yet, whether we experience them as complicated or simple, remember at all times that they still have only this one aim.

> *The mind is a nervous thief,*
> *the mind is a pure cheat.*
> *The ruin of sages, men and gods,*
> *the mind has a hundred thousand gates.*
>
> — KABIR

In our community, we meditate every morning and evening, so that twice a day we can express our intention to grow. We learn to do things like this because they help orient us as to what we will make of the day instead of leaving it up to our minds. The mind is populated by fifteen thousand thieves. There are another twenty-five thousand lurking in other places, but the mind has its own and we have to trick them.

Everybody would like to think that he or she is unique — "I am in a situation that is different from everyone else's, and all of my particular circumstances prove it." In fact, everybody is basically the same in this sense — we all have forty thousand different excuses. We all have forty thousand elements of uniqueness, which really means that we all face the same issue — who is in charge here? Are our intelligence, intellect, and free will in charge, or is it our habits, patterns, and the forty thousand thieves?

For most people, the forty thousand thieves tend to rule. They steal our lives. They steal our happiness. They steal everything and leave us nothing. So, we meditate instead. We practice Hatha Yoga. We do little things to remind ourselves that we are in charge and that we have the right to express what our lives should be. It is easy to forget, but that is why we start again and again and again. We often think: "I have to start over again — I must be so stupid." Not so. The person who joyously starts the day anew is free. Likewise, the person who pauses each evening to start all over again is also free.

Meditation technique itself is not realization. It is also not growing. Technique is just technique. The point of it is to bring us into the center of ourselves and to awaken in us the awareness both of a process and of the source of that process. For example, in music, technique is important. All students have to start with it, and elements of that technique persist in their playing even years later. At that stage, however, the musician no longer thinks about technique in the same way because it has become part of the structure. It is no longer what one does, exactly, but part of who one is.

The same is true of technique in meditation. We practice and become both familiar and comfortable with the various components — concentration on the breath, on the chakras, and on the flow within them. Once we master the techniques, we don't think about them much. They are just a part of us. It is something like learning to ride a bicycle or to drive a car. At first, we are preoccupied with all the separate movements, but after a time, we do these things without having to make them the focus of our direct attention.

While a technique by itself is not going to get us anyplace, that same technique — whether internal or external — is also a self-luminous expression of the divine. It is when we recognize the limits of method that we realize why we got involved in the method in the first place. At that point, we are called to transcend the method and examine its essence, which is our Self.

This recognition has far-reaching effects. In the process, we become more refined and sensitive people full of the strength and security that come from understanding our long-term place in Life Itself. We cannot help but be better lovers, truer friends, more responsible spouses, wiser parents, and more successful people in our work.

As we refine and extend our awareness, the quality of our actions extending from that awareness automatically improves. We become more efficient, and get closer to the point, which is to provide what is called for. Then, the feedback we get from others becomes more deeply satisfying as we discover that this flow of giving and receiving is nothing other than the flow of love.

This flow satisfies us so deeply that our awareness of all things changes. As we begin to experience this flow between ourselves and everything else, it reaches into the deepest part of us and addresses our deepest longing. We feel so nourished and uplifted by it that we realize there is no longer anything in our lives to be afraid of. In this way, a virtual Mobius strip extends itself from and comes back into that basic dynamic stillpoint within us, which is the essence of Life Itself.

Spiritual realization comes to us as the technique trains us to recognize the subtle experience of joy within ourselves. As we become aware of the ongoing presence of this joy, we discover that we can contact it at any time, in the midst of every activity. The experience of that subtle happiness is the link between our individual lives and infinite Consciousness. It is the core of every aesthetic experience and the power behind every desire. Experiencing it reduces all objects to one thing — a subtle, delicious unity.

As we become able to look deeply into ourselves and into every one of our experiences to recognize the extraordinary quality at the core of every one of them, we are permanently changed at every level of our chemistry. The opening of the heart imprints the resonance of universal consciousness on each one of us as we move through the world. Having experienced it, we can never see the world in the old way again.

Rudi used to say that the experience of it is subtle, like the taste of a pear or of a piece of lettuce. There are no real obstacles to experiencing it — we simply breathe in and out, and relax to let the creative energy of Life flow through us. As we do that, we will feel in our hearts a subtle joy arising out of that subtle condition. We allow that joy to flow within us and, as we move through our days and our lives, we carry it with us, exploring it as deeply as we can, as often as we remember to do so. It is that simple.

The power of Life Itself within us — *that* is meditation. To have a tangible, palpable contact with this Presence and to live with it every day — *that* is awakening.

REFINING THE BODY

Most human adults are like badly used soil. Many of their
natural resources have been sorely depleted and their
chemistry brought out of balance.
   Discipline is like crop rotation. When you stop misusing
your own resources and readjust your living patterns, a better,
more fertile balance is reached . . . . The harmony of the body
must be put in order on the most basic levels.

— RUDI

In laying the groundwork for our meditation and spiritual practice, we learn to pay attention to the state of our bodies. The first idea behind this is to sustain our vitality and refine our physical chemistry. The second involves the proper utilization of our resources. After all, much of how we feel is informed by two factors: diet and exercise. If we examine our diet and then look at the amount and kind of exercise we get, we will learn a tremendous amount about why we feel anywhere from a little tired occasionally to very tired a lot of the time.

To develop a constructive approach to these matters requires some discrimination. In my work with different people, it has become apparent to me that many health problems — including various mental and emotional problems — are greatly influenced by what a person eats. At the same time, I would say that being disciplined about what we eat and don't eat does not take the place of doing our deep inner work. For example, some people argue that a vegetarian diet is conducive to spirituality. I would not make such an assumption.

The same is true of many other assumptions people make about what is required to be a spiritual person. I would suggest that this represents a misunderstanding of what spiritual work really is. I personally happen to like vegetables and they constitute a fundamental part of my diet. However, not everybody will necessarily be healthy on a vegetarian diet.

Many nutritionists today claim that a diet tending toward less meat and lighter foods is generally better for you. I suspect that, if you were to practice vegetarianism for a while, you would notice your system beginning to feel finer, lighter, and more refined. You might also want to verify whether or not you are allergic to any of the foods you are eating. (There are people, for example, who are allergic to sugar and wheat and who find that eating these substances impairs their ability to think clearly and perform their work well). Still, we have to be careful about identifying one thing or another as spiritual. Nowhere in the *Shiva Sutras*, for example, does it say you have to eat vegetables to be spiritual.

Whatever the means, the more refined your system becomes, the greater your capacity to relate to different frequencies of vibration; the less refined it is, the more you are restricted to heavier frequencies of energy. It is the density of your inner, chemical atmosphere that affects the quality of your awareness. This is one reason why eating carefully has always been a part of different spiritual traditions. So, one of the points of these practices is general, systemic refinement.

The same general principle applies in every area of our lives. There are no rules and regulations that dictate how we have to live our lives if we want to do spiritual work. It is not the point to be married only once, to be celibate, or to observe a particular lifestyle. The nature and thrust of our spiritual work is not toward any particular form of self-discipline, self-denial, or any such thing; rather, a certain degree of understanding and awareness are necessary.

In general, for example, we must have some control over our senses. Our appetites cannot be in control of us. If they are, we are finished as far as any real growing is concerned. When we recognize that certain foods, substances, places, or kinds of relationships don't bring out the best in us, we may choose to avoid them. By doing so, we demonstrate the depth of our understanding as well as the recognition of what we can handle well or not so well.

A second element which influences the quality of our awareness is exercise. In the United States over the last few decades, we have seen a growth in the practice of forms of exercise and movement that originated in Asia — T'ai Ch'i Chuan, Aikido, and Hatha Yoga, for example. What distinguishes these different practices from many of the athletic disciplines of the West is the part they play in a person's spiritual work.

I myself have found the practice of Hatha Yoga particularly useful and meaningful. Broadly speaking, its purpose is to give the student access to the total range of motion available within a particular mechanism or set of muscles. This range of motion includes flexibility, strength, and stability. We also practice it with the idea of refining our total system.

Ordinarily, due to the shock, stress, and strain to which our biology is continually exposed, our cell walls thicken, their capacity for respiration is impaired, and their excretory functions become limited. This leads to the accumulation of toxins and tensions which crystallize in the form of the various chemical patterns that establish themselves in our muscles and tissues.

Practicing the *asanas*, or postures, of Hatha Yoga is not just a matter of refining our awareness. Each posture isolates particular muscles and, in doing so, brings that group of muscles into a state of stillness, allowing their chemistry to change. We are taking the crystallization that we have become, and releasing the pure ether that is its essence. We could say that the highest purpose of Hatha Yoga is to bring the fluctuation of our physical body to a stillpoint — to a point of perfect balance. When that occurs, the stillness is so clear that all fluctuation seems to disappear.

In the practice of asanas, both form and vibration are important. First, you master the form; then, you are able to relax into the vibration. You have to learn to hold the pose long enough and correctly enough for its vibration to interact with the basic vibration of your own system. The two knock around together and beat up on each other for a little while. Then, at some point, a certain stillness is established. At that moment the vibration of the posture absorbs your own vibration of individuality and resistance.

Often, when you are practicing asanas, you may go into a stretch and find that the first thing you encounter is your body's resistance to that stretch. You extend easily at first, but then your body may seem to kick back. If you work carefully in that stretch, feeling and becoming aware of the contraction, the tension, and the resistance in that muscle, you will notice that the contraction gathers into a point somewhere along the particular muscle you are working, and the muscle itself starts to tremble. What has happened is that you have caused the pattern — the chemistry — that has been held in that muscle to become highly energized.

You then wait until the muscles affected by that particular pose pass through a stillpoint. In other words, the muscles will react to the pose, they will contract to a stillpoint and finally release. The change in the muscles is the expression of change that has already come about in your awareness. It is also an articulation of that change that leads to even further expansion.

What you will have, as a result, is a definite physical change in the tissue — in the relationship between the cells and the whole structure to one another — and in the relationship between that structure and all the other structures with which it is involved. In the process, your cells throw off a lot of shock and strain. The crystallized pattern is released, and you have a muscle whose range of motion, even in the short period of such work, is extended into a new-found flexibility.

Because the shock is dissipated and the strain released, your system is more easily able to flush out the toxins that build up in the cells. With this, you experience a different quality to your emotions — that is, your emotions manifest a different frequency with an entirely different feeling behind it. Because of the improvement in respiration, your mind and emotions become quieter and, because they are quieter, you have the capacity for greater insight into the fundamental tides and pulsations occurring within the whole biological field that you are.

A few people find that, when they begin an asana and *pranayama*, or breathing, practice, they start to have physical problems. It is possible that their difficulties point to the presence of some previously existing dysfunction for which their systems have learned to compensate. When that compensatory behavior starts to be broken down, and as the compensatory pattern is rearranged into a healthier one, they may start to experience what seems to be a problem. This is a temporary event. When it happens to you, shift for a while to a simpler level of practice. Don't stop practicing, but rather, from this simplified level of practice, keep going and then build up again. Through practice, these levels of compensation — some small and some major — will be totally reorganized.

Real learning involves a change in our chemistry. Every truly progressive change is also a genuine change in that chemistry, and not just a shift from one thing to a subset of itself. The same is true of what our understanding, our minds, and our emotions go through in the practice of meditation. Indeed, the reason for doing Hatha Yoga is to support in us an awareness of what meditation is. In the course of dealing with our bodies and breath, we come to understand more about our spirit as well. In the process, the condition of all of them improves.

The whole point of asana practice is to awaken the dynamic stillness that we call kundalini. It is this energy that is the source of real change within us. All authentic change is based on our contact with that dynamic stillness. In our practice, we bring our breath and our attention to a stillpoint and there we find that this universal consciousness is always at the forefront.

It is this contact with the highest state, whether all at once or in stages, that transforms our minds, our emotions, and our physical bodies. At that point, we express our strength and flexibility mentally, emotionally, and spiritually. This is the deeper meaning of a total range of motion. It is what emerges as we refine our systems.

With this overall refinement, there comes a stage when we recognize that all forms of respiration are but one thing — the breath of God. Our practice of asana and pranayama, as with the other techniques we use, is intended to establish us in the pulsation of that breath. It enables us to experience something beyond the data provided by our bodies, minds, and emotions in a state where thought has no content. There, we discover and begin to participate in a profound renewal on every level. That is what yoga is all about.

GUIDED MEDITATION*

*When the yogin abides with his breath and mind absorbed
within, his gaze and pupils unmoving and, though seeing the
outside world, does not see it, this, then, is the posture of
Shiva arising through your grace, O Master. That truth free
of emptiness and non-emptiness is the state of Shiva.*

— ABHINAVAGUPTA

What follows is a suggested sequence for the practice of sitting in meditation. It consists of techniques and specific aspects to
notice as you practice. These points are dealt with briefly, with
the emphasis on what to *do* as you sit in meditation. The subsequent chapters will discuss in greater depth the meaning and
place of these different techniques in the practice of Trika Yoga.

Preparation for Meditation
We do not want the chemistry and the tensions of our everyday work and experience to limit our awareness, our flexibility,
or our range of motion. This is true not only in a physical sense,
but in a mental, emotional and spiritual sense as well. So, when
we sit down to meditate, we first take a little time to feel the different areas in our bodies, especially those areas where strain
tends to accumulate — the shoulders, knees, neck, and lower
back — and to relax them before we start. Then, as we sit, they
won't become more locked and therefore a source of distraction.
You don't need to do anything quite as elaborate as the process I
will give you here, but the point is not to assume that your body
is relaxed already because, in fact, often it is not.

Sit up straight. If you are sitting on the floor, try to sit up on
a cushion that is high enough so that you can comfortably cross
your legs. If you are sitting in a chair, be sure that your feet are on

---

* Editor's note: As a further aid to your practice, you may wish to refer to the
audio tape *Meditation: An Invitation to Inner Growth* by Swami Chetanananda
(Rudra Press, Cambridge, 1989).

the floor. Put your hands — thumb and forefinger together, palms up — on your thighs. This hand posture is called a *mudra*.

Start by relaxing your shoulders, pulling them back at the shoulder blades. Don't strain — just pull them back, and then let them drop. Let your head fall forward so that your chin touches your chest. Stretch out your neck, then sit back upright and let your neck relax. Swallow a few times to relax your throat. Then take a deep breath up your nose, and direct your breath into the top of your head — into your brain — and relax your whole head. Now relax the center of your brain again. As you do so, feel how your awareness extends itself.

Do you begin to get a subtle experience of the pulsation of your awareness? That pulsation is happening all the time because there is a continuous, reciprocal relationship between the deepest, simplest inner part of you and the total field of your activity. The more you relax, the more you begin to be aware of this dynamic interchange.

Now, take your attention down your back, relaxing each section — upper, middle, and lower. As you do this, also let your chest and your abdomen relax by tightening the muscles and then releasing them. Then, take your attention through your legs, starting with the feet and moving up through the ankles, calves, knees and thighs, up into the hips, doing the same tightening and releasing process. If you want to, you can rotate on your rear end a little bit, moving back and forth to loosen the muscles in your hips and buttocks, as well as the base of your spine.

Then, in the same way, move your attention through your arms, starting with the fingers and working your way up to your shoulders. Remember that the body responds to suggestion. If you tell it to relax, it will. Now, go back to the head, relaxing all the muscles in the face, and relaxing the brain once again.

Try to feel yourself letting go of all your worries and tensions. As for every desire, let it go. Relax your mind and your thoughts. These are not your life. Relax your body — it is just the tip of the iceberg. Begin to feel deeply within yourself.

At various points along the way as you are sitting, if any part of your body starts to be a distraction to you, just stop what you are doing, bring your attention into that area, relax it, and start over again. After a few weeks of sitting, the distractions posed by your body should become essentially irrelevant.

Breath

Breathing deeply will also facilitate this process of relaxing your body. Sit up straight and take a deep breath. Breathe simply, deeply, and regularly and feel your breathing. As you exhale, feel yourself becoming more quiet. This gives rise to a reciprocal event. As you become quiet, your body relaxes more; as your body relaxes, you are able to become more quiet and breathe more and more steadily.

Breathing slowly down from your diaphragm, take a deep breath and fill your whole body cavity. Feel the air come in and expand your abdomen. Breathe in until your breath naturally pauses, without being forced. When you reach that full point, the breath automatically stops and holds itself for a little bit. When it wants to come out again, exhale slowly and feel your whole body relax.

It may require a bit of practice but, as you sit, it is a good thing to re-train your breathing so that you are breathing from your diaphragm down into your belly, and not from your diaphragm up into your chest. If you breathe only with the top portion of your lungs, your breathing will make you tired.

Breathe instead from the diaphragm, making sure the diaphragm goes down as you breathe. In that way, the chest cavity fills quite naturally and you use your whole lung capacity. This will allow you to feel relaxed and energized. It is an especially valuable practice when you are dealing with tensions or experiencing a lot of stress.

As you inhale, hear in your mind the syllable *so*. On the outbreath, release the air slowly and hear — again, silently — the syllable *ham*, which is a humming sound. Feel the resonance of that *hmmm* in your throat and in the area of your heart, and notice how that resonance expands downward to the base of your spine.

Notice that when you breathe in naturally, there comes a point when the breath stops and is still for a moment before it goes back out. When you exhale, again it is still for a moment, before it comes back in. To pause at these points and notice the quality at the heart of them — this is what is known as stillness.

If you practice this particular technique, you increase your awareness of the various tides within your breath and your ability to attune yourself to the stillness at the center of them. The two points of stillness between the in-breath and the out-breath begin to merge and you come to experience the entire process of the breath as stillness. This brings all the disturbance and agitation — indeed, all perception — to that same, simple stillpoint.

The various breathing techniques, or pranayama, alluded to in different texts of Kashmir Shaivism have to do with stilling the breath. Once you are able to stabilize your awareness in those points where the breath is either fully withdrawn or extended, you have found the stillpoint. This is the pivotal point — the point from which the Breath of Life arises and subsides. It is the same as the highest state of self-awareness, in which the supreme creative energy Itself pulsates.

Chakras

As you sit, take your attention into the base of your spine. You will find that the base of your spine rocks gently backward on the in-breath, and forward on the out-breath. Keep your attention at the base of your spine until you feel a certain shift — something like a sense of opening.

With practice, you will notice not only the gentle rocking motion of the spine but also that inside that movement there is an even more subtle pulsation. As you come to experience that pulsation more definitely, notice, too, that each wave in the pulse moves completely up your spine. In other words, within the gross breath, there is another, finer, faster frequency — what I sometimes call the breath within the breath.

Next, take your attention to the *chakra*, or energy center, at the base of your sexual organs. Notice the difference between this vibration and the resonance at the base of your spine. Again, keep your attention there until you feel a shift.

Take your attention into your abdomen, two fingers down from your navel, breathing down from your diaphragm. (This is the same place which, when you get angry, becomes like a rock.) Tighten your abdomen, hold it for a moment, and then release. As you breathe, pull the air down and let your attention go into this center.

Breathing in and out, start to feel this center relax. As you do so, if you concentrate on that point, first your mind will become quiet; then you will feel your energy start to move down and settle there. From that, you will feel an expansion starting to take place in this center.

Breathe in again. Fill your whole body cavity with air. Take your attention deeper into the abdominal chakra and feel the same expansion process taking place again. Then exhale and relax. The more energy and attention you invest in this center, the stronger it becomes.

Notice how, as the base of your spine pulsates and the waves of that pulsation move up your spine, a slightly different frequency of vibration begins to happen there, too. Breathe into it and relax.

Notice how one frequency plays inside the next frequency, and so on. I like to think of it as a symphonic orchestra in which at the bottom are the drums, bass, and tubas — the heavier sounds. As we move up, there are the finer frequencies, until we get to the woodwinds at the top. Each finer frequency plays inside a heavier one, the grosser manifestations giving way on examination to the finer and finer ones. The harmony that establishes itself within these frequencies gives rise in us to the experience of deep, simple joy and complete well-being.

Next, allow your attention to rise up naturally to the center of your chest. Right there, we have not merely a physical pump but a profound energy center called the heart chakra. This is a powerful place from which and through which our inner spirit functions.

Breathing naturally, take a deep breath in your upper chest, filling the whole cavity with air. When your upper chest is filled, your breath will naturally pause and hold. At that point, take your attention into your heart chakra. First, it gets a little bit tight; then, it starts to relax, expand, and open. (If you can't feel this right away, don't worry about it. Simply continue to practice.) As you experience this expansion, notice the feeling of great sweetness that begins to enter there. Then exhale.

Take your attention now into your throat, and swallow to release any tension there.

Next, breathe up through your nose into the chakra between your eyebrows, relaxing your head as you do so. Can you feel a small point between your eyebrows? Notice that the feeling there is different from that in the other centers we have experienced.

Do nothing but be aware. If your mind wanders or your body starts to bother you, breathe for a few minutes, take your awareness to your breath, relax your body, and start over again. Try to maintain your contact with this trans-sensory awareness. From time to time, swallow to relax your throat, and direct your attention to your breath in order to allow this total energy field to flow naturally through your psychic and physical mechanisms and be absorbed.

Now take your attention to the top of your head. Breathe up, relax the whole crown of your head, and feel the many points on the crown of your head. As you breathe up, you may feel these points expanding and contracting, something like the movement of the petals of a great flower as they open and close in the wind. Each of these petals has a slightly different resonance, a different chemistry, a different content, that is released into your awareness.

Flow

Having opened these energy centers by bringing your focused attention to them, one after the other, you want to begin to train yourself to be aware of the flow of energy that is always circulating between them. Having brought your attention to the crown of your head, take it back into your throat, then into your heart and, after that, into the navel chakra. Sense the feeling in your head flowing down through the chakras as you move your attention lower and lower into your abdomen and then to the base of your spine. By drawing it back down through the chakras, you profoundly absorb the energy aroused in the experience of sitting.

Then feel that energy rise up your spine through the crown of your head again. This closes the circle. As you sit, continue to take your awareness down the front, through the chakras, and then up the back, through the spine. In this way, you become aware of the flow of energy which is the energy of Life Itself.

Presence

There comes a point, as we sit, when flow and chakras are no longer what we are paying the most attention to. Although we continue to be aware of them, we also experience an awareness of what I call Presence — a single, pure Presence which is both the perfection of Life and the highest state.

It is as simple as following the pattern from breath, to chakras, to flow, to presence. Just following our breath will unfold this progression for us. In that Presence is a stillness which changes the vibration of the field of our daily experience. This is real and sustainable change. When we open our hearts, this Presence can start to assert itself. The feeling that results is the spirit which informs us about ourselves as it informs us about itself and about Life and God.

Conclusion of Meditation

When you are ready to conclude your meditation, pull your shoulders back slowly as far as you can, and let them drop. Let your head roll forward, bringing your chin to your neck. Then, roll your head from side to side, or around in a full circle, in order to relax your neck. Roll down forward to stretch out your spine, especially your lower back. Take a deep breath and roll back up. Rock a little from side to side to loosen your buttocks, and stretch out your legs if you want to. This brings the circulation back into your muscles. Then, take a deep breath and relax.

Doing all of this brings your awareness back into your body. Each time after you sit in meditation, it is good to stretch a little, in order slowly and carefully to integrate the energy in which you have participated into your physical body and your waking state.

You also want to take some time to notice, aside from a little stiffness, how different your body feels from when you first sat down. This allows you to become increasingly aware of how you feel when you release tensions so that, in time, you can carry this experience into everything you do.

MANTRA AND THE BREATH

Student, do the simple purification.

You know that the seed is inside the horse-chestnut tree;
and inside the seed there are the blossoms of the tree,

and the chestnuts, and the shade.
So inside the human body there's a seed, and

inside the seed there is the human body again . . . .

If you want the truth, I'll tell you the truth:
Listen to the secret sound, the real sound, which is inside you.
The one no one talks of speaks the secret sound to himself,
and he is the one who has made it all.

— KABIR

A person who comes to a spiritual teacher is often given a *mantra*. This is a sacred syllable, a word, or even a series of words that the student repeats over and over again while he or she practices sitting in meditation. Classically, this practice has been understood as a means to help us focus our attention and support the mind in meditation. However, the point of such a word or phrase is actually more subtle than that. A mantra is also a living sound-force, the practice of which awakens in us a refined awareness of the nature of our own being and of the world.

The mantra repetition we do is only the first step in a great process of unfoldment. It is important that we practice it vigilantly as such, while paying close attention to what happens as we do so. In the process, we also discover that paying attention, in and of itself, is one of the most important parts of everything we do in our sadhana — our pursuit of an ideal, and our search for God and for truth.

In the early stage of our practice, we may repeat a mantra as a kind of prayer, attaching to this syllable our desires and aspirations for emotional satisfaction or even for material success and abundance. All of these things are bound up together as a part of this beginning stage of our practice. Over time, our understanding of the repetition of mantra will change, but at this stage it represents a part of the effort we make.

When a mantra is a single syllable, it is known as a *bija* (seed) mantra. One of the best known examples of this is the mantra "Om." Bija mantras, although there are principles of logic for their selection and use, have no particular meaning. Rather, they have a certain esoteric symbolism.

The practice of the bija mantra is aimed at leading us to experience the deeper aspects of the mantra, so that our awareness of it changes as we repeat it. We will not notice certain subtleties for a while but, if we continue to practice, eventually we experience actual shifts in frequency within the mantra itself. These are not shifts in any external sound that we can hear but actual frequency shifts in the energy of what we are doing.

Ultimately, our practice of any mantra is intended to refine our awareness to the point where we experience that pulsation going on within us all the time. When we can do that, we forget about the mantra itself because we are now aware, instead, of the dynamic event going on within and around us. As a result, the total vibration of what we are is changed. In the process, we transform ourselves.

There is no conflict between the different mantras, because they are all essentially one. In order for a mantra to *be* a mantra, however, it must be given by a teacher. Otherwise it is just a word. A mantra has force because it is practiced and passed on. It represents the exchange not of information but of energy between a teacher and ourselves. Thus, it is really a vehicle through which a particular teaching is transmitted. Therefore, throughout the whole Kashmir Shaivite tradition, the authentic mantra always comes to the student from the mouth of the teacher. If it does not, it is not effectively a mantra.

Mantra, as vibration, is the very nature of kundalini, the living energy which is the essence of our lives. It is the symphony of Life Itself playing in our hearts, our minds, and our senses. Mantra is the various frequencies that pulsate in the form of each one of us. So, we could say that each one of us *is* a different mantra and that when we receive a verbal mantra, it becomes individualized. Given the individual nature of our particular vibration, how could it be otherwise? Each mantra has a vibration at its subtle core that has an effect on the total field of energy articulated as you or I. Ultimately, mantra is our own life force, and to this we attune ourselves.

Likewise, every physical posture has a frequency. Basically, this is the significance of *mudra*, which means "posture." There are many such mudras, some of which involve the hands and fingers, while others engage the entire body. Their aim — indeed, the aim of the science of mantra and of mudra as a whole — is to put us more directly in touch with the whole range of the creative display manifested in and around us by the infinite.

Mantras and mudras work together. A mantra arouses a particular frequency by working to coalesce and draw together a certain energy. A mudra, on the other hand, by involving the physical body, grounds that frequency and translates it into a material event. Not only does this experience change the awareness of the person who is practicing; it also has an effect on the total field in which that person functions.

We can draw an analogy from the weather. When it is cloudy and we experience a low pressure system, a lower frequency of energy within the atmosphere presses down on everything. Because of the low pressure, the subtle pulse in the atmosphere is slower. What happens in that case? Everybody feels at least laid back and maybe even a little gloomy.

In contrast, when a high pressure system comes in, the clouds clear out and there is much less bearing down on us. Then, the frequency in the air picks up, there is a lot more light, and everybody feels more cheerful. Most people don't pay much attention to the difference. Their minds tend to be so tuned toward what they have to do during the day that whether it is cloudy or sunny is only one more background feature to their event. More to the point, they don't make a direct connection between the air pressure and their state of mind. Instead, they get caught up in their mood as if it were the whole reality.

Traditionally, however, it has been recognized that the nature of the frequency dominating our environment has a tremendous impact not only on our state, but on how we interact with and influence external events. This is why, in the training of individual students, different mudras were given and practiced to strengthen the character and disposition of each person and to counteract individual weaknesses. The same thing has been true of the practice of mantra.

As we practice, the process of focusing our minds on a mantra will take our attention off everything else going on between our ears. This gives the total field of our minds a chance to decompress and unwind. We start to relax, our muscles slowly let go, and the whole biological, chemical event changes. Thus, on one level, what we are learning is a set of techniques to help us stop repeating the mantra of ignorance — "What's going to happen to me?" — and to recognize, instead, the mantra of fulfillment which is pulsating inside us all the time. The mantra we repeat is only a technique for quieting our minds to the point where we can be in touch with that pulsation and maintain our awareness of it for increasingly long periods of time.

The person who comes to this with great sincerity, however, gets something else — that is, the real mantra — the living vibration that arouses our awareness of the life within us. It is the kundalini pulsating inside us as our Self. This mantra is the essence of initiation. It awakens us to the vitality of our inner nature and, as it pulsates inside us, begins to purify our bodies, minds, and emotions until, slowly, it reaches into the deepest part of us and tangibly reveals to our minds and senses the universal nature and power hidden inside us. This is what it means to grow.

Mantra repetition, as a stage in our practice, also helps to keep our minds from wandering. We discover, however, that as long as we think of a mantra as the actual sounds we repeat, we reinforce our tendency to stay at the level of vocalization. We also tend to stay stuck in our heads because this approach subtly reinforces the notion that we can *think* our way out of the contradiction we experience between our somethingness and our nothingness. Mantra is deeper than this. It is a pulsation of pure energy.

As the physical breath moves in and out, it repeats by itself the mantra *ham-sa*, or *so-ham*. This vibration is called *ajapa-japa*. *Japa* means the repetition of a mantra. Ajapa-japa is the repetition that occurs without the deliberate act of repetition. What does this mean? Since our breathing naturally makes the sound "so" as we inhale and "ham" as we exhale, we call hamsa the mantra that repeats itself without conscious effort. Therefore, I encourage people, instead of repeating a mantric syllable or phrase, to feel their breath and the flow of energy within themselves, and to let *that* be their mantra.

Think of it this way — the simplest and most fundamental movement that each of us *is* is respiration. This respiration involves three systems: 1) the combined cerebro-spinal and lymphatic system, 2) the pulmonary system, and 3) the cardiovascular system. These three respiratory systems, which are constantly pulsating, work together to manifest Life and are responsible for the support and maintenance of our biological existence. Although they do not have the same frequency, they are fundamentally connected to one another. The fluctuation of the energy in the cerebro-spinal system is the foundation of the physical breath which, in turn, is the foundation of our cardiovascular action. If there is no pulsation of Life Itself, there is no power by which the physical breath takes place; if we don't breathe, there is no cardiovascular activity.

It is the fluctuation within the cerebro-spinal fluid that is responsible for translating the energy of Life Itself into a biological event. This is the basis of our very manifestation. The breath of Life — referred to in the texts as *prana* — manifests on three levels: first, as the Absolute, second, as a generalized field of creative biological potential and, third, as specific individuals like ourselves.

Within the individual, it expresses itself as the pulsation that moves through the cerebro-spinal fluid, and so on. At the same time that it is the foundation of our manifestation, it is also the essence of all three of our individual respiratory systems. The fluctuation of this essence is known as the fundamental *pranic* tide.

The individualized prana pulsates some 21,600 times a day through the cerebro-spinal fluid. This happens every day, for every living person. Furthermore, the same type of fluctuation also manifests in every living event. This pulsation of Life Itself is the fundamental mantra that is on-going at all times. We are simply an expression of this mantra of the divine. The fluctuation happens and, because of it, we breathe.

The cerebro-spinal fluid is the medium through which the kundalini energy translates into a biological pulse — something like our biological battery. Are the biological pulse and the kundalini the same thing? Not exactly. They don't exist on the same level, in that the biological pulse is a material event, while the kundalini is not.

Kundalini as the energy that functions within the cerebro-spinal fluid is like the waves that travel through the ocean. The waves are not the same thing as the water, although it is hard to separate the two. Kundalini is the energy of Life Itself pulsating within us, motivating the involuntary nervous system to pulsate, and giving rise both to the voluntary mechanism and to our ability to feel, think, and do. This subtle pulse also translates into the various pulsations that are the foundation of our biological existence. This, in turn, is the source of the biological imperatives that launch us into the world in search of sustenance and the opportunity to reproduce.

There is but one highest, pure being which respires and whose breath we *are*. One way of looking at ourselves is as the word of God who is repeating us. We don't breathe *that*; rather, *it* breathes *us* because it is the fundamental power behind all the voluntary and involuntary nerve functions. The breath we are ordinarily aware of breathing is only an individualized expression of this.

Simply put, mantra is the Word that is spoken about in the Gospel of John. Ultimately, there is only one mantra, and that is the pulsation of Life. However, just as many frequencies arise from this one simple vibration, so the pulse of Life becomes the gross mantra that we can speak and hear.

Ordinarily, the energy pulsating deep within us becomes diffused as we direct our attention to all the things going on around us. One of the results of focusing our attention on our breathing is that we withdraw our senses from their usual degree of activity and involvement in these other things. The aim of all breathing practices is to cultivate our ability to experience the deeper pulsation within us. As we examine this vital process on the grossest level — namely, in our breathing and the different forms of respiration going on in our physical bodies — the understanding of the highest nature of reality eventually emerges within us.

Through our attention to our breathing, we begin to observe these various levels of vibration, consciously feeling and tuning into them. This doesn't mean that we space out or let just anything happen; rather, we train our senses, especially our sense of touch. By this I mean not only our physical touch but also our ability to touch things with our inner awareness, our minds, and our hearts. As we become more aware of our physical breathing, we will also begin to notice the pulsation of the cardiovascular system, the lymphatics, the electrical nerve impulses, and so on.

To become aware of the pulsation of the breath of Life is to attune ourselves to, and to participate in, the highest vibration. It is to understand the fundamental ground of all reality. By training this deeper ability within ourselves, we start to understand the very nature of the Self. We transcend all limitation, and the shackles of bondage are shattered.

As we become established in the awareness of this self-repeating mantra, we come to experience that *we* are not breathing, but rather that we are being breathed. Through our contemplation of this breath of Life, which is intimately connected to the highest creative energy of Life Itself, we become established in a tangible awareness of the divine. At that stage, we experience the joy of the infinite, highest state.

What really happens when we repeat a mantra is that, through our experience of the vibration, we become aware of the dynamic but subtly structured chaos that the whole universe is, and of which we are a part. Do you see how such awareness would put an end to your attachment to your own limited form?

To cultivate this awareness takes discipline and commitment as well as insight into the long-term effects of our behavior not only on others but also on ourselves. It requires that we let go of whatever has the potential to become an obstruction in the long term. This, in turn, requires a subtle, intuitive discrimination.

Our practice facilitates that process. The mantra stirs the kundalini energy within us, awakening and expanding it. Slowly, gently, just as the cleaning vat at a jeweler's gently shakes the dirt from even the tiniest pores of the gold or silver, so this mantra shakes from us all our negativity and tension. It shakes off the confusion, frustration, disappointment, anger, hostility, and bitterness. It shakes off the soil and the soot that cover our minds and our intellects, revealing to us the brilliance of our inner Self and its unlimited potency.

It is not a question of using one set of words to drown out another; rather, our minds become expansive, luminous, and clear. Our hearts become open, not crowded and cluttered with tensions. We can move around in our hearts freely without bumping into things. They are no longer like the closets in which we store our unused tennis rackets, the skis we haven't used in five years, the typewriters we had in college, the quantities of old clothes that have gone unworn for decades — they are not crowded anymore because we have discovered the vastness within.

As we train our concentration, our minds become focused inside ourselves. They become centered and still, as the mantra of the inner Self exudes its sweetness and radiance. Meditation then is effortless. At that stage, we are no longer trying to attain anything — there is no need. When we can simply tune into the mantra within, there is no higher attainment. We simply attune ourselves to that mantra and remember it. Then we will find the song of the secret Lord. From this, we go forward to the experience of the very Word of God because mantra, in its highest form, is nothing but the word of God.

As that mantra of fulfillment pulsates within us, it emanates waves of great beauty and joy that fill our hearts, saturate our minds and bodies, and overflow around us into the hearts, minds, and bodies of the people whose lives we share. Then, everything that we experience is mantra.

DYNAMIC STILLPOINTS: THE CHAKRAS

Don't go outside your house to see flowers.
My friend, don't bother with that excursion.
Inside your body there are flowers.
One flower has a thousand petals.
That will do for a place to sit.
Sitting there you will have a glimpse of beauty
inside the body and out of it,
before gardens and after gardens.

— KABIR

The Tantric tradition, as a whole, says that people are individualized expressions of the divine creative pulsation of Life Itself. Each person is like a wave on the ocean — an extension of the Supreme Self but not different from the Supreme Self in any way. This supreme creative energy in its absolute form is called *parashakti*. In its extended, individualized form, it is called kundalini. As kundalini, it is also known as the "garland of letters," a poetic way of referring to the vibrations inherent in the supreme Shakti, or the creative energy of Life Itself.

Trika Yoga is the practice by which we can come to know and understand this creative energy that is our very foundation. This practice is based on the fact that there are three primary channels of energy at the level of the subtle body. The first is located in the spinal cord and is called the *shushumna*. On either side of it, two other primary channels — the *ida* and the *pingala* — cross back and forth.

The seven points at which all three channels intersect form the primary energy centers, where the creative energy expressing itself as our bodies, minds, emotions, and spirit converges in a particularly dynamic way. These seven centers are known as the chakras. They are what Rudi used to call "the gateways to the soul," the areas where the basic creative energy of Life translates into action.

The word "chakra" means a circle or wheel; it can also mean a group or a collection. The chakras referred to in Trika Yoga represent the essential element in Tantric sadhana. There are quite a number of chakras, and different systems of thought take count of them in different ways. (Some texts in the Kashmir Shaivite tradition number them at 72,000.) We focus on seven primary ones in our practice.

There is a chakra in the base of the spine, in the vicinity of our sex organs, in the pit of our stomach about two fingers below the navel, in the middle of our chest, in our throat, between our eyebrows, and at the top of our head. Actually, the whole crown of the head is identified as a chakra.

These seven centers have a profound influence over our physiology, our mind and emotions, and ultimately our understanding. This is why we direct our attention into them in our practice. By doing so, we learn to expand and open them into something far greater than the body and more beautiful than anything you have ever seen in your life. Once we begin to experience this, we cannot help but ask, "Where does this come from and what is it all about?" As we attend to each chakra, we begin to understand not only how they are interrelated, but also how this interrelatedness constitutes *us*.

Since chakras, on one level, are differentiated events, it is possible for their functioning to become restricted. We can see this particularly when our systems are out of balance. Under the influence of our biological imperatives and the mantra of stupidity, we react to the circumstances around us by taking on tensions. This causes the energy centers in our system to contract.

We can say that stress and strain do not have a material reality, but their impact certainly has a real effect on our material system. Indeed, any attachment or tension can impede the functioning of this energy system. When the chakras are closed, the total function of our subtle body is impeded. At the level of our material bodies, the effects of stress and strain are the thickening of cell walls, resulting in their diminished permeability, in the decreased efficiency with which the cells exchange oxygen and fluids, and in the backing up of byproducts within the cells which cause them to die from constipation.

To a great extent, the cells sustain the patterns of strain that we take on because they themselves are not especially intelligent. They do whatever they are patterned to do. Thus, patterns of stress remain there until their energy has somehow been released, which can happen only when we condense the stress pattern itself to its fulcrum point and allow the basic respiration process to be renewed.

What does this mean? Our cells are constantly interacting with each other through different pathways, channels, and patterns of exchange. In each of these exchanges, there is a point of balance — a fulcrum point — between the two chemical valences of plus and minus. Thus, each one of the various flows has a center to it — a point of equilibrium.

This is true of every chemical pattern in our system. Every relationship within the biological entity that we are has a fulcrum point where the two sides of the interaction are equal. There are billions of such fulcrum points, but seven primary ones relate to the total field of our functioning, from the simplest level of manifestation within us to the most complicated biological process. These are the chakras.

A currently popular line of understanding suggests that the chakras are related to specific zones of physical functioning, and that this is what is important about them. This, in turn, leads people to talk about having "a problem" in one of their chakras — the most frequently focused upon being the sex chakra. This is misguided thinking and indicates confusion about the true nature of the chakras themselves.

Each chakra is an energy center that expresses itself in particular ways both within our systems and in relation to the environment around us. In this sense only can we say that each chakra has a relationship to some aspect of our physical, intellectual, and emotional lives. Likewise, certain aspects of our understanding are direct articulations of the vibration of a particular chakra.

This is a much more subtle and complex phenomenon, however, than the cause-and-effect relationship suggested by the "problem" approach. Instead, the energy in one of our chakras may become dense and contracted because of our inability to absorb one tension or another. This contraction obstructs the energy of that chakra from fully articulating its potentiality on many levels. It might manifest as some form of dysfunction or give rise to some dissatisfaction.

At the same time, in a deeper sense, there is no "problem." This is an important distinction because, once we start thinking that we can fix specific "problems" by "working on our chakras," not only are we buying into the idea that we have real problems in the first place; we are also falling into the trap of spiritual materialism — that is, of trying to *use* God instead of trying to *know* God. At that point, we have ceased altogether to engage in authentic spiritual work.

As we work with them, the chakras open naturally. This is not a process we can force. Nor is there any reason to think of the chakras as something to cultivate for any other purpose. They simply flower within us. The experience, in itself, is reason enough.

When we first hear about the chakras, they can seem like some mysterious, even improbable, phenomenon. *We* have never noticed anything like that in ourselves — or have we? Think of this: Has your heart ever been broken, and did that experience change your behavior, both in the short and the long term? Probably it has, and probably it did. It affects us powerfully to have our hearts broken, and we don't usually forget the experience.

Of course, when we say that something or someone has broken our hearts, we are not talking about anything physical. After all, when the heart is physically broken down, that is a heart attack. So, we mean something different. The term "heart" actually refers to three levels of experience: the individual experience we have of our own heart chakra; the heart as our center in the stillness of the mind; and the absolute essence of all reality.

When these hearts of ours are affected, we feel it deeply. We may be in pain or we may be ecstatic, but whatever the state of our hearts, *they* define how *we* feel. The paradox is that we define our mental and emotional state by them, yet know so little about them. Indeed, we spend little time even thinking about them.

The heart and how it is responding on any given day constitutes one of the most powerful influences over our psychology and our behavior. Depending on what is going on in there, anything can be happening in our minds — nice thoughts as well as wild ones. Our behavior can be relaxed and encompassing of others or downright brutal and cruel. I find it truly remarkable that, based on whether or not the heart is open, we decide whether we are having a good day or a bad one, are nice to others or withdrawn and agitated. Whatever is happening in the heart is just that essential to our experience.

In various ways, this is also true of the other chakras. For example, have you ever been so afraid that the pit of your stomach twisted like a knot? Doesn't that also change your behavior? Or have you ever been so emotional that you felt completely choked in your throat and couldn't talk? These energy centers profoundly affect our minds and emotions, our thoughts and behavior. Everything we feel, think, and do, in some way manifests first through these centers. So, in the exploration of our inner Self, we take our attention into these centers and begin to look through their windows into our soul. But to do that, we first have to open them.

This can take a little while. After all, how many of us ever actually stop to pay attention to these energy centers? At certain moments, we may notice that our hearts feel open, but that is usually the end of it. It is like looking outside and noticing that the sun is shining, but simply taking it for granted. When we neglect our hearts for long periods of time, as we often do, they don't just open up immediately when we ask them to. It may be that they once did, but after a while they stop thinking that we are sincere when we ask. When this happens, we have to direct the warmth of our attention to them for some time. Then slowly, just as a garden responds to the light of the sun, so the inner heart slowly responds to the light of our attention — our consciousness — first by expanding, then by releasing into our awareness the fragrance and sweetness which are the love that sustains our human existence.

The frequency of the energy vibrating in the heart is finer than any you have felt before. You might at first experience some kind of spasm — some spontaneous body movement — as this force starts to awaken within you, but you will also feel a sweetness slowly starting to fill your heart, drop by drop. Feel that, breathe into it, and let it expand.

When you work with the heart chakra in your meditation, release all your wants and needs, all your cares and worries. Your desires and fears are the logs that keep the fire of agitation burning inside you. Let them go — feel them fall away. Instead, sincerely ask to grow, until you feel an inner shift. Stay focused on that wish until the shift occurs and supports you. This is something that you can do again and again.

If you only keep feeling into that fine, subtle point, gradually it will become bigger and, in time, can become great. Indeed, the center of some great beings is as big as the manifest universe. Wherever they are and whatever happens, they are at ease in the experience of "I am That."

The center of the head is, paradoxically, a center of gravity. Compare it with the structure of a flower. If we look at a flower, we see that the top of the stem is also the base of the flower from which all the petals come forth. The spinal column is suspended from the base of the skull, a neat little hanger that allows the spine to hang in space and affords it range of motion. It is at this point at the base of the skull that we experience the kundalini energy — the energy of our individual creativity — as it rises up to meet the descent of the divine creative energy. We practice maintaining our awareness of that space.

While our gross senses can function only within a limited range of frequencies, there is, within all of us, the potential to resonate on many more frequencies than we are ordinarily aware of. Indeed, in the crown of our head, there is the potential to resonate with all of the energies that manifest as this universe.

This highest chakra has to do with liberation, the freedom from and transcendence of the entire field of individual human endeavor. It is in this center that the stream of our individuality merges into the ocean of pure, undifferentiated awareness. When we direct our attention outward, we forget about that subtle space. Our minds run on and on, and we are never still enough to get there in the first place. However, if we focus on opening the chakras in the head, we increase our capacity to restrain the impulse to direct our attention outward.

Within this system of chakras, there are also what various texts describe as three knots, or *granthis*. These are sometimes described as the knuckles in a stalk of bamboo. In some schools of Kashmir Shaivism, these knots are considered to be more important than the seven chakras, although they are intrinsically part of the same system. In any case, they, too, can serve as points of focus in our practice.

One of these knots lies at the base of the spine, the second in the heart, and the third in the chakra between the eyebrows. These granthis are given the names of deities (as are the chakras). There is the *Brahma granthi* in the base of the spine, the *Vishnu granthi* in the heart, and the *Rudra granthi* in the head.

In Hindu mythology, Brahma is the aspect of God that brings the universe into manifestation out of God, Vishnu is the aspect that sustains the universe for a time, and Rudra (another name for Shiva) is the aspect that destroys it, drawing it back into itself. This process of expansion, pause, and contraction is nothing other than a way of talking about the pulsation of Life Itself.

The Brahma granthi is related to the chakras at the base of the spine, in the sex area, and below the navel. In time and with practice, we discover that while these three lower chakras have subtle differences, together they play a unified role in the manifestation and strength of our individuality, along with the qualities of our character. Both the Brahma granthi and these three chakras have to do with our physical nature, our biological processes, and our movement in the world. In martial arts, this is the primary chakra where practitioners center their attention.

The Vishnu granthi is related to the heart and throat chakras and involves the mental and emotional aspects of our existence, including our capacity for compassion. The Rudra granthi, which is related to the chakras between our eyebrows and in our head, has everything to do with the transcendental aspects of our existence and with what I would call wisdom and understanding. We could also use the term "wisdom" in connection with the heart, but that would be the wisdom related to life as a creative process in the context of our manifest human existence. In contrast, the chakras in the head have everything to do with the wisdom related to self–realization, liberation, and stabilization in the highest state.

As we deepen our spiritual work and develop a more penetrating awareness, we pierce these knots and dissolve these fundamental structures, because they are the basic points in the mechanism around which various tensions condense. Piercing them is what allows the kundalini energy to move unrestrained through our whole system. As it does so, it alters and finally dissolves, transforming the structure itself.

Some people ask what to focus on during meditation. When you sit down to practice, start with the base of the spine and work your way upwards, focusing on wherever the strongest feeling happens to be. If you feel a great tension or a strong knot in your stomach, for example, take your attention there and breathe into it until it relaxes and feels focused. Then, move on to the next thing.

If you feel an overwhelming joy or something almost like a sweet nectar emerging from your heart and starting to flow through your whole system, keep your attention with it until it subsides. If you feel the whole pattern of your mind and brain starting to dissolve in your head, and if that has a different *rasa* (a texture and flavor) of sweetness to it, keep your attention with that and enjoy it.

In some cases, you will feel tension and constriction that you will have to breathe into; in others, it will be some wonderful experience, and you will also breathe into that. Some of it will be profound and, when it is all over, you will recognize your unity with the fundamental process of respiration which is the essence of everything that is. Whatever you feel, though, continue to practice the same thing over and over, coming to it on each occasion as though it were the first time.

Take your attention into each of the chakras successively and feel the pulsation there. Keep your attention at that point until you feel a shift — a subtle expansion — taking place. Breathe into that and open to it. Then, go to the next chakra, feeling each of them successively, from the base of your spine to the top of your head. Once they are open, then begin to move your attention down the front of the body from the top of your head to the base of your spine, and up the back to the top of the head. This is the same circle of energy we talked about in the discussion of flow. As you do that, keep your body relaxed and your breathing regular, but don't fall asleep. Don't take a long time — just a few moments in each place — until you feel the subtle change happen. Then move along.

Each center has its own nature and, in a sense, you can start with any one of them that you want. The point is that, because this is a whole system, wherever you start is not where you will end up. Furthermore, each individual point is completely one with the field in which it is articulated. This means that we cannot open one part without, at the same time, having every other part of the system change. It is a whole event in which everything that happens affects everything else. You need only take your attention inside one of these centers and begin to feel an expansion within it to feel an expansion beginning to happen in all the other centers as well.

By withdrawing your attention into each of these chakras successively and staying there until you feel this process of contraction, shift, and re-expansion occurring, you begin to experience directly, on the different levels of your individualized manifestation, the functioning of this vast and subtle creative power. By being aware of your breathing and feeling the effects of the breath in each of the energy centers as you breathe, you will notice how your breath extends from and retreats into each of them. It is much like the way the tide pulls in and draws back.

As you feel each of the different energy centers, you will also experience more and more palpably that each one has a different vibration. Together, they generate a resonance which is the symphony of your individual existence. It is the magnetic field that shapes all experience for you. Over time, as you become quiet and centered, increasingly subtle vibrations and resonances will become accessible to your awareness until, finally, you become established in the dynamic stillness which is the source of your being and the power behind all change.

We cultivate our capacity to concentrate by moving our attention from chakra to chakra and by beginning to be aware of the basic flow of energy that manifests on the physiological, mental, emotional, psychic, and transpersonal levels. As each of the chakras starts to resonate and expand, we feel the flow that connects them all — the tide that surges subtly forward to encompass each chakra and then subsides into the dynamic stillness of pure consciousness, the highest state.

Try to feel in yourself this flow of energy and open to its nourishment. Allow your awareness to follow it deeply inside you and feel the simple joy hidden in its depths. Breathe from that joy and to that joy and feel it expand. As you sit quietly, aware of the fluctuation of your breath and of the flow of the energy within you, you may also become aware of what I call the breath within the breath. This is the subtle pulsation within the pulsation of your breath. As you cultivate your awareness of it, it becomes stronger and stronger. It becomes your strength and your clarity, your support and, eventually, your awareness of the divine.

This takes practice, and you will probably find that your attention wanders from time to time. When you recognize that you have gotten lost in some thought, come back and start again. Relax your body, focus on your breath, feel the flow, and take your attention from chakra to chakra, following your breath down the front and up the back. Relax, allow your heart to open, and let this higher creative energy begin to work deeply within you.

If you are so wound up that you can't do that, then think of something simple like a flower or a place that you associate with stillness. You can also think of your teacher. If none of these things helps you to open, at least sit down, watch your breath, and *feel* what it feels like to breathe. After a short period of time, if you simply pay attention to how good it feels to breathe, that happiness will be with you, within you, and around you. If you practice this a lot, you will be able to connect to and participate in this extraordinary experience, no matter where you are or what is going on.

There is something so rich about just breathing. If, every day — for a little while or for as long as you can — you take your attention inside, relax your body, and feel the pulsation of your breathing, you will begin to feel, first within the chakras and then within your system as a whole, a resonance like a great symphony unfolding within you. It is as if God is singing to and through you — as if everything that you are and do is nothing but the song of God.

It is always our awareness, and never our effort, that influences whether or not the flow is impeded. We certainly put our energy into cultivating our ability to pay attention, but our actual awareness of the different chakras will emerge when *it* wants to.

It is like gardening. We create the environment — the field within ourselves — where this awakening is possible. Some of it will come up quickly; some of it will take a long time. After a while, it all just shifts into place.

The chakras will awaken themselves, and we are not going to have anything to say about how or when it happens. Some of them are going to jump out at us hard and even bite us. With others, we are going to sit there for years and think, "That place in me is dead." Then, one day that same place will break open. All we can do is train ourselves to pay attention and practice focusing our awareness.

In the beginning, we make this happen by taking our attention along the line of the chakras. The equipment is there; we just have to develop our awareness of it. By taking our attention there over and over again, we develop our ability to feel the whole thing until eventually we feel the substance of the vitality all at once. Then, the entire mechanism springs open with our conscious attention, which is also energy. This is why the chakras are often drawn as lotus flowers, which open in the light of the sun. Similarly, all we have to do is shine our attention upon them and they will unfold.

The different textures we experience in the chakras — the fabric, or the creative expression, of our individual lives — are something over which we have influence and in which we have complete and total participation. We are not dominated by them. Given that, our lives really become creative — we could almost say, artistic — expressions. These textures are our medium, and they are infinite in their potentiality.

A musician has a somewhat limited medium with which to work. The violin, for example, has its limitations. It is not a wind instrument, and there are certain sounds it cannot make, simply by virtue of what it is. The same is true of a piano. By contrast, when we have total influence over our own creative mechanism, we have an extraordinary range within which to evoke and compose the textures of our various relationships and of the creative activities we unfold. Furthermore, we can do so without becoming entangled in the events.

We feel the reciprocal relationship between the individual and the universal in ourselves. As we take our attention through the chakras, their various energies expand to participate in the full range of expression of Life Itself. Simply because of our quiet participation, Life Itself brings about a complete change throughout this individuated expression that we are.

Because we offer ourselves into Life, Life penetrates us. In this dynamic, reciprocal interchange, our work is to find balance and harmony. We understand that balance and harmony are an extension of our relaxing, our feeling, and our turning inside to allow all these energies to assume their proper places. Then there is no separation between ourselves and Life, between ourselves and God. There is only this reciprocal relationship — this identity — between our individual nature and the divine.

FEELING THE FLOW

Opening the Heart: Further Thoughts

The mystery of spiritual emptiness may be living
in a pilgrim's heart, and yet the knowing of it
may not yet be his.

Wait for the illuminating openness,
as though your chest were filling with Light,
as when God said,

Did We not expand you?

— RUMI

The main obstruction to our being in continual contact with the depth of our minds and emotions is that we close our hearts. This is why the most important effort we have to make is to open our hearts to this depth, in order to be in touch with the flow of creative energy within us. Then, there is no forcing anything, no creating or manipulating any energy. Our task is to open ourselves, to be in touch with that flow, and to have the strength and courage to live from it.

It amazes me that we will fight and work, worry and strain, and then exert ourselves some more, only to attain some extraordinarily stupid things in the world. Yet, when it comes to making the effort to feel our own hearts, we refuse. Instead of taking our attention inside and really relating to Life, we relate to the reflections of Life going on around us. Since we don't relate to Life Itself but only to the superficial dissatisfactions we experience, we react by thinking that we have to do something about them.

For many people, this requires entering into a little psychopharmacology, so they can put themselves out of their misery. "I don't want to feel my heart. I can take care of it with about that much gin." Then, of course, we don't feel our hearts — for that matter, we don't feel anything. As I suggested earlier, that is a good part of what tobacco, alcohol, drugs, and a lot of over-eating are all about.

Some of our inner work *is* going to hurt. Still, we must search for a deeper understanding of our resistance and the power it has to limit our existence. When we experience pressure, the challenge is literally to open ourselves to it and drink it in instead of resisting or fighting it — instead of thinking, "Oh, God, I've got to do this, but it's so hard and I can't take it" — we all know the script.

Most of us have so much resistance to discomfort that we fail to recognize we have a choice in the matter. Instead of resisting, we can choose to become centered and quiet, and simply open ourselves to absorb the pressure. Then, we are able to absorb the energy within the pressure. This fuels a total change in the pattern of creative expression that we are and allows us to address our discomfort in a completely different manner.

We cannot force the flow, nor is there any need to — it is always there. It is only that sometimes we have to force open the doors to our hearts, our brains, and our minds in order to get into a position where we *can* experience it; where the understanding, which is a part of it, can extend into our hearts and minds, into the lives we lead, and into the energy field that we project around us.

Most people are fundamentally interested in certainty. Openness and certainty, however, are polar opposites. If we use the word openness, we are actually discussing the absence of boundaries, which also implies total uncertainty. It is difficult for the cells to exist in an atmosphere of uncertainty — indeed, they require certainty. They have a program, and they all get together to share this program with one another. The more we expose them to uncertainty, the crankier they are likely to get. Thus, without a lot of training and preparation, it is difficult for a person to feel comfortable with things being up in the air.

Every time our lives turn out differently from what we expected or thought we wanted, the best response is to continue to do our practice. This means opening our hearts every day to our lives as they *are*. Doing so puts an end to every kind of mental disturbance caused by our likes and dislikes and by what we want or don't want — by the whole boat-load of *samskaras* (the residues of our past experiences).

Each person has his or her own life, and there is a kind of finiteness to it. The opportunities we have for growing may be the very ones we always wanted, but they don't necessarily come in the packages we insist upon. This alone may keep us from recognizing and responding to them when they finally do appear. We can sit and wait for the package of our choosing to come, and we may wait twenty-five thousand years. Or, we can take what does come, work with it as it is, and grow from it.

This is true in all arenas of our lives. If we choose to grow, we can only open ourselves to and embrace our lives where and as we find them. We can only cultivate them and see what grows. Then, even though the form of our lives doesn't necessarily become what we thought it ought to be, it does become its own highest expression of itself.

To that, I have to say, "Hallelujah," because what we think our lives ought to be is, in every case, only an expression of the limits of our imagination. We cannot imagine the extraordinary potentiality of the Life that we are. We can only unleash it and learn from it. Put most simply, being open means that we suspend our judgments and truly embrace what *is*.

Learning to open our hearts, no matter what the situation we face, is the deepest challenge we face in our practice. This became clear to me shortly after I went to New York to find Rudi. It was my second day at his house, and I was sitting downstairs in the meditation room after class. I closed my eyes and felt myself literally sinking down. I kept my physical eyes closed, but opened my eyes internally and found myself standing in a musty, foul-smelling cave. It was dark, with light flickering in the background. In short, it was my vision of what hell must be like.

Suddenly, an immense, horned figure — blue in color, with the head of a buffalo — started to lumber toward me. I said to myself, "What did I do to deserve *this*?" A great fear welled up inside me. (Much later, I saw Tibetan paintings which led me to recognize this as a vision of Yama, the lord of hell — the lord of death.)

At that moment, though, as I looked at this figure, I thought, "I got here by doing one thing and I'm going to continue doing it, no matter what happens." All along, I had been making the effort to focus on my heart — to open it and try to respond to everything around me from that openness, with love. So, at that very moment I opened my heart as wide as I could and loved that character for everything I was worth. With that, I felt a great love and sweetness come through me.

Then, I felt myself rising up and floating out of the event. Suddenly, a great light burst in my head. I fell down and came to some time later, only to find that I was back on the floor of the meditation room at Rudi's house. It took me a few minutes just to figure out where I was. After a while, I crawled upstairs and sat down.

Rudi was there having supper, and maybe an hour had gone by since the end of class. He just looked at me, smiled, and said, "Very good." As I thought about it later, somehow I never felt there was anything particularly odd about any of it. Rather, I thought to myself, "I've just learned something. I've had an important experience here."

Indeed, that episode helped me learn to respond to all change with openness, love, and gratitude. I have attempted to encounter all the different people and circumstances in my life in the same way. The experience taught me to meditate on opening my heart to that powerful energy, to meet it with love, and to let that love guide me. I think this is why not only fear, but also the frustration, anger, and bitterness which are the harvest of fear, have never taken hold of me.

Along your own way, some powerful things may happen to you. You should keep your response light and simple and endure everything with love. Then, it all becomes something wonderful. I have lived by and from that experience for the last eighteen years, and it has never let me down. Not even once. I may have let *it* down a few times, but when I've realized that, I have made the effort to turn myself around.

Some people assume that having an open heart is identical to some ecstatic state, but the two things do not necessarily go together. Sometimes, we tie them together and, in beginning a spiritual practice, that is alright. As we grow, however, we have to develop the subtle capacity to discriminate and to understand that there are times when the feeling of total well-being, which is an expression of an open heart, will not necessarily gush all over the place. When a person has the experience of something gushing, although it may be the gushing of a good thing, it can also be a hemorrhage.

Sometimes we have a tight feeling in our hearts and get caught up in thinking that they are not open. Yet, this is not necessarily the right connection to make. Some of what we feel may just be atmospheric pressure. Such pressure can mean nothing more than that it just happens to be a heavy day. At other times, we may find ourselves in pain and feel a great lump in our hearts. That does not necessarily mean that they are closed, either.

So, in an early stage of our practice, an open heart may mean feeling blissful. At another stage, it may not. I have seen people who were blissful and ecstatic but who had no clarity whatsoever. Indeed, the pursuit of ecstasy can sometimes bring about the fall of a person, if we confuse it with knowing the Self.

Ecstasy does not necessarily imply clarity. Clarity, together with an open heart, is a simple event. It is a subtle, intuitive experience that occurs when all the elements come together and we recognize that, because of our effort and concentration, the creative energy arising in that moment is leading us to a refined expression and higher understanding.

This is progressive and promotes transformation, while ecstasy sometimes does nothing but promote confusion about what we really want. Furthermore, as we go along, we may have any number of such experiences. In every tradition with a strong mystical element, there are powerful spiritual experiences that can occur as our chemistry is transformed.

It is like this: Suppose we take a chemical compound and simply shine light through it. What happens? It changes. Similarly, when this deeper energy is released from within us, it changes our physical, mental, and emotional chemistry. We might express this by saying that we are restored to a different level of health. The point is that we are going to go through a lot of changes, some more ecstatic than others. We can note them and note our reactions to them, but we don't need to think about them much or get stuck in them.

The second thing we want to do — and this is more important — is to change our own vibration. In other words, the mass or bundle of energies that composes an individual should be transformed by this experience. It should be refined and purified so that, like a fine violin string, it holds the subtle vibrations and tones much longer. This is another way of talking about what it means to return to our original simplicity. It is the point of clarity.

It is always true that when our hearts are open, our minds become quiet — just like that. What it comes down to, though, is something even simpler. The ability to open our hearts and minds resides in the simple decision to be happy. In that decision, a further chemistry change takes place. Instead of being filled with the heaviness of our ambitions, desires, fears, and worries, a lightness within us allows us to let these things go.

The chakras cannot flourish in a cloud of poisonous gas, fog, and smoke. They do not open their petals to darkness — like flowers, they close at night. But when we fill ourselves with light, these flowers within us bloom and flourish. The light is our decision to be happy, no matter what. When we make that choice, no separate effort is required to bring about an open heart or a clear and balanced mind. They are one movement and, in their presence, everything within us opens.

The Rising Up Of The Energy

To bring your Shakti under control is samadhi.
Samadhi is the upward breath, the God within.
When the upward breath is established,
all of the universe is inside you.
The upward breath is the same in all creatures.

— NITYANANDA

The elegance of Kashmir Shaivism lies in how it explains the process of manifestation. It asserts that, from the simplest to the most complex levels, the same fundamental process repeats itself over and over again. Thus, the process of manifestation in the universe is the same as that which occurs in our individual lives and experiences. In every case, we see the pulsation of Life Itself at work.

The term prana, discussed earlier in connection with mantra, designates the life that animates all beings. It is present and most discernible, on a gross level, as our breath. On a more subtle level, we experience it as the pulsation of the kundalini energy in the cerebro-spinal fluid around our brains and spinal cords. Herein lies the fundamental spark of this tide, which pulsates in a constant expansion and contraction. It is a dynamic event that continues throughout our lives from the moment we appear as an individualized expression of it through our dissolution. In fact, we can say that this energy *is* Life, or the energy of Life Itself.

If this kundalini energy were not active, we would not be. It is not that we would be dead, because what we mean by "dead" exists only in relation to what we describe as "alive." The kundalini energy is beyond all limited discussions of life and death. If that force were not active, we would simply not come into being. There would be no life, no death, no anything, because the appearance as well as the disappearance of our bodies happens within something infinitely greater than these.

172

Kundalini is another name for this basic breath of Life. It is the energy that connects us as biological events to the highest level of Self-awareness. It is always present in us but, because of the inner atmosphere with which we identify and the heaviness in which we become entangled, its functioning becomes constricted and limited. Then, this deepest part of us is not at the forefront of our awareness. Still, kundalini is the natural condition of Life Itself which, when aroused, manifests as an aware and responsive human being.

People sometimes talk about "awakening" the kundalini. This is not exactly how it works. Kundalini, as the essence of our biological, as well as of our intellectual and emotional lives, cannot be asleep. When we talk about awakening it, what we mean is that we bring our concentration to focus on its ongoing flow. Then, what we are doing is arousing it, or causing it to rise up within us.

The human body is said to be made up of seventy-two thousand combinations of sound vibrations. Trika Yoga involves being in touch with these vibrations in order to intensify them as a whole. The process churns and refines us, as the gods of Indian myth are said to have wrapped the serpent Shesha around Mt. Meru — the mountain at the center of the world — to churn the ocean of milk.

Some of the gods seized his head, others his tail. They pulled back and forth, much as my grandmother used a paddle churn back in Kentucky to churn the milk into butter when I was a boy. The serpent, of course, is the kundalini energy, while the ocean of milk is the inner Self. The "butter" that is churned up consists of the physical abundance, the emotional and intellectual maturity, and the spiritual satisfaction that come from our deep awareness of that energy.

This energy is aroused when we start to look within. As this energy is released from its inhibited respiratory condition and starts to pulsate with increasingly higher frequencies, it begins to rise up. As it does so, it changes our chemistry, causing everything to loosen.

On rare occasions, this happens because of a spontaneous awakening through the grace of the Divine. Usually, however, it occurs through contact with somebody in whom this energy is already aroused — namely, a teacher. This contact is shaktipat, the descent of grace. Thus, the descent of the energy is called shaktipat, while the corresponding rising up from within us is called kundalini.

The union of ascending and descending energies begins the fulfillment stage of our meditation practice — the natural movement of the energy toward its original state is the process that begins to awaken us to our true nature. With this simple rising up of the energy, we become energized and begin to experience the beginnings of the joy and well-being that emerge from this upward movement. The purpose of having an accomplished teacher is to facilitate this process and convey to us the highest possible awareness of it. This is the teaching. After that, it is up to us to cultivate our own awareness of the experience.

For that matter, an accomplished teacher is constantly transmitting the highest teaching. It remains a secret only because the people who come cannot see it, even though it is right there in front of them. They cannot hear it, even when it is explained to them. Even if they do hear it and get it, or see it and discern it, they walk out the door and twenty minutes later become so distracted that they forget all about it. So we practice, in order to shift our awareness — to perceive increasingly finer vibrations in the context of the creative energy, until we come to the point of stillness. Then we practice some more, to learn to establish ourselves in this awareness.

The fundamental energy of Life has a spiral manifestation — what the osteopath Dr. Rollin E. Becker refers to as a spiral tide. It is actually a tide within a tide within a tide that continuously folds in on itself, which is why it is described as a serpent coiled at the base of the spine. This is not merely a metaphor, but a description of the actual experience. Our breathing twelve times a minute constitutes a tide, within which there is the tide of the fluctuation in the cerebro-spinal fluid. Within that, there is yet another tide. The spiral energy of kundalini is constantly unfolding and rising, then contracting and descending, and within *that*, there are other currents still.

Relative to each level of breath, there are corresponding levels of materiality. On one level, we are attuning ourselves to the energy of our physical existence, called *prana-kundalini*. At the level of prana-kundalini, our sense of corporal materiality dissolves, and our awareness of the flow takes over. We don't notice our bodies so much any more.

By bringing a rhythmic movement to prana-kundalini through our concentration, we intensify its function and it rises up. Moreover, when we practice different breathing exercises, we can speed up the rate of the fluctuation in the cerebro-spinal fluid and bring it to a stillpoint. It condenses and then goes quiet. The process is one of following the energy to its source, which we do by observing it as it arises. Through this rising up and intensification, we begin to have access to the energy of our individualized consciousness, or *citta-kundalini*, which we experience as the pulsation of the mind and emotions.

If we were to reduce the aim of our practice to one central issue — one central activity — it would be to bring about the upward movement of the energy. When we talk about releasing tensions and allowing the creative energy to flow, or about experiencing the energy of Life Itself, or about knowing Shiva and Shakti, all of these are consequences of the upward movement of the energy. It is from this that we discover their nature and hence our own.

The bottom line for us in our practice must be the upward movement of the breath or energy, and the impact this has on our experience. Moreover, it is not simply a matter of the energy rising once. It does no good unless we facilitate its rising over and over again. It is because of the upward movement of the breath that all the other things we discuss in our practice become accessible to our awareness.

The upward movement of the energy is a simple thing, and we don't have to strain to experience it. It is neither esoteric nor mysterious. I do notice from time to time, though, that people are not aware of this upward movement when they take a deep breath while sitting or doing other things during the day. This is simple enough to correct.

Whenever you take a deep breath, exhale slowly and be aware of the upward movement of the energy as you breath out. Notice that if you exhale quickly, without drawing the breath up the spine through all the chakras to the top of the head, it becomes draining instead of energizing. Any kind of fast exhalation will actually bring the energy down. Likewise, any kind of unconscious exhalation will not have the same effect as a slow and conscious one. If you want your breath to uplift you, then you must draw it consciously, in a way that allows the energy to move up.

At the end of an exhalation, if you really relax, you will feel the upward movement of the energy. As it takes place, you will feel a slight release, or shift, at the base of your spine. You don't have to spend a great deal of time focusing on any of the chakras, but should instead feel the flow rising up through them, all the way to the top of your head. It rises not like the mercury in a thermometer, but more like a pyramid out of the depths of you. It should rise all the way to the top of your head, so that at some point, you will feel your attention totally absorbed there. Do this for as many breaths as you can follow with your attention. When your mind starts to wander, come back and do it again.

The fundamental difference here is that the one breath is an unconscious act, while the other is conscious. The conscious act increases the frequency of the energy in you, whereas the unconscious one only makes you feel heavier as you move toward a lower level of functioning. Thus, it is important for you to have this basic awareness not only when you sit, but whenever you draw a deep breath. Essentially, what you are doing over time is facilitating the upward movement of the energy.

As you work on this more and more, you will notice that the chakras open and, in a way, cease to involve an effort. You will experience them as something like open doorways. You will also be aware of the total mechanism at all times, so that you will not have to pay particular attention to any one part of it. As you sit, your awareness may circulate through the whole system, but even this becomes an aspect of the continual deepening that takes place in you as the energy rises.

This rising up of the energy will extend your capacity to tune into what, in the *Vijnanabhairava*, is called "the unstruck sound." In fact, to attune ourselves to that unstruck sound is the same as attuning ourselves to the fundamental rhythm that we are. In that state of attunement, all seventy-two thousand energy points in the head start to awaken.

When the energy rises and pierces the crown chakra, it is not that you strike the unstruck sound, but that you enter into its field of resonances. You will experience this as a subtle shift. Then you become aware of a resonance with a number of levels to it. When you experience it, shift your attention to the back of your head, to the point where the brain stem enters the skull, and start to listen. (As discussed earlier, this is a particularly strong point because it is where the spinal column and the brain come together in the brain stem.) If you work on that for a while, you will start to hear a number of resonances, one of which is a low-pitched, almost rumbling sound.

These are points of reference for you in your meditation. Especially if you sit by yourself a lot, you will find them meaningful. Again, the rising up of the energy is the fundamental issue. When you sit, this is an important thing to focus on. As you observe your breath and relax, concentrate on the expansion of the energy — its upward movement, the thawing out of the various energy centers, and their extensions.

Sometimes, you may feel that you have gotten stuck in this process. Do not become concerned about this. It is better just to keep working. What is important is the upward movement, and not anything else. All of the wiggling and jiggling that goes on in the process is where the getting stuck comes from. Various episodes of this will occur but there is no reason to be concerned about them in the slightest.

Whatever agitation we feel as the energy rises up is a natural, systemic purification. It informs us of the process as it transforms our total pattern, releasing tensions and reorganizing what we are. Our only job is to relax and let it do whatever it wants. If it is intense, that is fine. Moreover, just because we feel heat and agitation does not necessarily mean that we are not relaxed. Indeed, it means that our relaxation is effective. We should have as little resistance as possible to the rising of the energy. Think of it this way: The energy structure of a human being is not that much different from the structure of a tornado — dynamic stillness surrounded by tremendous activity.

Kriyas

Just as the deep glow of pure gold is revealed
after repeated heating,
so the inner is made luminous through the
heat of concentration.
Let the world be illuminated within.
This is one means: the way of Buddhi.
Perfect one-pointedness, dharana, is understanding;
it approaches the Thought of the Atman.

— NITYANANDA

Kriya is a classical Sanskrit term for the ways people experience the kundalini energy becoming active within them. We experience kriyas in our meditation practice as a sudden trembling of the body, as spontaneous physical movements, or as a strong emotional release. In a broader sense, though, a kriya is what happens when we release tension through our practice and experience the flow of our creative energy in new ways to which our system is not yet accustomed.

Think of it like this: If I were to hit your arm hard, creating shock and strain at the point where I hit you, some residue of that shock and strain would inevitably stay in the tissue for some time. The same is true on an emotional or psychological level. If a person gets hit hard enough, the tension stays in the system, impairing the respiration of the cells and muscles, or maybe even of the system as a whole.

The impairment of the respiration creates a buildup of toxins and causes a great inefficiency in the cells. It may not kill them, but they may function at only a fraction of their actual capacity. Therefore, one of the basic physical manifestations of the awakening of the energy within us happens when our bodies, minds, and emotions begin to release these shocks and strains.

As the deeper creative energy starts to function in us, other little interesting things may happen as well. We build up so much internal congestion in our everyday lives that, on every level, it suppresses the natural respiration which is, in fact, our life and which sustains our bodies and minds. Generally speaking, we become so compressed that we reduce the capacity of the energy of Life Itself to function freely within us.

As we release those tensions, enabling the energy to flow unobstructed once more, the first thing that happens is that we begin to flush out the congestion. So, when we have been sitting in meditation and working to release tension, our bodies may fall over; they may twitch a bit; we may have strong emotional spasms, during which we cry a lot for no apparent reason. These different experiences are all referred to as kriyas.

Every such manifestation of that energy is just fine and perfectly normal. It is like when we have been sitting for a long time and one of our legs falls asleep. When we get up off of it and the circulation starts to move again, the first thing it does is tingle and twitch. Similarly, if you sit on your arm for an hour, what happens? After a while you don't feel anything. The arm becomes completely insensitive. Isn't this something like the experience that many of us have of life? It rolls over on us for about five years, and we don't feel a thing after that. Of course, when we finally roll out from under it and the flow of energy starts to come back into the tissue, we are likely to shake, rattle, and roll a little.

I'll tell you a story about this. When I first met Rudi at his shop, I had never been out of Indiana except for that one hour following my arrival in New York. Remember that I was terrified of New York because, in Indiana, we knew for sure that hundreds of people were killed on the streets there every day, and that the trees had all died ten years earlier from the pollution. In any case, when Rudi closed his shop that night, we went around to his house, as was his custom. The other people living there all came to sit with him, too, while another, larger group came in later on.

I had been there for almost no time when somebody came in and sat down behind me. I wasn't looking at the person — I was too busy looking at Rudi because I myself was having an extraordinary experience. All I noticed was that somebody sat down. The next thing I heard was a blood-curdling yell. I suddenly became aware of a man shooting up behind me, starting from a full lotus position. His body planed out in the air, then hit the floor flat, his arms and legs flying in every direction. Now *that* was a kriya. I thought to myself, "Hmm — there is something unusual going on here."

This is an extreme example, of course. More likely, what you will experience is just some twitching and subtle shaking. In either case, this process of kriyas — of irregularity in our breath, additional heat in our bodies, and agitation in our nervous systems — is not an activity of the mind. Rather, it is a change of frequency setting itself up within the involuntary nervous system. The part of us that breathes and moves the fluids around is going through a genuine and necessary shift. This is a shift of frequency that expresses a deeper contact with the Self and results in the refinement in our systems.

It is like the agitation we feel as we take our attention away from a desire and focus within, instead. Any time we let go of a desire, a certain agitation occurs. The same thing is true when any level of frequency shifts. Whenever we change a vibration from one level to another, we experience the period of agitation that accompanies the shift, as one frequency or pattern is disrupted and replaced with another.

As we go through the oscillation and movement toward a stillpoint — the quiet moment when there is no pattern at all — different patterns will come up. We just have to hang in there with them. We let them wiggle and jiggle around a little and try to keep from paying too much attention to the wiggles and jiggles themselves. Then we can watch as they cool down in an entirely different way.

All of this is a good thing. The agitation we experience is a natural part of any inner change. We simply have to keep our guts and our attention together as these energies shift around so that we don't get splattered all over the wall during whatever changes are trying to happen.

It is also quite common for people to get sick during periods of powerful change. Our systems, as they go through such changes, begin to drop all the garbage and congestion under which they were struggling to function previously. Any massive release like this may very well manifest as some kind of health problem, and yet, we are not sick in the traditional sense. Indeed, this can be an expression of the fact that we are being refined and getting stronger.

So, agitation is not a bad thing, nor is being agitated the negative state we usually think it is. At the same time, even when we are agitated, it is still important for us to control ourselves and be thoughtful. We can't just explode because, when we do so, we only pump the poisons right back into our systems.

When we experience a kriya, it has no real meaning or purpose and we accomplish nothing by giving it any serious attention at all. Instead, we have only to take our attention inside, relax, and allow these energies to flow within and through us as we focus on our wish to grow. Then, the presence at the core of the kriya — the very essence and epitome of what is special — reveals itself to us. As we recognize that this essence permeates our entire existence, slowly its beauty and vitality become apparent to us, and we discover them to be our own.

PRESENCE

*Here, bliss is not like the intoxication of wine or wealth,
or even like union with a lover. The emergence of the light of
consciousness is not like the light produced by a lamp,
by the sun, or by the moon. The happiness of release from
accumulated differentiation is a joy like the removal of
a burden. The emergence of the light of consciousness is
the recovery of a forgotten treasure — the abode of complete
non-duality.*

— ABHINAVAGUPTA

The discipline by which we live is our way of channeling our energy. If we do not, it is like pouring water on the ground and having it go in every direction. However, if we channel it and give it some structure to follow, it flows in the direction we want it to. This allows it to become organized enough for us to appreciate its presence and to understand and experience its power. If we can't recognize and respect that power, how can we grow?

Meditation is a vehicle. It is the time we take and the system we use to touch the untouchable, to feel the unfeelable. This is the presence within and around us that, in at least some moment of our lives, we have all experienced. I say that it is unfeelable because we do not feel it so much as it is what feels us all the time.

Meditation provides us with amazing mental and emotional benefits, but the most extraordinary benefit lies in finding that quiet place within where we can begin to experience the presence of the divine. We sit down, quiet ourselves, take our attention inside, and keep it there for a while. As we turn our attention inside, our energy slowly starts to organize itself and to contract. After a while, it comes to a point of maximum contraction that we might experience as something like an intense loneliness. Yet, if we hang in there a little longer it will shift and expand once more. Then, we reach a point of steadiness from which a certain sense of flow starts to emerge. From that place, we understand the process and unity of all of Life.

This takes the capacity to open ourselves with love and devotion, and to stay open no matter what dance the world is doing around us. Whether that dance looks terrifying or alluring, it is up to us to stay within the awareness of our own creative flow and to allow that flow to extend itself.

As I said in the Guided Meditation, there comes a point in time when flow and chakras are no longer what we are paying attention to. Although we continue to be aware of them, at that stage we talk about an awareness of what I call Presence. This is a single pure Presence which is both the perfection of Life and the highest state.

Presence has two aspects. One is our intimate experience of it as the essence of what we are. This, however, is not distinct from the other aspect, which is infinite and in every way transcendent and unlimited. When we experience the Self in this way, we experience the power that has given rise to our bodies, our minds, and our breath. Thus, there is no denial of body, mind, or emotions. There is no end to breathing. Instead, deep nourishment flows from this contact — a nourishment that dissolves all the boundaries that have kept us from recognizing and experiencing Life as it really is.

If Life is an infinity and there is such a thing as eternity, there is no question of getting closer to it or farther from it. It just *is*, right now. This means that there is only one thing — our joyous awareness of infinite Presence which pulsates as every experience that *is*, in every form and facet that we can feel.

Grace is infinite Presence. It is not restricted by time, and it is always present in our lives. Our work consists of refining ourselves enough to participate in it fully. Most people don't participate in it because of the degree to which they are tense and contracted around their own point of view. We all know what this sounds like: "I want this," "I deserve that," "This person did that to me," and so on and so forth. These are the tensions that deny us full participation in the grace that permeates our lives. This is true for every human being.

The cloud of hormones that fogs our inner atmosphere also keeps us from experiencing that Presence. It keeps us locked in the fear of what might happen to us, unable to participate in the simple happiness that is within us all the time. Usually we get so involved in struggling with Life that we can't extract ourselves enough to pay attention to it.

So, we do Hatha Yoga to stretch our muscles and get our breathing going in a different way. This relaxes our physical systems, which makes it easier for our minds to relax and for us to have easier access to this inner spirit. We also do breathing exercises to promote relaxation and awareness on another level. Our real work begins, though, when we just drop the struggle. Even if we have to drop it five hundred times a day, that is all right. If we keep on dropping it, eventually it will stay dropped.

In our practice, we learn to go beyond the influence of our hormones. This does not mean that we suppress or get rid of them. Instead, we make an additional effort to open the doors, to feel our breathing, and to let the sun shine in a little more every day. That warmth and light will dissipate the dense atmosphere of the hormones and burn off their fog. Then we become free of our bodies and they are simply there.

Our real work begins when we release the struggle and allow for a change of vibration to take place within us. Again, it is something like gardening. In the beginning, we break the ground, haul out the rocks, fertilize the ground, turn under the soil, and plant the seeds. Next, we keep the weeds out while the seeds sprout and become strong enough so that they can take care of themselves. Finally, we harvest. The first stage is strenuous; the second, somewhat tedious. Both of them are real work. In the end, when we look at the garden itself, we cannot exactly say, "I did this." We just appreciate something alive that has emerged and that was not visible before.

In dealing with our tensions, in facing our fears, and in understanding, through careful observation, how the pure Presence of Life Itself manifests as every kind of distinction and differentiation, we finally arrive at the shores of creation and attain a sweetness and a peace that are enduring. In attaining this happiness, every pressure disperses and there is no such thing as isolation. In fact, there is only the one thing into which everything has merged, which is the same thing out of which everything came in the first place. In this state there is no such thing as dependent or independent — there is only one.

The more we become established in this Presence, the more all issues like coming and going, back and forth, or past and present become irrelevant. Our thoughts no longer arise in the same way and ultimately we experience whatever we see as something like the aurora borealis — curtains of light of many colors and densities. Human beings, chairs, dogs, buildings — all are simply waves of light, reflected through different vibrational atmospheres, taking on different qualities. They are all nothing but energy, to be appreciated, admired, and enjoyed.

A teacher gives us endless demonstrations of how this works in the context of a finite biological envelope. Something is happening there that has nothing to do with the individuality of the teacher. In this regard, when Jesus says, "I am the gateway," he is talking about two things. One is, quite simply, that a great spiritual person is, indeed, a gateway because he or she is a living manifestation of that highest state. Thus, the notion of Jesus as a teacher is consistent with the Tantric understanding that the fastest way to attain that highest state ourselves is through a mediator, a person who awakens that understanding in us and trains us in it.

But let us take this a step further to the second point — namely, that what a mediator actually does is awaken us to the divine Presence that is continuously within ourselves. Then, the person who loves God, God, and the love of God are recognized as one. The subject, the object, and the relationship are all one thing. This is why Rudi used to say, "God is love." That love exists within each of us equally.

As we come to understand and to experience this, we do not have to change the form of our lives; we do have to change our relationship to that form. We have to change the degree to which we pay attention to it. Then, the form transforms itself because of the Presence of this conscious energy.

Moreover, by our contact with and participation in that energy, something starts to happen in us. We feel it, we watch it, and we sense it. We see it happening in us and in our lives. As it happens, we have the practice and the training to allow it to keep going and to learn something from it. The more we learn, the more we relax and trust it. Then, the more it happens.

Over time, we do the work appropriate to our own condition that will allow us to participate in this visceral and palpably joyous Presence as it asserts itself. It is more than a spirit — it is the opportunity to experience the identity of our individual spirit and the divine spirit. That is real happiness, and it is permanent and enduring.

Through our practice of meditation, hopefully we will mature into people who understand their practice simply as the awareness of the Presence of God, or the state of pure happiness. Everything we see and feel, everything we think we know — indeed, everything we think at all — is nothing but a shadow. It is all a reflection — an indication of the real Presence which has nothing to do with what appears to be. We see it clearly, not with our physical eyes but as we quiet our minds. Then, we see the real behind the shadow.

At this point, there is nothing to accept or reject, nothing to embrace or avoid. Within a state of total well-being, what need can there be? Instead, a person established in this Presence understands the whole world as a celebration, as an expression of the love of God. Slowly, the many cease to be at the forefront of our awareness. Instead, we see only the One.

~~~~~~

Extending The Energy

LOVE AND RESPECT

Love is reckless; not reason.
Reason seeks a profit,
love comes on strong, consuming herself unabashed.
Yet in the midst of suffering,
love proceeds like a millstone,
hard-surfaced, and straight-forward.
Having died to self-interest,
she risks everything and asks for nothing.
Love gambles away every gift God bestows.
Without cause God gave us Being,
without cause give it back again.
Gambling yourself away is beyond any religion.
Religion seeks grace and favor,
but those who gamble these away are God's favorites,
for they neither put God to the test nor knock at the door
     of gain and loss.

— RUMI

Living in the world imposes pressures on us that slowly
cause us to be less than lovers of life, and sometimes even cynical
about it. Indeed, if there is any real struggle in our spiritual work

it is the struggle to maintain our appreciation and our love for the creative power of Life. We are challenged to maintain a degree of passion for it that will allow us to drop the tensions and rise above the pressures — to find in our lives, even as they demand tremendous work, a sense of mystery that compels us to further understanding.

Many people think they understand love, but few really do. Love is so big that, in the process of trying to wrap our minds around it, our minds will break. There is a song by Bo Diddley in which the chorus asks, over and over again, "Who do you love?" This is a big question. It concerns our basic orientation. What do we care about in our lives? The truth is that our lives, in the form of every tension we ever experience, are always asking us the same question. "Who do you love?"

If we truly love God — if we love Life — then each of its pulsations is a source of excitement and exuberance — a condensation of joy. If we love something else, then each pulsation, each ripple in the force will be the source of our misery. When our minds are set on something other than the highest, whatever we care about will seem to be approaching us or drawing away. Since what comes closer also goes away, we drown in questions of gain and loss.

All too often we assume that the emotional flutters we have every now and then are true love. There is a big difference, however, between what I would call love and what the songs on the AM radio talk about as love. The latter promote what I would describe as a hormonal surge, or "l-u-v." *Love* is something else. There is a lot of hormonal surging going on in the world but little of it actually gets to the point of becoming love.

The difference is important. Love is the fundamental power and, whether there are a hundred thousand people in the picture or one, this power itself remains one. The highest understanding of love lies in its power to transform lives, restore health, and bring about a sense of total well-being. It is the other end of the spectrum which is directed by desire — the limited, contracted form of love — that has a tremendously destructive potential.

In our personal relationships, it is true that there may be some limits to our capacity for loving. But within the depth of our Self, in relation to the human beings whose lives we touch, we have an endless power to give. Furthermore, if we don't explore what we truly are and learn to love *that*, we will never find out what it is we have to give anyone in this life.

Right now, we may think about love in terms of exchange, as a process of giving and receiving. At a certain point, though, as we look at it more carefully we will start to understand that we are neither giving nor receiving anything. We are simply participating in the vitality of Life Itself. *That* is what gives everything. When we understand this, we see that love is an endless giving that never diminishes its source and has no need for any kind of return.

Love has no perfect behavioral program for us. It accepts us as we are here and now, and allows us lives that we can really live. These cannot be lives circumscribed by rules and regulations because it is impossible to be orthodox and free at the same time. If we require rules and regulations to play by, then we remain spiritually infantile.

In its highest sense, Life installs in every one of us, as individuated expressions of Itself, the ultimate freedom to choose. Our own bottom-line freedom is what makes it necessary for us to feel and demonstrate a deep respect for everybody. This respect has nothing to do with a moral stance but is simply the recognition that whatever we encounter in someone else is an expression of the same Life that expresses Itself through us. Rumi notes this by saying that the ability to respect and love others, and to be loved and respected by them in turn, is maybe the greatest of treasures. He says, "A circle of lovely, quiet people becomes the ring on my finger."

Acting with love and respect toward others is often difficult. Even *understanding* the meaning of love and respect is a continuous challenge. Growth and understanding are the conscious expressions of what we value. We work to create balance and harmony by treating everyone and everything else with love and respect. Furthermore, we take responsibility for acting in this way without getting caught up in how other people behave.

We do not have time to worry about how other people are working it out for themselves. We do not have time to give grades to anybody else. More to the point, this is not our job. It *is* our job to look within ourselves and, as much as humanly possible, to rise to this understanding every day, whenever and wherever we are. Only then do our relationships with one another genuinely live on through the years; only then does the love between us attain a real longevity and maturity. Only then are our lives an experience of joy and richness independent of, and never conditioned by, our physical or material circumstances.

To experience profound joy in life, I think, is possible only if we master an understanding of love. If we can do it well in one setting — if we can serve that creative interchange in one relationship — we can serve it everywhere. This is what we are trying to learn.

Few people are able simply to love themselves and even fewer are simply able to love life. So, in the beginning, in order to learn what it means to love, it is necessary to have an object for that love. For this reason we have a teacher. We cultivate our capacity to love through this interchange.

This is why, in every Tantric tradition the guru plays a crucial role as the living demonstration of the creative power of Life Itself. We have a teacher to support us as we stabilize our minds, our emotions and, in some instances, our physical lives. Having attained stability and understood about nourishment and inspiration, we rise to a different level of understanding about the form of the guru. Then he or she becomes the creative energy of Life Itself.

As we begin to understand what is taking place in this creative interchange, we see our own place in the fabric of Life as both significant and not significant. We see ourselves as junction points for the creative energy. We understand about all relationships in the context of this relationship. Having understood that, we rise to the level where love no longer has anything to do with individuals. We understand, at a certain stage, that love wears many faces in our lives and that the important thing is not what face it wears but its enduring Presence.

"Love" is one of those words human beings sling around a lot that means something different every time we say it. Its meaning is often so nebulous that it gives us the opportunity to read into it whatever we want. For me, it means that I have a permanent commitment to sustaining my connection in particular relationships. It means having the willingness to give of myself entirely for the sake of cultivating the unity that exists there.

If we commit ourselves to a life of loving, we commit ourselves to loving no matter what happens in our lives. We may not always experience the happiest of situations but, if there is only one thing, then there is no true possibility of ever coming apart from our connections. Consequently, a spiritual person does not think about breaking his or her own relationships or those of others. We are not interested in separation but in unity. Only in cultivating this condition of unity in our lives can we ever develop the maturity to rise above the tensions that exist in every relationship. Only in this way do we become mature people connected to the infinite resource which grants us the capacity to love in the first place.

When Rumi says, "Love is reckless," he means that love holds nothing back. At the same time, "love proceeds straightforward and steady as a millstone." This implies several things. First of all, it tells us to do the little things well. If we concentrate on doing these well, the big things will take care of themselves. The person who looks only to the big things is a chaser of mirages.

The second point is not to hold anything back. We can think, "Does this mean that if I fall in love with someone, I shouldn't hold anything back?" I would say, yes, absolutely. Put it all out there. If it works, fine; if it doesn't, fine. You will know the difference.

You see, there is a trick here. We cannot hold anything back, but the trick is that we will either learn something or we will get lost. One thing or the other, and there is no getting an angle on it ahead of time — no figuring it out or being clever. We simply have to learn what it means not to hold anything back, even as we remember why we are there in the first place.

If we remember that our lives are for growing — that our actions must promote everyone's best interest and not just our own— if, in speaking our minds about joy or distress, we remember that we must attempt to serve the situation as a whole, then whatever we do is likely to be an act of real love. This is one of the little things we have to learn to do well.

Love is bigger than anything we can talk about. We can discuss human love and we can see small demonstrations of it, but love itself is bigger than this whole earth — which gives everybody a lot to work on. Whenever I hear people say that life is not fair, I say, "You're right. It's not." That still does not limit us, because we have inside us, at every moment, a happiness which is an extraordinary source of strength.

If we cultivate that happiness and recognize the completeness that is within us — indeed, that *is* our life — the happiness itself matures into love. That love is beyond all time and space. It is infinity which gives of itself without ever being reduced. It endlessly creates from within itself without ever being externalized. It is endlessly uplifting and endlessly in harmony.

If we devote ourselves to understanding about love and to articulating that understanding all the time, we are not denying our egos. There is, after all, no need to reject or deny the ego. We are only challenging our current state of awareness, questioning our choice to focus on certain aspects of our lives over others. In this process of challenging and questioning, we expand our egos until finally they become identified with love and with the whole of Life. Slowly we come to understand that Life is one thing, not ten thousand.

The truth is that growing is real work. Being a big person is work, made all the more difficult by the fact that nobody is going to give us a nickel for doing it. The bigger a person we are and the stronger we become, the more burdens Life will give us to carry. But because of the power of love within us, these are actually no burden at all. Rather, they become the joy of participating in and observing the unfoldment of the most wondrous and amazing power of Life Itself, with its endless vitality and freedom to change.

The only thing that has ever been truly important in our lives is the love. Even if we have to rip our guts out for it, it is the only thing that sustains us and the only thing that makes our lives interesting in the slightest. It is the one miracle that enlivens and revitalizes the whole program. Furthermore, I am not spinning these things out of some *How to Be Happy, Healthy, and Holy: The Saddhu's Guide to Self-Realization*. This is something my teacher went through hell to give me, and that his teacher went through hell to give him.

The way I would say it to you is this — love Life Itself. Love the divine. When you do, the only things you will ever put at risk are your limitations.

SERVICE

Giving food or money to charity is not devotion.
Universal love is devotion.
Seeing God in all beings is devotion.
Looking with equal-sightedness is devotion.

— NITYANANDA

Within the realm of the change we are attempting to arouse in our lives, we strive to cultivate a pure, intensive awareness that is also non-reactionary. By "non-reactionary" I mean that we cease to react to the circumstances we encounter. Rather, we respond to the potential for growing that we recognize within ourselves. That is all. The actual activities in which we do this are of secondary importance. They are only extensions of something going on at a deeper level.

If we are not in touch with the rhythm of a given event, we may be caught off guard and fall into a defensive, reactionary mode even though we have no real cause to do so. Instead of bringing the situation into a new balance, we complicate what was really a simple change. We allow our attention to be dragged into everything going on around us instead of staying focused on our inner work.

In cultivating change and in keeping our attitude strictly progressive, we must do our best to control our minds and emotions and to keep our attention inside. Otherwise, we will react to every new reverberation in the field of our experience, and step on one land mine after another in the process. As we change, corresponding changes get set off throughout the field of our lives. This in itself is wonderful, provided we remember that as these reverberations spread through our lives they will do so initially as dissonant feedback. We are, after all, changing our tune, and it may take a little while to establish a new harmony.

We demonstrate our awareness of what is really going on by releasing our tensions and allowing our creative energy to flow freely. We could also call this giving of ourselves; internally, we might think of it as learning and growing. We could also call it continuous improvement because it is something that happens within us and that we demonstrate all around us. I would call it serving the situation in which we find ourselves.

Service is the way we extend these shifts in our own energy and ground them in the total field of our experience. When I talk about grounding, I mean that we allow this new awareness — this new creative capacity — to fill our lives. Through our attitude of service, we support the movement of this wave through our lives and allow it to do its work of transforming everything that it touches.

Creativity and service are really the same thing. Both are infinite. They can go in many directions, and will. Only our attachment to the biological imperatives, and to wanting things to be as *we* think they should be, will limit our ability to follow, tune into, and be aware of this creative power within us as it opens and expresses itself.

Self-expression and service are two aspects of a single process. When a musician performs, for example, this is self-expression. People come to hear the performance because the experience in some way serves them. Something touches them. We may think that unless we are involved in some kind of artistic project, this can have nothing to do with us. When we understand, however, that our entire lives are a process of self-expression and that we can make them as creative and artistic an undertaking as we choose, the connection is not so remote.

To talk about what service *is*, we first want to talk about what it is *not*, and how the two things become confused. I would say that we undertake a spiritual search because we intuit (or at least hope) that there is a certain great sweetness buried within us. We look for ways to know and serve *that*, even though we may not know quite what to call it.

Many religious traditions start with this sweetness as their basis and with a vital spiritual wealth behind them. Over time, however, we have seen many cases in which the organization promoting the tradition develops the need to survive as an institution. Then, the needs of the organization become more important than the needs of the individuals it is called to serve. These needs take on a life of their own in ways that have nothing to do with the spiritual growth or development of the individuals involved.

To define themselves more clearly — to establish who belongs and who doesn't and to clarify their boundaries — many organized religions develop lists of do's and don'ts that crystallize into codes of behavior or systems of ethics. These may accompany an established, structured belief system or ideology. The problem is that ideologies have no more relation to that original experience of great sweetness than ash does to a fire. They cannot promote the kind of self-knowledge that unlocks our real possibilities.

The difference between an organized religion and a spiritual practice is often that a religion, when it lays down a set of beliefs, circumscribes what individuals can aspire to instead of leaving that open to the unfolding of Life Itself. In so doing, it orients the individual toward serving the religion rather than the Self.

In a very real sense, we should not consider Kashmir Shaivism a religion any more than we should consider it a philosophy. It is neither. What the practitioners and philosophers of Kashmir Shaivism hoped to do was share their experience of sweetness and provide a training that would allow others to become established in that highest state. For that matter, meditation is not an ideology or a belief system, but a lived-through experience. It is our own discovery of the power that is the Life within us, and our direct contact with and unfoldment of that power.

Whatever concepts a spiritual practice may give a person should be only the vehicle for obtaining the experience of this infinite resource. A spiritual practice teaches us strategies for awakening to our own infinite creative capacity, in order simply to be and know ourselves. In knowing ourselves, we will also know God and come to an understanding of what it is that we are truly serving.

We look for something to support us in our exploration and discovery of what is infinitely beautiful and of immense value within ourselves. As we do so, we discover that what we are seeking is not something we have to search for anywhere else except within ourselves. It is simply there. Finding that, living from it, and serving it is the quintessence of all religion. It is the only thing that gives real value and meaning to our lives.

It seems to me, however, that all too often we see religious organizations going out into the world with one kind of mission or another. Implicit in this approach is the conviction that the given group has a greater purchase on the truth than anyone else, if not downright ownership rights. The objective then becomes one of "sharing" that "truth" with everyone else, while giving out presents of one kind or another to make the whole event more appealing on the front side. This is what is often thought of as service — a notion I would suggest represents a real misunderstanding.

In the first place, we have to be extremely careful to avoid systems that present themselves as the only vehicle by which we can grow. This is because as human beings we all have within us the same resources for growing. So, every religion and every spiritual practice should simply be an attempt to awaken us to these resources and to demonstrate how they can be used. Any such system must be universal, and not the private domain of one group over another.

Any group of people who decides they have the inside track on "the will of God" is turning spirituality into a power game and setting up the people over whom the group has influence to live in fear and guilt. It trains people not to question, thereby denying their innate freedom, and sets the stage for every kind of manipulation. We have seen many examples of this in recent years in many different religious groups. We have also seen that it serves no one.

[handwritten marginalia:] People should not bother with their religions but seek the Self, the BELIEF that God is everything.

[handwritten note at bottom:] How can one say "religious convictions" are disdainful, and each should seek his own religion? All religions have DIFFERENT ideas of God — pantheism, polytheism, monotheism. seperate

The reality is hidden underneath the flow. It is not in the ideas or in any set of beliefs. For that matter, we can hold any beliefs we want to. It is how we *act* that is our real concern. Many people have believed all kinds of wonderfully idealistic things — among them, the people who brought us some of the more interesting periods in history such as the Crusades, the *jihads*, the Inquisition, the pogroms, and the witch hunts.

It is not our job to be concerned with judging the behavior of others or trying to decide who is or is not a sinner. Better to treat everyone as a friend of God. I say this because I see a real contradiction in putting our hands around somebody else's throat with threats of damnation, and trying to tell them, at the same time, "God loves you." This is serving the truth?

It reminds me of when I was in college and involved in campus politics. One day, as I was about to give a speech at a political event, some of my friends handed me a button that read, "Support mental health, or I'll kill you." We laughed about it at the time, but it has struck me ever since that there is something completely warped about going out and killing anyone in the interest of whatever we define as Life. Something like, "Kill a heathen for Christ." This is craziness.

I am generally suspicious of any missionary effort that claims to serve others by "spreading the truth." My favorite case is someone who says, "I want to grow — then I can help all you other people get over *your* ignorance or *your* problems." It is the second step that always pitches such a person into deep muck. What he or she is often really saying is, "And, by the way, if you don't buy into my program, you can count on being damned."

I find there to be something subtly cynical about this kind of evangelical event, whatever the movement. Sometimes it is expressed in the thrust to go forth into the world, set up missions, and convert pagans. Sometimes it happens when we buy into the idea that people *have* problems in the first place, and that it is up to us to "help" them solve these problems.

Instead of thinking that anybody has a hold on the truth, I would suggest that we cultivate instead our capacity for being open to everything. The process of absorbing and distributing throughout our system the different energies we encounter will make of us a different kind of people — people capable of responding to whatever we meet up with and thereby able to serve any and all of it. *problem again. Pantheism is contradictory. One cannot believe in two types of theisms.*

Genuine service has nothing to do with *getting* anything — not even with the satisfaction of knowing that we have modified a situation so that it now conforms to our image of how we think it should be. Any time we try to "improve" a situation — to make it over in our own image — we can only do so by imposing our will on it. This does nothing but create a new tension, yet it is what most people have in mind when they talk about helping others.

Doing somebody a favor, for example, implies a *quid pro quo*. On some level, we remain concerned with what we anticipate getting back from the interaction. The test for this, of course, is to check how we feel when nothing is forthcoming from the other person. If we feel somehow offended or ripped off, we can be fairly certain that we entered the situation stuck in our own interests. This is not service. When we genuinely serve someone, we give them what *they* ask for, if possible, and not what we think they need. We extend ourselves to support a change that someone else is trying to make from within him- or herself.

True spirituality is not something that we sell, nor is it anything about which we have to convince anybody else. It simply resides in our heart and becomes something that we share with other people in the quietest of ways. The more beliefs we tag on to it, the more trappings with which we surround it, and the more we make it into a project of convincing others, the less spiritual it is and the more it becomes just another wholesale outlet in the religion business.

There is no need to get into any of this. We have more than enough work to do within ourselves for quite a few years before we try to take on anybody else and do *their* work. Better to do our own first. Before we try to convince other people, better to become the living example of what we are talking about. Then, we discover that we never have to say a word to convince anybody about anything. Those who want to know will seek us out, and as for those who don't care to know, we can sincerely wish them well.

In a way, this notion of service is not altruistic at all. It does not grow from an interest in charity. I do think that genuine sharing and service have a definite impact, but I would still hesitate to say that we are "doing" anything for anyone else. Service is simply the attitude we take toward every activity and interaction in our lives. This is what supports the extension of our own creative energy.

Thus, service has nothing to do with serving another individual or a group of individuals, although it may look like it does. If we try to serve without understanding this, we will turn into single-issue politicians. We can serve ideologies and belief systems, and end up serving nothing but our own egos. So, it is crucial for us to understand that we do not serve individuals. Rather, we attempt to serve Life Itself as we encounter it within the individual.

In service of this kind, there is no limitation, no barrier, no boundary. There is no group of people whom it is for, and no group of people whom it is against. There is no idea that it serves and none that it opposes.

You are cold, but you expect kindness.
What you do comes back in the same form.
God is compassionate, but if you plant barley,
don't expect to harvest wheat.

— RUMI

People who are confused about the meaning of service often fall into the attitude that they are not getting what they deserve from life in return for whatever they feel they have contributed to it. This always suggests to me that such people view service as a business investment. It also says to me that their view of reality is not exactly accurate.

We are, in each and every moment, a product of our past action. No matter what our propaganda about ourselves may be and no matter how wonderful we may think we are, our real position — while it may not always be clear to *us* — will always be clear to everyone around us. If for some reason we think we are not getting what we deserve, it is probably because we don't deserve it. The extent to which we are continuously looking for pie in the sky is the extent to which we are avoiding whatever we are really supposed to be doing now. To go on in this way guarantees that we will not grow.

People who give with the idea that this will bring them some variation on gold and riches search and search, even as they miss the richness already present in their lives each and every moment. They miss the opportunities to extend themselves in a simple way toward another person or even just to sit down and become quiet. They fail to understand that there is a simple rule here, and that it works on every level: The more you give, the more you get. The more you are able to open and give of yourself genuinely, the more you will be able to participate in the finest levels of the infinite vibration of Life Itself.

When we contemplate this idea, the feeling we have in our hearts all too often is one of, "I can't." Nonsense. The extent to which we resist participating in the flow of give-and-take represents the extent to which we deny the infinite nature of our own awareness. What understanding can then possibly reside in our hearts?

Many of the opportunities for giving that present themselves are counter-intuitive. Most people's instincts and intuitions run in the direction of self-preservation. All too often, our instinct for self-preservation dominates us. We find ways to justify serving *that* instinct by convincing ourselves that we are giving something to somebody else when, in fact, we are not.

This is the logic by which we engage in the game of winning and losing — what I think of as the Game of Life. It is the general logic of the world. However, there is, at the same time, a different logic — what I call the Logic of Love. This is the logic by which we transcend our instincts and cease to be concerned with self-preservation.

We can operate on the assumption not only that real giving takes many forms, but that most of these forms, in some measure, will be difficult and will hurt. Before we batten down the hatches, spin the turrets, and load the guns, however, we just might want to consider whether or not we are blasting an opportunity to give. Are we shooting down an enemy or a friend?

I tell you that sometimes giving hurts. But the pain it brings is merely our own crystallization dissolving. It has nothing to do with anything anyone else is doing to us. The pain we feel in this life is really Life doing us a favor because some kind of illusion and misunderstanding — some skewed perspective — is being resolved. As it is resolved, it may sting a little or even a lot, but the depth to which we are able to eat the pain is the extent to which we are able to rise to the infinite moment.

Our giving must be genuine and without any expectation of a return. We must give with the understanding that giving of ourselves is the only way we can be filled by spirit. In other words, we have to give of ourselves in order to arouse the flow. It is not as if something else will enter into us to get it going for us — we start it by giving deeply of ourselves.

We give of ourselves in order to create the opportunity to realize the infinite nature of our individual awareness. If we do this in a genuine way — without reservation, but with an enduring commitment to growing and evolving — there is nothing to prevent us from arriving at the shores of creation.

Rudi used to say that a superior person serves in a superior way. We grow based upon our capacity to tune into and support the unfoldment of the total program in any realm in which opportunities appear for us to do our work. One such opportunity lies in our relationship with the teacher, because a real student serves a teacher. Indeed, this is one of the important steps toward self-fulfillment in all the Tantric traditions. If we don't have a mentor and serve him or her well, we are unlikely to learn much of what that person has to share with us.

Service to a teacher has nothing to do with giving the teacher any *thing*. Rudi used to say that it is ridiculous to come to a great being who is already full of the divine and try to tempt him or her with one thing or another. After all, when a person is in a state of completeness, what more does he or she need? People used to see Nityananda surrounded by piles of food which he simply allowed to decay. It never entered his mind that he should do anything with it — he simply observed Life. This is the fullness at work. There is no place to go, nothing to prove, and nothing to be done.

A great deal of the inner work we do will manifest in the form of some interaction with the teacher, in which our understanding will be tested over and over again. This makes it crucial for us to be well-established in the understanding that there is only one thing and to have a sense of its vitality. Our contact with a teacher — indeed, our service to a teacher — is simply our joining and communing with the teacher in this one spirit. It is our respect for the understanding we experience within that communion. This contact is what we can also call love.

It is up to us to cultivate and internalize this love. As we do so, it becomes our permanent state. Then, it becomes an energy we can share with whomever we meet, wherever we are. We live permeated with love, joy, and great vitality. So, this should be our objective in the student–teacher relationship.

When a student, for one reason or another, chooses not to make service a part of his or her practice, it is unlikely that the relationship with the teacher will become deep and strong. It is like this: Suppose someone works for you and you give that person a job to do. Suppose, too, that he or she repeatedly doesn't do the job. What conclusion can you draw? You might decide that the person is not really interested in the job. My feeling is that when people take their practice and use it, they are opening their hearts and minds more and more deeply and living from their own center more and more powerfully. This is the real service that the student undertakes and it begins in the interaction with the teacher.

What does it mean to serve a teacher well? It means to take the teaching and use it well by doing our work to the best of our ability. This is what allows a creative interchange to take place — an interchange that draws us closer not to the personality of the teacher but to a deeper participation in the creative flow. Supporting the expansion of that creative flow on all levels is what deepens the connection. Moreover, when we take what we have learned and use it well, who benefits? First of all, we do. When we approach service in this way, we generate the capacity within ourselves to serve not only human beings but Life as a whole, in an infinite progression.

Some people say, "That's all very fine, but I don't have any real opportunities for service." This always makes me reflect back to the years when we were first setting up the ashram in Bloomington, Indiana. I had returned from being with Rudi in New York with five dollars in my pocket. Before leaving, I had asked Rudi if there was more money to be had, and he had said to me, "Any fool can do it with money." So, I went back to Bloomington to figure out what to do — because it was apparent that something had to be done. Just to be earning some money to get things going, I went out and found work as an appliance salesman in a hardware store. It would not have been my first choice in jobs, but I didn't care. I did it anyway.

After one week, several of us worked out a way to buy our first house. The following week, we took on a defunct restaurant, and a week or so after that, we opened a bakery. When I told my father about all this, he said, "Now son, be careful. You've worked hard and you don't want to lose money here." I said, "Wait a second. All I can lose is five dollars. That's all the money I had when I started, so that's all I can really lose."

The point is that there is always something we can do to serve the situation in which we find ourselves. There is always an opportunity for us to extend ourselves in the direction of another human being or somebody whom we say we love. It doesn't matter how humble that opportunity might be. What does matter is that we recognize, even in humble circumstances, the potential for growth. What is more humble than a seed, and what is more bountiful, if properly tended and appreciated? One seed, after a few seasons, generates a hundred thousand more.

What we experience in the teacher is a living embodiment of the awareness that absolute freedom is intrinsic to the divine. This freedom expresses itself in each one of us as the power of free choice. The range of expression available to us can be greater or lesser, but power of choice itself can never be obstructed or diminished. Every human being's permanent condition is absolute freedom. We are all free to come and free to go. We are free to explore the reach and range of our own innate, creative capacity.

In order to develop the proper respect for other people, it is essential for us to understand that every human being is endowed with the power of free choice, including ourselves. We must respect this power absolutely in everybody. The authentic recognition of everyone's freedom and essential independence is what allows us to generate and exist in an atmosphere in which we can begin to recognize the real interdependence between all things. Without a full recognition and acceptance of that freedom, a person cannot attain the highest state of awareness, because that *is* the highest state. That is what we serve.

In these increasingly difficulty times, each of us will be called upon in some way, determined by the quality of our individual lives, to serve those around us even more. This will take work. To be able to do this work well, we must learn early on to maintain our equanimity, along with our inner openness and joy, no matter what difficulty we face.

Turning to face the difficulty requires courage. But when we center ourselves, open our hearts, and allow our creative energy to flow, then, without any act of bravery, we find within ourselves the strength, the depth, and the support to go forward in whatever act of service we are called upon to undertake.

For this to happen, we must also be well-grounded in our attitude of service toward the people with whom we work and those we say we love. When someone else is agitated, for example, we don't respond with agitation. We maintain our calm and openness as best we can and speak in ways that will facilitate the other person's finding some peace of mind and stability in whatever direction he or she is reaching.

Most importantly, we don't allow ourselves to become magnetized by the lowest level in the environment or entangled in the tensions going on around us. Rather, we work to bring peace, stability, and love to our environment every day. In this way, we create an environment in which something wonderful can come forth.

Our response to the people and situations in our lives has to be progressive, not reactionary. The solutions we come up with must not be repressive but must allow the creative energy of everyone concerned to flow. We do this in two ways: by examining the long-term best interests of every person in the situation and by maintaining our own balance and harmony. Indeed, our only code of action must be this: to function in the service of the best interests of everyone concerned.

When we serve, as one way to find meaning in our lives, we also connect to and promote the highest interests of everyone else because we are serving the Life that exists within all of us. This service can take many forms but, in every case, it reaches into individuals and transforms them from within, even as it transforms us. Then, we see in the process that we have done nothing but remain open. Life Itself has brought about the change.

The wish to serve is a crucial attitude to have because there is no avoiding or denying our involvement in the world. Ultimately, it has everything to do with our happiness. To find permanent happiness and real meaning in our lives is to understand the significance of service and to live from that understanding. The paradox is this: We can be truly and permanently happy only when we recognize our own nature. At the same time, we can discover the vastness of our inner potency only in a state of happiness. It is when we are light and simple, resting in the awareness of our infinite nature, that our highest creative capacity can unfold.

Every endeavor that becomes permeated with consciousness and joy as a result of our inner work is transformed into a spiritual endeavor — an endeavor that serves a teacher, a teaching, humanity, and ourselves all at the same time. If we genuinely want to grow, we take service as our effort in every arena of our experience. Then, we will get over all the difficulties, bridge all the gaps, and be able to make the quantum leap whenever it presents itself.

A person who has attained the experience of the highest state requires nothing from anybody else, but is willing to be a resource to others simply out of his or her own interest in sustaining the flow. Rudi once asked the Shankaracharya of Puri, who was quite old by that time and a deeply spiritual person, "Why, at this stage in your life, do you keep practicing?" The Shankaracharya said, "To keep the circle closed." To keep the flow circulating.

We have to look for ways to extend the flow — that is, in the beginning, we have to look. After a certain point, however, it all kicks in on its own and we don't have to go looking for anything at all; we simply draw to us ways to serve. As that happens, we find more ways to serve than we have holes in our body. We find ourselves giving from places in ourselves we didn't even know were there.

Thus, it is the people who don't really know how to serve who are running all over the place trying to do so; the people who *do* know just sit in one place and opportunities for serving come to them. Because we are participating in a real, palpable force that goes beyond any of us as individuals and encompasses humanity, *it* is the arbiter of our destinies.

To people who truly want to know about the energy, the energy shows itself. We extend its flow throughout the course of our own activity by maintaining a balanced orientation toward what is internal and what is external to us, and by moving in the stillness of that equilibrium. As we do so, we are truly serving not only the teacher but Life Itself.

A person who experiences the fullness of his or her creative energy cannot but demonstrate tolerance, patience, openness, persistence, love, and respect toward other human beings. This is no platitude, nor is it something we can fake, because real love and respect — as well as true patience and tolerance — will always test us, giving us the opportunity to demonstrate the degree to which we understand the fullness within us.

We find, in the process, that our practice benefits us by enabling us to think more globally. Consequently, we find within ourselves an increasing willingness to embrace whatever calling presents itself before us, to complete that calling, and to undertake increasingly finer ones.

This entails discriminating between what truly serves our inner work, and what leads us away from it. "Who do we love?" The inner or the outer divinity? The outer divinity is success, style, fashion, and whatever follows those lines. It is whatever directs our attention to things outside us. The inner divinity is the joy, fulfillment, love, compassion, and sharing that come from dwelling in the heart of the inner Lord.

We have to decide which of these will bring us fulfillment. Which one will we serve? Then, we have to work to serve it. There will be periods of pressure to give in to one thing or another and abandon our commitment. This makes it necessary for us to learn to focus on that inner divinity and to sustain our equilibrium in our approach to it every day.

Implicit in service of this kind is an understanding about Life. I mean "understanding" not in the abstract, but as something that comes from our experience of the vitality and power that are the source of our physical nature, our senses and feelings, and our intellects. We have to understand that power from within ourselves. Then, from our understanding and our palpable contact with it, we extend our awareness and begin to participate more broadly in that Life manifesting as other individuals. This is a real form of service.

As we cultivate that understanding, a kind of purity emerges within us that dissolves our egocentricity and makes our perspective profoundly expansive. We start to experience the unity of everything and to stabilize ourselves in it. Then, we understand that there is no such thing as an "other" and that we really serve the whole — the Self, the essential reality. Furthermore, the more clearly we understand service, the fewer limits there are to our awareness. The boundaries of our awareness and our identity will tumble before our expanding knowledge of the power of Life Itself.

It is this understanding that allows us to get out of the way of the program Life has set in motion. It allows us, in every sense, to identify with that program and become established in it, so that we become the vehicle through which it unfolds. In this, we find true and lasting liberation. We are released from the bonds of the biological imperatives, and of biological life itself.

Our willingness to be utterly open to Life's program makes it possible for us to serve Life without reservation. It reveals the meaning of our lives because our existence becomes an ongoing act of service to the only reality there is. Then, the meaning we serve is yet another expression of the creative energy of Life Itself as it rises up and manifests simply and purely in the state of total well-being from which we live every day.

*The universe came into being gradually
over six days. God could have just commanded,
Be!...*

*Constant, slow movement teaches us to keep working
like a small creek that stays clear,
that doesn't stagnate, but finds a way
through numerous details, deliberately.*

*Deliberation is born of joy,
like a bird from an egg.*

— RUMI

We make two types of effort within ourselves. One is the effort to cultivate our deep desire and commitment to grow. In India, this is called *Bhakti Yoga*. This yearning to grow becomes the devotion to finding and being with the inner master. The second type of effort involves the thirst for knowledge which, as it matures, evolves into understanding and wisdom. This is called *Jnana Yoga*. Both Bhakti and Jnana Yoga, according to Abhinavagupta, are like the two wings of a bird — our ultimate realization depends on the rhythmic interaction of the two. We cultivate within ourselves the deep desire to grow and the understanding of what it means to be the best person we possibly can be. To these ends, we put forth as much effort as we can.

Effort is sometimes called the will of God, or *iccha shakti*, with iccha meaning "will." This is a way of saying that whatever effort we make is an expression of vitality which, ultimately, we undertake for the joy of it and not for any particular purpose. Indeed, the sense of well-being we have every day is directly related to the effort we make in any area of our lives.

In one sense, there are many levels of effort. For example, there is the effort involved in physical self-control, emotional stability, mental commitment, and spiritual awareness. We have to build upon each of these. As we work and get a handle on one level, we become aware that there is yet another. We get a handle on *that*, and discover there are still more.

The important thing is to have a certain quality of life, action, and relationship. We strive to discover this quality within ourselves and to share it with the people we love. This is mind-breaking, heart-breaking, body-breaking work, all of it. Furthermore, we discover in the process that the things from which we learn the most — those that teach us the most about ourselves and about life with other people — are, on the face of it, going to be the most disappointing to us.

This is because the myth we create and strive to maintain about ourselves is, in a way, the myth of the immortality of our individuality and of our personalities. When we see through this myth and recognize it for what it is, we cannot help but be disappointed. Yet, such disappointment is also a release. If we can let go of it, we can see what we *do* have once the smoke clears. Then, what we need to know comes to us in its proper time. After all, if everything we hope to know were to come to us at once, the input would probably overwhelm us. Indeed, without ongoing self-cultivation, we wouldn't have the capacity to absorb it.

It would be like taking a corn seed and pouring the Colorado River on it. All it really needed was a few drops of water today, a few tomorrow, and a little more the next day. That rate would allow the seed to soak in the nourishment and make it possible for its highest potential to emerge. Put it under the Colorado River and what happens? What was nourishment becomes the source of its undoing. Better to be patient.

In talking about this process, I use the term "work" because I don't like the term "spiritual path." If there is but one infinite, pure awareness that is the source of all of our lives, then there is no path from one place to another. In an infinity, where is there to go? Each person works out his or her awareness of the highest state, and each person has his or her own *way* of doing this. In this sense, I suppose we could talk about there being a path. Even then, each person's way is and must be different. This is why Confucius said that the Way is as broad as the number of people undertaking it. I prefer to say that, for each of us, there is simply work to do to discover the vastness of our inner spirit.

Each of us has already had a taste of that experience, whether we have recognized it as such or not. Think of those days when you have gone out early on a fine, clear morning and felt how good it was to be alive. The taste of our inner spirit is that simple. What usually happens, though, is that instead of going through the day full of that clear awareness, someone comes along, we get into a discussion, and immediately we get distracted. Two people later, somebody says something that sends us off to the races, and we forget the feeling entirely, not to mention how to sustain it.

It is like having a fine meal on the table and yet, for some reason, insisting on getting down on our knees, crawling over to the corner where the dog bowl is, and eating from that. We cannot raise ourselves up to sit at the table and be simple, authentic human beings. We go off course and forget what we are. Yet, if we could stay in the state we were in when we first met the morning — if we could sustain that awareness — then the power within that awareness would completely change our understanding of who we and other people are, of what truly composes our relationships, and of what Life is about. We would see that it is very, very big.

It is, in some ways, much easier to accept dog food from this life; to do otherwise requires an act of will. This is the effort that we make.

In his book, *The Book of the Five Rings*, the seventeenth-century Japanese master swordsman, Miyamoto Musashi, says over and over again, "You must practice this constantly." If becoming a master swordsman or a consummate anything in this world requires that much practice, concentration, devotion, and one-pointedness, then what kind of concentration, one-pointed-ness, and devotion are required to know and master the energy of Life Itself?

Real spiritual understanding of this kind is not all that com-plicated. Even attaining the highest state is not all that complicated. It is a few simple things done over and over again, each time, with a new mind and new eyes; each time, with a new awareness that allows you to see, within that simple effort, the power from which that effort emerges in the first place.

The techniques that you practice help you to cultivate your concentration so that you can sustain a simple connection to this energy, which allows you to participate more and more deeply in it. These techniques are not recipes, rule books, or the manual for a home computer. Rather, they constitute a series of activities that guide your attention to the different linkage points where the energy changes its frequency. This helps you to appreciate more deeply the dynamic circumstance that you are.

Sometimes, in the process, you will feel as though you are sitting there and nothing is happening. At other times, you will feel that all hell is breaking loose. One of the reasons for sitting regularly is to find within yourself the balance between emptiness and fullness — between the feeling that nothing is happening and the experience that too much is happening and you wish that some of it would stop.

The point is to be patient and simple and to let it slowly hap-pen. Life has its own way of turning. Things happen, just like that, and then everything is different. It is remarkable how every-thing can look bleak and dreary and, just when you are getting used to it, change in a flash. One small event — say, a glance or a touch — can turn everything. So, your task is simply to keep an open mind and see what happens.

Every difficult situation you have faced in your life, however long it may have dragged on, was really dealt with in the first fif-teen minutes. This is true of every crisis, every disaster, every tension, and every conflict. Sometimes it is even the first two minutes. My point is that everything is decided quickly. It is how you deal with the first seconds or minutes of a potential conflict that determines whether it will promote or entangle you.

This is why practice is so important and why a real commitment to it is essential. Either you surrender in the first few minutes and begin the process of finding a stillpoint, changing yourself to have a higher vision of the situation, and extending that vision through the event, or you operate from your ego and your misunderstanding. That leaves you fighting and resisting, trying to dominate a situation and impose your own will, until finally the whole thing has brought you down to the lowest common denominator available in the event. This happens faster then you can imagine, which makes consistent practice all the more necessary.

You can study with a teacher and learn how that person behaves; you can learn how a group of people explain what they are doing by spending time with them; you even can work a little more and study their ideas and practices. Nevertheless, only when you set those ideas and practices in motion in your own life does it become possible for you to bridge the gap between your separate physical, mental, and emotional existence to an enduring experience of unity. There is no substitute for doing. *Thinking* about doing will not get you anywhere. *Doing* is what makes progress.

If someone were to give you a hammer, a saw, or a knife, and tell you to work with them, you would probably not master the tool instantaneously. (The first time that most of us used a hammer, we went slowly and still probably hit ourselves.) With practice, however, you can sink a nail in two or three hits, fast. In the same way, you now have in your hands a solid method. So, practice. Just the doing of it will answer many of your questions.

This process of self-discipline — of controlling your mind and emotions, checking your desires, and living a simple, disciplined life — creates in and around you an atmosphere in which you can begin to sustain your awareness of true subtlety. You can then go more deeply into it and extend your awareness of it to the point where you actually start to live from it. In this way, your life becomes something magical.

One thing to avoid is the temptation to evaluate your own process. Keep it simple and don't think like that. Simply keep on working at it. Just because the superficial shell of tension you feel around yourself is not getting blown off in one intergalactic explosion doesn't mean that your practice is not sinking in. Actually, it is a good thing if this shell cracks naturally from the inside, because that means you have grown from within.

Many people suffer from self-doubt not only in their lives but also in their meditation practice, and from the fear that they are not working hard enough. In either case, self-doubt is not helpful in any way. In fact, it can only take us into strange places and wrap our heads around a bean pole in no time at all.

At least part of the reason people experience self-doubt in their practice is because they bring into it the values, standards, and expectations of all their previous experience. For instance, if we are used to getting A's, being on the honor role, and getting a lot of attention, we may start in with the idea that meditation will be the same kind of experience. Then we find that we don't get A's out of it — that it doesn't even work that way. Pretty soon, this has us beating our heads against a wall. Yet this is only because we are looking for a kind of confirmation that is meaningless in the first place.

Once we recognize what we are doing and stop struggling for a recognition that is impossible, the issue of self-doubt becomes equally meaningless. This is one of the things we face in our practice that will affect the degree to which the whole experience of meditation will change our lives.

Whether we are or are not working hard enough is an interesting issue because too much meditation is just as useless as too little. Practicing is really a question of preparing ourselves properly, training our concentration, keeping our attention focussed during the day, doing the tension-release exercise, sitting — and sitting completely when we *do* sit — and then taking some time to reflect on what is happening. When we do these things, the process becomes one of experience and reflection that will teach us a lot about ourselves.

The problem with trying to evaluate our spiritual work is that we then jump onto the pendulum of thinking, "I'm open,

I'm not open, I'm open, I'm not." When feelings arise, we become entangled in their reverberations. The next thing we know, the whole event is getting noisier and noisier, tighter and tighter, instead of becoming quiet.

Even when we have practiced for a long time, our sense of direction and purpose — the place from which we live our lives — is not something we can take for granted. We never become established in a state of understanding that is permanent. It is never the case that we can just relax and forget about it. All of us have challenging lives that put pressure on us in many ways. Even though we may think and talk about our practice somewhat regularly, it is still a good thing to stop for some period of time every day and become quiet in order to listen to Life Itself directly and intensely again from within.

This is necessary because any understanding we develop and cultivate from within ourselves is a dynamic, living event. Either it deepens because we want it to, or it is being dissipated. This is true whether we are fifteen or twenty-eight, forty or seventy. There is never a point when we can allow ourselves to walk out on our lives. Cruise control is strictly for cars, not for human beings.

Through steadfast, devoted, one-pointed attention to the pulsation of Life Itself within us, we train our senses and intellects to perceive the light and experience the warmth that are the essence of the mirage we call our lives. No amount of practice can prepare us for the extraordinary things that will take place as we begin to pay attention to a different level of the dynamic event that we are — as these energies start to awaken and shake off their crystallization, and as the various tensions that we are composed of start to break down. At the same time, our practice becomes our rudder for navigating through the remarkable, multi-dimensional experiences we have to undergo as this total event unfolds.

As we experience this, we discover that our work is not to *get* anything but to unfold what we already have within us. Understanding that we have a great treasure within us, we attend to it with care, allowing that creative potential to support us in whatever monumental work we must do in our lives. If great people rise in the face of adversity and if that greatness is within all of us, then adversity itself is the opportunity each of us has to rise.

What is alive in us is always alive. What is not living about us never was alive and never will be. It is our confusion about why we do the things we do — indeed, about why we perform any action at all — that causes us endlessly to mistake what is merely dust for what is important. This confusion is the cause of suffering in our lives.

To deal with this confusion — to cultivate within ourselves the proper understanding — is a serious effort. It is the work of a lifetime and establishes us in what is truly vital, delicious, and nourishing about life. It is what raises us above the level of the superficial, the dull, the repetitive, and the dead. It is a serious effort, which frees us from the tensions within ourselves and the tensions around us. It frees us from all resistance to the flow within, allowing us to be at ease inside ourselves and in contact with the power of Life, which is elegant and gracious, giving and receiving, and continuously Self-renewing. There is no finer thing we can do with our lives than this.

SURRENDER

To become a devotee
is to surrender one's devotion.
To become a fit man
is to surrender one's fitness.
To enter Union
is to surrender one's ego.

Self-surrender must be
in everything.

The worth of this surrender
the Lord of the Meeting Rivers
alone knows.

— BASAVANNA

In many spiritual practices, we encounter the term, "surrender." This refers to the process of learning to let go of our worries, tensions, attitudes, and opinions. It is the process of releasing the mental and emotional limits within which we confine our energy and through which we require it to work. At this level, surrender means taking a deep breath, relaxing, and letting go of whatever obstructive feelings, ideas, or attitudes we may experience.

Yet the whole also goes beyond the sum of the parts. Surrender is more than just taking a deep breath. Every day, I watch people take a deep breath and not let go of their tensions. I watch them instead take a breath in order to re-organize their inner resources and enter the fray once more. Under the guise of surrendering, such people are simply trying to find some leverage in an argument. Ironically, the same people often imagine that they are practicing surrender. In truth, however, much of what we are doing when we think we are surrendering has nothing to do with surrender in the slightest.

Surrender is much more than relaxing; it is even much more than letting go. There is no method for achieving it, nor is there any technique for teaching it. There is only our commitment to growing which combines with something indefinable. Together, they allow us to grasp the essence of surrender itself. The process by which this happens is, in its entirety, something truly mysterious.

When I say that surrender involves letting go, people sometimes think this gives them license to withdraw or escape from their responsibilities and commitments. Not so. Our capacity to surrender has nothing to do with being relieved of our responsibilities and commitments. We don't walk away from anything. Rather, we learn new ways to live with our obligations as we do the work we must in order to fulfill the requirements of our lives.

Many of these requirements will not be ones that we would have chosen, but are simply those that have presented themselves to us. They are the work Life has given us to do, that we *must* do. To try to evade this work is something only fools attempt. Instead, we are called to face our lives directly and openly, and to live them as we must.

It is living life as we must that opens us to a great inner depth because we develop the strength, the sensitivity, and the thoughtfulness to recognize who and where we are in every circumstance. Then, confusion cannot blind us as we do the work that confronts us. Furthermore, we bring that work to its full completion as we come to understand that, first and foremost, we must live in a state of surrender.

Is there anything in our lives that does *not* have to be surrendered? Think about this question for a moment. If there is only one, pure, dynamic event — the essence of Life Itself — and if there is nothing outside of that, then, when we let go of something, have we really lost it? In an infinity, where can it go?

I will tell you this now, although it may not seem clear for some time: Every person and every situation that comes into your life is there for one reason only, and that is to be surrendered. The sooner you understand this, the more deeply you will understand Life Itself. Some people will understand this with you and, in that spirit, will share a long and profound communion with you. Many will not.

The circumstances in your life fall away from you like dead leaves off a tree, returning their material content into the soil of your life and becoming part of the compost from which you continue to grow. There is no need to resist or fear this — it is simply the natural way of life.

The point is not to become entangled in your various experiences — not to become enmeshed in the disappointments or deluded by the successes. Simply understand that every experience that manifests in your life does so for one reason. It is not there to *teach* you to surrender but simply to *be* surrendered. Either you will learn to do so or you will suffocate in cynicism, tension, and disappointment because these are what being entangled in the world is all about.

At the same time, to surrender something doesn't mean that it is going to leave you or even that it *has* to leave you. Every time you surrender into the flow of real love, nothing is diminished. Instead, everything gets bigger. You find yourself more filled, again and again renewed. So, understand that surrender is not like dropping something, although some things do fall away in the process. Even then, their essence and reality are not lost to you. This is why we say that the real key to authentic growth is surrender.

As you go through the joy and the suffering you encounter during your life, your understanding of surrender is what allows you to find within yourself the strength and purpose to absorb each experience for what it is and then to allow it to drop away. It is thus that all experience — no matter how difficult — becomes nourishment that adds to your strength and increases the richness of your life.

Learning to absorb our experiences in this way doesn't come easily, and everybody is clumsy about it at one point or another. If we don't learn to do so, however, our inner constipation will only increase. Since we don't want to get stuck in this, we have to be honest with ourselves about our own shortcomings and make a real effort to extend our skills through practice. We could call doing this the science of spirituality; we could call it the science of Life; we could also call it the science of surrender.

This is not an intellectual process, nor is it some understanding that we can articulate as a set of rules or guidelines. We can only say that there is always a reciprocal relationship between consciousness and surrender because absolute consciousness *is* pure surrender. Furthermore, surrender never happens by accident and it never happens by itself. It is always intentional insofar as we have to *want* to understand it and practice living from the heart of it for anything to happen.

In this regard, the will is involved: We will ourselves to let go. This is much more difficult than willing ourselves to hold on. After all, willing ourselves to hold on comes naturally — even if it is a complete illusion and the only thing we really end up holding onto is our misunderstanding. This is why Rumi says:

If they ask what Love is,
say, the sacrifice of will.
If you have not left will behind,
you have no will at all.

Someone once asked me, "If the same principle in life repeats itself over and over again, then why is it that surrender can't be taught? It seems as though it should be everywhere and immediately apparent." In one sense, she was right. Surrender *is* everywhere, because surrender is the nature of the highest reality and of all manifest reality through which it expresses itself.

Surrender is the essence of our bodies and minds; it is the essence even of something as dense as a rock which slowly, over billions of years, spends itself. This essence is not immediately apparent to us, however, because of the ways in which this consciousness conceals its true nature. So, in our case, the question is how long we want to take to recognize and experience it. Do we want to take lifetimes or only a little while?

When I say that surrender cannot be taught, I don't mean that it cannot be learned. I mean that the experience of its essence is inexpressible and that we can learn about it only through continuous concentration and attention. Only those people who really want to understand it are ever able to do so, and even they tend to forget about it two days after they figure it out. Thus, the process of learning surrender is one that generally takes a long time and requires coming back to again and again before we become established in our understanding of it.

We can never assume that we have mastered it once and for all. This holds true of most things, but it is especially true of surrender because the power of Life is unfathomably more vast and awesome than the human mind is capable of encompassing. People who assume that they understand surrender are always the ones who forget to do it. Either that, or they fall into the other trap: They try to give themselves a grade. They want to know, "Am I making progress? Am I really doing it?" The problem is that, in our attempt to inventory with our mind that which is *beyond* the mind, we only end up taking inventory of those things from which we were hoping to be free.

When we do this, we become confused about the significance of these things to our spiritual work. We start holding onto them and confusing surrender with acquisitiveness — confusing letting go with holding on, opening up with closing down, being still with running around, growing spiritually with ambition and worldly accomplishment. This is a strange phenomenon, but it happens all the time.

We will not grow in any meaningful way if we do not understand surrender. Moreover, growing is not represented by our capacity to carry more bags. At some point, even the strongest person in the world will collapse. Rather, growing is our capacity to put down our baggage and sustain the flow of creative energy within ourselves.

Something special resides within us. Indeed, everything we could ever possibly know is already within us and, if we have not found it, it is because we have become so stuck in tension that we forget to look. We can find that treasure within us whenever we have a problem, whenever we are in pain, and whenever we are besieged by doubt or confusion if we give it all back to the higher power within us. We let go of the whole thing and say to that essence within us, "This is not my problem, God — it is *your* problem." We give it back, we remain open, and in giving it back, we slowly unearth that treasure.

Over and over again we have to learn to appreciate the enormous creative capacity hidden within the energy of our lives. It is that creative capacity that sustains our bodies moment by moment and by which all of our experiences and feelings are demonstrated. It is that creative capacity that endlessly shows its power throughout our everyday lives. Yet, we rarely have the trust to open ourselves to it — to take the time to allow it to demonstrate the depth of its creative and re-creative capacity.

When we are able to do this, however, we find that subtlety is attained through surrender — the quantum leap in our awareness that we can make daily. It doesn't happen accidentally, and it is not the same thing as relaxing our bodies. It *is* the same thing as totally stilling our minds. In the stillness of surrender, we become able to appreciate a subtle extension which is the essence of our growth.

To grow as a person requires a tremendous balance between sustaining our daily lives and, at the same time, going into the depth of those lives and unfolding the potential that exists within every one of their experiences. It involves opening out and exploring the subtle dimensions of what we are. To do this, we must have the capacity to be energetic, expansive, spacious, and, at the same time, quiet, simple, and steady. Indeed, the strength we hope to attain in our spiritual search is first to hold ourselves steady and then to hold the universe around us steady. This strength we demonstrate in our service to all those whose lives touch ours.

When we are a vehicle for the energy and when we understand that the deeper energy of Life within us is the agent by which all action is accomplished, then we live in peace. Whatever problems ripple the surface of our lives are neither to be solved, nor even really addressed, because they simply arise and subside.

When we are attuned to the flow of Life Itself within us, *that* is the tide that changes the landscape. Then we are able to absorb the understanding that Life is trying to communicate to us. This is what allows us to change deeply.

Ultimately, there is nothing I can tell you about surrender except having nothing and wanting nothing; not keeping score, not trying to be richer, not being afraid of losing; not being particularly interested in our own personalities; choosing to be happy, no matter what happens to us. These are some of the clues. The rest we learn with practice and grace.

GRATITUDE

*I have often said that the person who wishes to begin
a good life should be like a man who draws a circle.
Let him get the center in the right place and keep it
so and the circumference will be good. In other words,
let a man first learn to fix his heart on God . . .*

— MEISTER ECKHART

The first moment I saw Rudi — as well as every other moment I was with him — was, for me, a moment of devotion. Witnessing the sacrifice he made in himself and the way he cared for other people, I was so amazed by it that I had no choice but to try to live up to what I had seen. Seventeen years have gone by since he passed away, and I find that I respect him even more now than I did then. I couldn't grasp it all at the time, because I was bringing my bottle-cap mind to an ocean of love.

In his talks to us, Rudi used to say, "Feel gratitude." I sometimes say the same thing. The reason for this is important. To feel gratitude is to remember what we have and to feel the great richness within us. If we remember, every day, that something special is happening within us, then and there we find something for which to feel grateful. This, by the way, is neither as easy nor as simplistic as it sounds.

The alternative to feeling gratitude is to think either that we are inadequate or that something is missing. The Zen master Suzuki Roshi says something rather interesting in this regard. He says that whenever we ask for more of something, we automatically lose whatever we had in the first place. This is so because the same power that has created the whole universe is also within us. What more can there possibly be? To think that we require "more" only demonstrates our misunderstanding of the resource we already possess.

The very idea of wanting "more" really becomes a way of avoiding whatever circumstances we face as part of the experience of being ourselves. Much of what we face, we may not particularly feel like doing, but it is like changing a diaper: If we don't do it right then, before we know it we have an angry baby, we still have to change the diaper, and now we also have a rash to treat.

To land in Rudi's house was an interesting experience. I didn't much care for working in the sub-basement of a building with a plumber who spoke no English, or for fighting off rats the whole time, but I did it as well as I knew how because I was so grateful to be where I was. I thought, "I had better do a good job with this, and then I'll have the chance to grow here." The quality of our effort in every area counts. It may be a lot of work; at the same time, it is the only way we can test and begin to understand the wide range of creative energies within us. It is also the only way to discover that there is no situation where we cannot experience gratitude for something.

The reality is that we all have a lot to be grateful for. It is fine if we don't feel grateful every day. I can understand that. If we feel terrible on some days, I can understand that, too. What I don't understand is how we can accept the lack of gratitude in our lives without making even a simple effort to find it within ourselves, nourish it, and allow it to grow and flower.

Sometimes, when we are all heated up and agitated in the middle of a lot of change, we may find it difficult to feel gratitude. (I'm supposed to be grateful for *this*?) So, we can try to be just a little grateful, without pushing things. On the other hand, we will find that there are other moments when gratitude wells up and spills all over the place. In the moments after meditation, I try to take a few moments to feel simple gratitude and joy for the opportunity I have to participate in the broadest, finest field of potentiality that is.

To grow as a human being requires that we develop the capacity to rise above our tensions and the struggles of our daily lives. It compels us to become established in the quiet within ourselves, where we can begin to absorb and digest the various pressures that function within and around us and find even therein a certain harmony.

Only in this harmony — this quiet, simple richness that is both our own essence and the essence of our practice — is it possible for our understanding and experience of the highest part of us to become clear. As long as we are thrashing around in the stresses and strains, in the temptations and tugs that pull us in every direction, we have no capacity to do anything but endure. In that endurance, we only create further problems for ourselves.

To persist in going beyond our tensions is a commitment that binds us further to the pursuit and demonstration of our own infinite resource. It is something that, paradoxically, we do for ourselves, reinforcing and making visible for ourselves our own empowerment and, hopefully, using well what has been transmitted to us. This is what demonstrates our love, our respect, and our true gratitude.

Only if we persevere in this pursuit do we have the capacity to rise above the apparent and experience the obvious. We are constantly being deluded by the apparent and failing to participate in the obvious. True genius is the capacity to recognize the obvious, which is that our lives are articulations of the richness, beauty, and unity that underlie all manifestation. Each of us has a place in this symphony of Life. As we dissolve tensions and allow the creative energy to flow, we experience the fulfillment of being fully alive as conscious participants in the drama of the whole.

In doing this, we cannot worry about where we have been or about whatever pain we have undergone in getting to where we are. Better to be grateful to everybody who has ever hurt us because it was they who showed us where and under what conditions the truth does not persist. So, they have done us a favor. They were also the ones who pushed us to keep growing. When we understand this, we can be grateful for the role they have played in our lives. We accept the pain and allow it to happen (which is *not* to say that we go looking for it). We can be grateful for this understanding, even as it puts our experience into perspective.

More importantly, we look at the work we have to do and at the richness and quality of the sharing that takes place in our lives every day and tend to these things. We cease to worry about

whatever tensions we encounter, taking them as new opportunities to extend and deepen the quality of our experience and to
share that new depth with the people who are important to us.

We live in this world to learn how to bring our existence to
life. If we are drowning in our sorrows, desires, needs, or anything else, we cannot possibly be doing this for ourselves or for
anyone else. Instead, we are perpetuating the unhappy condition
in which most people find themselves.

We do, however, have a choice. We don't have to stay the
same; we can change. It doesn't matter where we start or what
we think our problems are. It only matters that we do our quiet
inner work with love and devotion every single day. In this way,
we will transcend ourselves. It is only this kind of life that brings
us to the point of allowing our egos to die into the fullness, the
joy, and the gratitude for this experience, full of enthusiasm for
further exploration of this extraordinary expression of Life that
we are.

Both Nityananda's and Rudi's whole reason for existing
was to transmit their understanding and to share the tools by
which we can undertake our deep inner work and transform our
own lives. The truly great people we meet do not want anything
from us. They do not have any agendas or plans. Instead, they are
simply, completely, and deeply present, and willing to share that
essence of Life Itself with us.

So, to whom or what should we be grateful? For one, we can
be grateful to Life for affording us the opportunity to participate
in it in this most extraordinary and wonderful way. Life, of
course, sometimes wears peculiar faces. On one occasion, I was
sitting with Rudi. My chakras were shaking, tears were running
from my eyes, and I thought, "How can I possibly thank this person? How can I show the gratitude I feel?" After all, saying thank
you seemed so trite — so insufficient. To have only that fall out
of my mouth felt, in a way, almost insulting. "Oh hey, thanks!"
For me, the idea that I could give anything of meaning to Rudi always felt somewhat like pissing into the ocean to try to add some
depth to it.

It occurred to me at the time, and I have felt ever since, that there is really only one way to express such gratitude, and that is to live what we have learned; it is to be the best person we can possibly be. The only way we can thank people is, in some way, to understand the contribution they have made to our lives and to show value for that — not just in this moment, but from moment to moment and throughout the tenure of our presence here. We can try to live in a way that reflects our appreciation for this richness. This means carefully trying to understand what it is to be in balance within ourselves and within all our relationships and responsibilities.

This does not mean that we must suddenly become perfect people. Personally, I wouldn't much care to be surrounded by pure and perfect people — to tell the truth, I even find them somewhat boring. I am much more concerned with being surrounded by growing people, in which case one expects that mistakes will be made. From a certain point of view this is a problem. From a broader perspective, however, we see that these mistakes enrich our lives.

A perfect diamond is never going to change. It may be beautiful but it is not alive. Life is permeated with assymetry, imperfection, and disharmony. This is a wonderful thing, not a bad one. If we can continuously connect to the fundamental ground — that creative power underneath every event — then regardless of whether it is assymetrical or disconsonant, sharp or flat, we are in harmony with it. We are not fighting it.

The understanding of how to be the best person we can be emerges as we cultivate one-pointed concentration on growing. Then, there is no need to judge our lives because whatever we need to do just happens. There is no need to step away from it and ask, "Was I the best person I could have been?" When we are one-pointed about growing, we simply release ourselves into the moment. In a way, it becomes an infinite moment. Then the best that is there happens, and we do not have to think too much about it.

What gets in the way of our doing this is our constant need to judge ourselves. This is not the point. In a very real way, the eccentricities of a particular performance, though they may not always be technically up to standard, can add real depth and richness to the event. People prefer going to live performances over sitting and listening to a recording because even though tapes can be made cosmetically pure, they lack the vitality and spontaneity of the live performance — that is, they lack the mistakes. They also sometimes lack the quality of a certain inspiration.

This means that we have to be careful about judging ourselves. I would say that judgment and total concentration do not exist in the same place. We are either doing one or the other. What we really want to do is take this question of being the best person we can be beyond the issue of performance. Rather, we want to ask ourselves to what spirit or state we aspire, in order to allow that maximum quality within ourselves to show.

We spend long hours training, so that our bodies and our minds will not be the limitation of our capacity to serve this deepest inspiration. When we have connected to that vitality within us and aroused it, when we have brought it to the forefront of our awareness, we step aside and let it do what it wills. Our ability to do this is our real expression of devotion, of sacrifice, and of gratitude.

Conclusion

What shall I do, O Muslims?
I do not recognize myself. . . .
I am neither Christian nor Jew,
nor Magian, nor Muslim.
I am not of the East, nor the West,
not of the land, nor the sea.
I am not from nature's mine,
nor from the circling stars . . . .
My place is the placeless,
my trace is the traceless.
It is not the body nor is it the soul,
for I belong to the soul of my love.
I have put duality away
and seen the two worlds as one . . . .

— RUMI

Everything we have discussed to this point has been an attempt to present an overview of what we are likely to experience as we begin to pursue our own wish to grow through the practice of meditation, and as we continue to explore this question of "Who am I?" Yet, the awareness that emerges in us as we do this is just the beginning. It is the stage of practice known, in Kashmir Shaivism, as *anavopaya*.

There are basically four stages of awareness in spiritual development. In the *Shiva Sutras*, these are called anavopaya, shaktopaya, shambhavopaya, and anupaya. Anavopaya is the first of these stages. *Anava* refers to what is individual, and *upaya* means "strategy" or "skillful means." So, anavopaya is the strategy of individual effort. It is called this because, in the beginning, our practice *is* an effort. As we have discussed, it is the work we do to attain something. We experience the teacher as effort and we work to master the techniques of our practice. We engage in service as actions that we perform. All the aspects of practice we have discussed in the preceding chapters come under the heading of anavopaya.

Part of this effort involves our work in the world as we pursue our desires. This work helps us come together as an entity, giving us a sense of what we like and appreciate, and what we don't. At this level, we also pursue our emotional needs and various forms of recognition. We may achieve a certain level of material fulfillment as well as a confirmation of our individual worth and capability. We come to understand what it means to accomplish things, which refines our sense of who we are and what we are capable of doing. Indeed, the challenge at this level of practice is to emerge with a positive feeling about ourselves and a sense of our own competence. In the process, we learn to respect our creative energy in basic ways.

Furthermore, we begin to understand the whole world — our experience of this body, our relationships, and everything we do and everything that surrounds us — as nothing but an overlay on the surface of Life Itself which is unlimited in any way. We explore the process by which Life has taken on the appearance of matter and experience without ever losing any of its vitality, potentiality, or internal wholeness and coherence.

The culmination of this stage is the realization of the things we have pursued and worked for. We get them and, in the getting, recognize their ultimate unimportance. It is not, however, that we reject or suppress our desires. Indeed, we first cook them, even as they cook us. Ultimately, we recognize that it is not we who are fulfilling anything.

This recognition is the linchpin. It signals the second stage, called shaktopaya, the strategy of awareness of the energy of Life Itself. This stage evolves when we begin to understand everything we experience not as matter but as energy. We may not always live in that understanding, but it is always accessible to us. It is not that we lose our perception of material reality but that we see through it. As a result, the geometry and physics of our experience undergo a quantum change. Furthermore, we come to this stage of awareness not by getting serious or heavy but by becoming light and simple. So, this is a stage of less effort and a more refined awareness.

Shambhavopaya is the instantaneous and full recognition of the infinite — of the Self. At this point, we recognize everything as the Self, although there are vestiges of self-awareness. There is a stage beyond that, called anupaya, in which one is totally immersed in the infinite. This full awareness of infinity and dwelling in continual contact with it is the highest state. Then, we observe the activity of the world without ever losing our connection with infinity.

This is the progression of the upayas, each stage of which represents a different aspect of consciousness. Anavopaya, which we have discussed in terms of the personality, involves effort. It involves the quality of energy required to deal with the material world. Individualized consciousness, on the other hand, is conscious energy as articulated in individual form. This is shaktopaya, or awareness of the energy. Finally, there is unbounded, infinite consciousness, which is shambhavopaya and then anupaya.

In a critical sense, we do not go from one stage to the other or leave one and merge into the other. As long as we have bodies, all four stages are present in us at the same time. It is simply an issue of which one dominates our awareness. In the beginning, our individual effort dominates our attention. Yet, at some stage, we recognize that all this individual effort, even though a necessary part of our training, is not the ultimate point. Then, our focus shifts. It is not that we cease to make an individual effort, but within the context of infinity our individual effort takes on a kind of effortlessness and we experience our unity with Life Itself.

These shifts in our awareness, which are represented as these different stages, evolve over the course of our practice. They do not come about without practice because, even when a certain fine energy manifests before us, our ordinary patterns of tension and lack of awareness tend to reassert themselves. Consequently, we forget all about what is fine because we have not refined our inner capacity to retain that understanding. We can have extraordinary experiences and deep insights which we have no capacity to retain because our minds and our senses are undisciplined.

As we learn to retain these insights and carry them into our ongoing experience, we become able to deal with tensions differently. We see our patterns and recognize our ways of limiting ourselves. Then, we can allow the energy within us to unlock these tensions, releasing them for us so that we become finer, bigger people.

Understand that this effort is required every single day in both our inner and outer lives. If we hope to recognize that our whole existence is nothing but creative energy, we will have to pay attention to all facets of that existence. This, as we have seen, is real work. Sometimes it is tiring, sometimes painful, and sometimes frustrating — especially when we are beating our heads against the wall — but it is still a profoundly wonderful and important endeavor. It is certainly the only thing that will always add value to our lives. Indeed, any endeavor that we undertake without this effort can only depreciate our lives, regardless of what we may think.

This does not mean that we shouldn't relax and have fun. In fact, an important part of our spiritual work lies in making everything — no matter how difficult — as much fun as possible, and in finding the joy in every situation. It is wonderful to experience that joy and to allow it to permeate every event that we engage in, as long as it is not at the expense of our attention. In that spirit, we absorb this material, we come to understand and articulate it, and we learn to digest whatever experience we encounter. We become able to rise to any challenge that confronts us, having the understanding, the method, and the techniques to do so.

Rudi's statement that spirituality is a question of depth over time means that we work to become established in that state permanently. We extend our center further and further, thereby creating an environment in which increasingly subtle and sophisticated energies can manifest and be sustained long enough for us to appreciate their presence. Releases of tension occur that allow us to think increasingly in terms of the big picture. This is not an issue of recognizing existing patterns but of expanding the capacity of the mind.

It takes time for this expansion to work itself into our brains and change the chemistry of our thinking and our emotions. This is because the mind, being a pattern recognition mechanism, will ignore everything it doesn't recognize as part of an existing pattern. Only when that element has been around long enough does the mind make a shift and appreciate the new pattern. It takes time for us to recognize the changes that happen within us. Indeed, the mind is usually the last to know. This is what makes it so important to sustain a centered state and continue to allow the creative energy to flow, even when we think that nothing is happening.

When we can stop our minds and be quiet in complete surrender, then we have gone right through the maze — straight through all the levels to infinity. If we can stay there long enough, this awareness will sink into our brains and start to explain its own nature to us. Since we and it are really nothing but the same thing, a flash of recognition occurs that liberates us instantly from our misunderstanding. The point is to remember this long enough to allow it to happen.

We are not always going to remember to keep our attention focused inside on our wish to grow. Repeatedly, we find ourselves having to bring our attention back from one thing or another. This is why I return again and again to the words over the gateway to Rumi's spiritual community — "Come, come to the *semna*[6]. Even if you have broken your vows a thousand times, come, come again. Ours is not a caravan of despair." Our practice is a celebration of Life. It is a philosophy that urges us to find beauty and truth in everything that happens.

S ome people come to this work with the idea that they have to reject some aspect of the world. In India, spiritual seekers have traditionally renounced everything and gone into the forest to live off the land and from what they could beg. This practice, known as taking *sannyas*, is a way of putting one's belief on the line — of saying, "I trust God to provide for my life."

From the perspective of Kashmir Shaivism, however, it is not possible to reject the world because we are always interacting with one aspect of it or another. That is why ours is a non-rejectionist tradition — we reject no aspect of human experience. Furthermore, by learning to interact in the world with a refined awareness, we come to understand where the true source of our fulfillment lies. We come to a radical trust in Life Itself because we have experienced it as our Self.

In a very real sense, the highest level of our practice is to recognize that our individualized consciousness is God. To be still and become aware of the multiplicity of ways in which this consciousness expresses itself — this is our work. When we know this, we see that there is nothing particular to change about ourselves. The point is simply to understand who we are. That understanding will effect every change that is required.

We come to the awareness, then, that God does everything through our lives — indeed, that God *is* everything in our lives. As personalities, we ourselves do nothing, whatever we may imagine. This awareness is surrender. It is called detachment and renunciation; it is also called sannyas.

True sannyas involves understanding that our individualized consciousness is God, which is the source of our life and from which we are never apart. God's infinite fullness is never absent from our lives. If we follow this line of thinking, we realize that everything in our lives has come from God — that God is our support and our sustenance, and that what carries us is grace.

The fundamental thing we hope for is an understanding of the absolute — an understanding that we are an individualized manifestation of the same vitality that has generated the whole universe. Our only purpose is to realize our highest creative potential. Consequently, we need not be anxious about anything. This is really what sannyas is about.

The fortunate person has the opportunity to understand that what we really wanted all along, when we first felt that vague and undefinable sense of longing, was happiness. We understand that the happiness we have pursued through one accomplishment or another was never really there in the first place. We recognize that authentic happiness has nothing to do with what we get or don't get, with what happens or doesn't happen, or with who likes us or doesn't. Instead, the happiness we have looked for is inside us and always has been.

How is this possible? The Self, being infinite, is also infinitely free and infinitely creative. This being so, it is also pure and dynamic joy. If the Self is the essence of what we ourselves are, then our very essence is this same joy. We intuit this in our yearning for happiness. We sense its possibility and we long to enter into it fully.

Through our practice, we come to recognize that all this requires is a simple, conscious decision — one that we can make and renew every single day. This is the decision to be happy, no matter what. It is that simple. At the same time, it is difficult to sustain this decision. It requires a steady commitment and ongoing concentration. In other words, it requires that we continually release tensions and allow our creative energy to flow. So, while it is not a heavy endeavor, it is a serious one. While it is simple, it is not so easy.

Yet if we have everything in the world but are not happy, what do we have? Our trip through this world is so short that if we are not happy, we are going to miss it. Our lives happen in a flash. Once we are no longer busy trying to make money or struggling for one thing or another, we can just stop for a minute, take a breath, and clear our heads. Then, we will see how fast it all goes.

If we don't seize the extraordinary opportunity we have right now to engage this happiness — to embrace it and allow it to embrace us — then it is lost, and our opportunity for liberation has passed by. I assure you that few people have this opportunity, and it is more than priceless.

When we choose to be happy, our boundaries loosen because they are no longer limited by our perception of matter. As they loosen, we understand how the energy crystallizes as matter and then releases to become pure potentiality once again. In this way, we set the stage for the unfoldment of shaktopaya, which we can call the real awareness of the energy. This arises when we recognize that *we* are not matter, since all matter is also energy. We experience ourselves and everything around us as nothing but creative energy.

As I have said, the key throughout the whole process is surrender. This is what takes us from one step to the next. In order to go beyond suffering our lives as a series of problems, we make a commitment to whatever program Life has for Itself from within us. This necessarily means that we surrender our limited desires over and over again. Then, even more than the surrender of our desires, this commitment becomes the continuous sacrifice of our physical lives and our egos into the creative flow of Life's unfolding from inside Itself.

The work we do and the things we pursue in the world are meaningful and valid to us. So, we should work hard, with integrity and courage. As we work and face the tensions that arise before us, we must do so not from a position of weakness but from a strength based on our recognition of the importance of happiness and our acceptance of our absolute inability to control anything that happens to us in the world.

If we think we know what we want when we start out, we limit where we can end up. This is fine and appropriate from a worldly point of view because any project we are involved in needs definition and limits. But in our spiritual work, if we think we know where we want to go we have already closed down our possibilities. Facing uncertainty may be frightening, but it is utterly necessary if we aspire to the highest levels of Self-awareness.

As we empty ourselves of all our tensions, the creative energy rises to fill us as guidance, as inspiration, and as the capacity to *do*. Indeed, it is this fullness that manifests as knowing what to do, how to do it, and when. Intuitively we know how to handle situations that have previously always overwhelmed and confused us.

Understand that great people rise in the face of adversity. If that greatness is within everyone, then adversity is the opportunity for each of us to rise, if we have the training, the skill, and the understanding to utilize it properly. Tension becomes an extraordinary opportunity when we begin to address it, tune into it, and pay careful attention to it from this perspective. When we can be present with it and flow within it, it becomes a source of a profound creative power. This is not a creative power that dominates anybody but one that uplifts us and everyone whose life we touch.

It is not that the struggle ever goes away but that we have transcended it so that it no longer affects us as it once did. In this second stage, courage, virtue, and nobility predominate, and we face our experiences with a happiness that is not undone by anything we encounter. As this happiness works its way through us and this stage matures, it merges into infinity, which is also love. It is boundless giving in which there is neither receiving nor the need to receive. After all, what can we add to infinity?

Spiritual teaching and spiritual awareness are the same thing — a living, dynamic, conscious Presence. This Presence is the source of words but also goes beyond them. No idea or concept can contain it; rather, all ideas and concepts are contained within it. When we are able to open ourselves to this Presence, we recognize teacher, teaching, and disciple to be one.

Although we use the name "Kashmir Shaivism" as a point of reference, our practice transcends all names. In a way, what we are doing here is demystifying mysticism. Through practice and surrender, we come to understand in a simple and natural way that the most extraordinary magic in the world exists within us. This is who we are. We learn that realization and liberation are not remote states beyond our reach, but are our fundamental condition. Realization is always there, all the time. It is we who confuse matters by involving our energy in every possible distraction.

We simply *are* Life, just as we are. There is no need for us to look outside ourselves for anything. Consciousness itself has brought us to this point and consciousness will carry us on. Nothing else is necessary. This means that, just as we are, we are complete. Maybe the range of our creative power has not yet been fully expressed, but nothing external is necessary to satisfy the situation.

If our individualized consciousness is infinite and divine in nature, we *can* come to realize and experience it *now*. There is nothing we need to have added to the equation. We need only to surrender, to open, to flow, and to realize. This is what it means to grow.

If everything is only one thing and our individual consciousness is, in fact, infinite and one, then it is true that we have no real problem. There is no need that the power of our own consciousness cannot fulfill. So, our practice — and the whole idea of growing — has nothing to do with attaining something that we don't already have. Rather, it is a process of facilitating the unfolding of what is within us — of demonstrating the divine.

What do I mean by "demonstrating the divine?" I mean allowing the full range of our creative energy to unfold and demonstrate itself — we could say "to reveal itself" — within our individual field of expression. We want to demonstrate fullness. It is the continuous dissolving of tensions that allows for the experience and the demonstration of this fullness.

This is necessarily more than a discussion of personal attainment or the acquisition of something for the individual. If it were only that, it would be nothing but an egotistical endeavor. Rather, it must be about the relationship of individual human life to Life Itself, and about the place in which our personal willpower and behavior fit into the fabric of that experience. The endeavor is a value statement about the meaning of human life, its highest potential and purpose, and the role therein of social interactions and their cultural forms.

When we go on to look at the implications of this discussion for contemporary culture we recognize that if we have human beings in balance with themselves and in harmony with their environment — if the ultimate creative potential unfolds from the individual through a humanity in harmony with the world around it — this then gives rise to a cultural and social statement different from what is currently being produced.

In the cultural, social, economic arena, we begin to understand that linear thinking can no longer play the role it has hitherto enjoyed. We see that, not only for the benefit of our individual selves but also for all of humankind, we must develop a systemic point of view based on the understanding that everything emerges from one thing. We realize that Man is not the lord of nature but merely one of the threads in its fabric — a fabric in which all forms of life are interdependent. It is through our practice that we come to know this reality experientially.

As we know and understand it, our existence becomes an extension of love, which is the foundation of Christianity; it becomes the end to suffering and the fulfillment of compassion, which is the foundation of Buddhism. It becomes the recognition of the creative pulsation of the Self — of God — which is the foundation of Hinduism; it is the state of the uncarved block, which is the foundation of Taoism; and it is an expression of the harmony of Heaven, Earth, and Human, which is the foundation of Confucianism. In this sense, we accomplish and attain the end of each spiritual practice. Established in the highest state, we are universal.

Appendix

KASHMIR SHAIVISM AND TANTRISM

The term Tantrism refers to a current found in both Hinduism and Buddhism — a current which is, at the same time, distinct unto itself. The emphasis in Tantric Hinduism differs somewhat from that of Tantric Buddhism but the two also have elements in common that remain outside other streams of thought and practice in Hinduism or Buddhism as larger traditions.

In general, Tantrism is extraordinary in its acceptance of the world, and the events and experiences that happen therein, viewing these as complete and appropriate aspects of Life. Therefore, all of a person's life experiences become the arena within which he or she cultivates spiritual understanding. Unlike many traditions which set up taboos and ritual prohibitions, the Tantric traditions recognize that no area of life is to be rejected.

There are two general traditions within Hindu Tantrism. One is called "Shaivism," the other, "Shaktism." The term "Shaivism" derives from the name "Shiva," one of the names of God, and refers to God as pure awareness. "Shaktism" derives from the term "Shakti," and refers to God as a vital, creative impulse, or conscious energy. The different monistic Tantric practices have paid greater attention to one aspect or the other. "Shaivism" and "Shaktism," therefore, simply refer to the aspect of God a given group has emphasized in its practice and discussion.

At the same time, Shiva and Shakti are recognized as ultimately one and the same. Shiva, originally known as Rudra, is one of the most ancient deities of India — that is, one of the oldest human experiences and expressions of God. He is God as the lord of creation and destruction, and his dance is the fundamental rhythm of all Life. Shakti is often depicted as his consort, as a way of suggesting that pure consciousness and creative energy are inseparable and ultimately one and the same. The thirteenth-century Indian saint Jnaneshvara says:

> *The difference between Shiva and Shakti is merely in name and form; otherwise, they are of the same essential "substance" …Just like the sound coming out of two sticks striking against each other, similar fragrance out of two flowers from the same plant, the same light out of two lamps, the same word emanating from the two lips, the same sight from the two eyes — the basis of both Shiva and Shakti is indeed the eternal unicity.*
>
> *Shiva-Shakti enjoy the experience of manifestation in duality without ever losing their oneness.*
>
> *The devoted couple are inseparably attached to each other and neither can exist even for a moment without the other.*

All branches of Shaivism, in the most general sense, derive from various understandings of God as Shiva. Kashmir Shaivism is a branch of Tantric Shaivism that emerged in Kashmir, in Northwest India and is a general term referring to both dualistic and non-dualistic schools of thought. From the seventh to the eleventh centuries A.D., Kashmir was a meeting ground for some of the most sophisticated spiritual practitioners of the time. Their careful articulation of their inner experiences produced a unique and highly refined organization of a number of strands of Tantrism that had existed in India from ancient times.

The practitioners of non-dualistic Kashmir Shaivism built on the Shaivite teachings of antiquity. They came to view the world as absolute consciousness, which they called Shiva. This consciousness is both one and free, creative and self-reflective. It is the fundamental, basic person in each of us — the fundamental "I," or divine Self. Thus, Kashmir Shaivism emphasizes not a devotion to Shiva as a personal god nor to Shiva represented as the *lingam*,[7] but to the inner Self.

Trika Yoga is essentially a Tantric method, and is aimed at coming to know the energy of Life Itself as we experience this at the individual level. Trika Yoga is a practice intended to develop our awareness of this energy to the point where we experience it not merely as our finite self, but as the infinite Self, the power that underlies all of reality.

The philosophical and practical currents within Kashmir Shaivism expressed themselves first in the agamas, texts which were accepted as divine revelation without human authorship. These took the form of dialogues between Shiva and his consort Shakti. By the eighth century, so many agamas had been written that it was difficult to master them all. So, a teacher by the name of Vasugupta recorded the *Shiva Sutras*. This was the first text associated with a particular individual, and was still considered to be revealed. The purpose of the *Shiva Sutras* was to present the gist of the tradition and practice as a whole, in a limited number of *sutras*, or verses.

The systematic growth of Kashmir Shaivism unfolded as the Kashmir Shaivite practitioners reflected on the nature of the highest reality, describing it as pure consciousness always in a state of pulsation, or *spanda*. The spanda texts that discussed these matters were attributed to human authors. It is likely that Vasugupta also composed the *Spanda Karikas* to elaborate on the shakti side of the tradition, and to make clear the place of human experience within the context of universal consciousness.

From Vasugupta and the *Spanda Karikas*, the spanda tradition was further elaborated by Somananda in the *Shiva Drishti*, and by his disciple Utpaladeva, the writer of the *Ishvara Pratyabhijna Karikas*. With this latter text, we see the emergence of an emphasis on knowledge and some recognition of the role of the intellect in a person's practice.

Prior to this, in earlier schools of Shaivism, practices had emerged that made deliberate breaks with conventional values. Individuals, for example, lived in graveyards and smeared the ashes of the cremated corpses on their bodies as a way of demonstrating that they themselves had died to this world and its constraints. These practices were also radical assertions of human liberation and ultimate freedom.

With the emergence of the *Pratyabhijna* schools — another major strain in Kashmir Shaivism — however, these earlier practices were transcended. At the same time, the spirit so integral to Tantrism of going beyond the bonds of convention persisted. There was a move to expand the intellectual base of Kashmir Shaivism and to articulate more clearly the experience to which the Shaivite teachers hoped to direct a person.

Another development, referred to as *Trika*, began in the tenth century with Abhinavagupta, the most illustrious of the Kashmir Shaivite teachers. Abhinavagupta studied not only the Shaivite, Buddhist, and Vedantic traditions but also aesthetics, poetry, and drama. Indeed, he is still well known in India as the most important theoretician of aesthetics.

What is less well known is his role in the development of the Kashmir Shaivite tradition. Although an expert in the field of ritual practices, he was primarily concerned with the practice of yoga and of *jnana*, or knowledge. As a teacher, he was interested in going beyond both ritualism and intellectualism in order to put a person in touch with the pure, innate experience of the divine. In his work, we find a continous and significant attention to the sensual, or experiential side of a human being — precisely those aspects which were rejected or denied in the mainstream non-Tantric schools of Hinduism and Buddhism.

Abhinavagupta's student Kshemaraja wrote a number of commentaries on earlier texts. After Kshemaraja, however, there was only one other writer of importance, the twelfth-century teacher Maheshvarananda who wrote the *Maharthamanjari*. By this time, however, and in the centuries that followed, Kashmir had been overrun by Muslim invasions. By the twelfth century, Islam was on the ascent in Northern India. Even so, the tradition of Kashmir Shaivism has persisted, although never again on the scale or with the sweep of influence that it held in earlier centuries.

Endnotes

[1] *Cf. Mālinīvijayottara Tantra* (MVT), 4/40.

[2] *sarvam svanubhavasvabhavavimalam, Anuttāraṣṭikā,* Abhinivagupta, verse 3.

[3] *Īśa Upaniṣad* 1.

[4] *Anuttarāṣṭikā,* Abhinavagupta, verse 5.

[5] Renee Weber, *Dialogue with Scientists and Sages,* Penguin Books, London and New York, 1986, p. 8.

[6] In my view, the conception of *upāyas* in the context of Intellectual Ignorance assumes added significance. I am not certain how far my conclusion is tenable, but I suspect that in the traditional thesis of Patañjali, Yoga is cessation of mental activities (*cittavṛtti*) while here, intellect — by virtue of its refinement, or sublimation — is transformed into a vehicle for self-transcendence, *i.e.,* realization of the Absolute: *vikalpasaṃvidabhyāsasya avikalpantatāparyavasānāt, Tantrasāra,* Abhinavagupta, KSTS, p.4.

[7] Each type, except *anupāya,* comprises several sub-upāyas of cognate status.

[8] *Cf. Vijñāna-bhairava Tantra,* verses 19- 20.

[9] *Cf. Tantrāloka* (TA), Abhinavagupta, 1.245.

[10] *Cf.* MVT 2.21-23.

[11] *Cf.* MVT 4.34.

[12] *Cf.* MVT 4.4–8.

[13] *Cf.* TA 3.272.

¹⁴The treatment continues right up to the fifteenth chapter, with the exception of the thirteenth and fourteenth chapters, if Jayaratha is any guide.

¹⁵This accounts for the feasibility of liberation based on an identification of the intellect with meditation, the vital breath with the quinary upward movement (*uccāra*), and the body with the objects of the senses. The doctrine of *sthāna-prakalpa* (projection of one's concentration onto another place) is also an auxiliary of *anava*. The "place" is considered to be one of three types: the vital breath, the body, and that which is exterior (*bāhya*). The vital breath is five-fold, the body two-fold, and the exterior eleven-fold. The six paths (*sadadhva*), cycles (*cakra*), seat (*pīṭha*), and half-seat (*ardha-pīṭha*) are all subsumed under this notion of place.

¹⁶*Cf.* TA 1.138.

¹⁷*Cf.* TA 1.205-6.

¹⁸*Cf. Īśvara-pratyabhijñā-kārikā*, Utpala, 1/1/1.

¹⁹*Cf. Anubhava-nivedana*, Abhinavgupta, verses 4-5.

TEXT

¹*Pratyabhijnahrdayam: The Secret of Self-recognition*, trans., introduction, and notes by Jaideva Singh (Delhi: Motilal Banarsidass, 1980), p. 51.

²*Cf.* John Roper, *Testament* (New York: Henry Holt and Company, 1988), pp. 54-63.

³See, for example, the work of Rudolf Bultmann and Norman Perrin, and the studies by the proponents of redaction criticism over the past fifteen years.

⁴Quoted in "First Word," *Omni*, October, 1988, p. 8.

⁵*Siva Sutras: The Yoga of Supreme Identity*, trans., with introduction, and notes by Jaideva Singh (Delhi: Motilal Banarsidass, 1982), Sutra III.28, p. 192.

⁶*semna*: The turning meditation originated by Rumi.

⁷*lingam*: An upright stone smoothed by the flow of a river current, which represents the dynamic and creative energy of God, and which figures in devotional practices in many Shaivite temples.

Suggested Reading

Alper, Harvey, *Understanding Mantras* (Albany: SUNY Press, 1989).

Bharati, Aghehananda, *The Tantric Tradition* (New York: Samuel Weiser, 1975).

Chatterjee, J. C., *Kashmir Shaivism* (Research and Publications Department, Srinagar: 1st edition, 1914; 2nd edition, 1962).

Dyczkowski, Mark, *The Doctrine of Vibration: An Analysis of the Doctrines and Practices of Kashmir Shaivism* (Albany: SUNY Press, 1987).

Easwaran, Eknath, *Dialogue With Death: The Spiritual Psychology of the Katha Upanishad* (Petaluma, California: Nilgiri Press, 1981).

Gnoli, R., *The Aesthetic Experience According to Abhinavagupta* (Benares: Chowkhamba, 1968).

Hatengdi, M. U., *Nityananda: The Divine Presence*, Foreword by Swami Chetanananda (Cambridge, Massachusetts: Rudra Press, 1984).

_____ and Swami Chetanananda, *Nitya Sutras: The Revelations of Nityananda from the Chidakadash Gita* (Cambridge, Massachusetts: Rudra Press, 1985).

Kabir, *The Kabir Book: Forty-Four of the Ecstatic Poems of Kabir*, versions by Robert Bly (Boston, Massachusetts: Beacon Press, 1977).

Kramrisch, Stella, *Manifestations of Shiva* (Philadelphia: Philadelphia Museum of Art, 1981).

_____, *The Presence of Śiva* (Princeton, New Jersey: Princeton University Press, 1981).

Lalla-Ded, *The Ascent of Self: A Re-Interpretation of the Mystical Poetry of Lalla-Ded*, trans., with commentary by B. N. Parimoo (Delhi: Motilal Banarsidass, 1978).

Larson, Gerald James, "The aesthetic and the religious in Abhinavagupta's Kashmir Shaivism," *Philosophy East and West* 26, April, 1978, pp. 236-239.

Maharthamanjari, French translation by L. Silburn in *Le "Maharthamanjari" de Maheśvarānanda, avec des Extraits du Parimala* (Paris: E. de Boccard, 1968).

Mishra, Kamalakar, *Kashmir Shaivism: The Central Philosophy of Tantrism*, Ph.D dissertation, Benares Hindu University (currently in press).

Muller-Ortega, Paul E., *The Triadic Heart of Śiva: Kaula Tantricism of Abhinavagupta in the Non-dual Shaivism of Kashmir* (Albany: SUNY Press, 1989).

Musashi, Miyamoto, *A Book of Five Rings: A Guide to Strategy*, trans., Victor Harris (Woodstock, New York: The Overlook Press, 1974).

O'Flaherty, Wendy Doniger, *Asceticism and Eroticism in the Mythology of Śiva* (Delhi: Oxford University Press, 1975).

Padoux, A., "The Fourfold *Upāyas* According to Abhinava's *Tantrāloka*," In *Abhinavagupta and the Synthesis of Indian Culture* (currently in press).

_____ , *Le Symbolisme de L'energie de la Parole dans Certains Textes Tantriques* (Paris: E. de Boccard, 1963).

Pandey, K. C., *Abhinavagupta: An Historical and Philosophical Study* (Benares: Chowkhamba Sanskrit Series, 1, 1935).

_____ , *Indian Aesthetics*, vol. 1 of *Comparative Aesthetics* (Benares: Chowkhamba, 1950).

Potter, Karl, *Presuppositions of India's Philosophies*, (Westport, Greenwood Press, 1976).

Pratyabhijñāhṛdayam: The Secret of Self-recognition, trans., with introduction and notes by Jaideva Singh (Delhi: Motilal Banarsidass, 1963).

Rastogi, Navjivan, "Concept of Śiva as a Category in Kashmir Shaivism," *Indian Philosophy and Culture*, vol. IX, no. 3, 1964.

_____ , "The Contribution of Kashmir to Philosophy, Thought, and Culture," *Annals of the Bhandarkar Oriental Research Institute*, vol. LVI, 1975.

_____ , *The Krama Tantricism of Kashmir: Historical and General Sources*, vol. I (Delhi: Motilal Banarsidass, 1979).

_____ , *Introduction to the Tantrāloka* (Delhi: Motilal Banarsidass, 1987).

Rumi, *Open Secret*, versions of Rumi by John Moyne and Coleman Barks (Putney, Vermont: Threshold Books, 1984).

_____ , *The Ruins of the Heart: Selected Lyric Poetry of Jelaluddin Rumi*, trans., Edmund Helminski (Putney, Vermont: Threshold Books, 1981).

_____ , *This Longing: Poetry, Teaching Stories, and Letters of Rumi*, trans., Coleman Barks and John Moyne (Putney, Vermont: Threshold Books, 1988).

_____ , *Unseen Rain: Quatrains of Rumi*, trans., John Moyne and Coleman Barks (Putney, Vermont: Threshold Books, 1986).

_____ , *Rumi: We Are Three: New Rumi Translations*, trans., Coleman Barks (Athens, Georgia: Maypop Books, 1987).

Sanderson, Alexis, "Mandala and Agamic Identity in the Trika of Kashmir," In *Mantras et Diagrammes Rituels dans L'Hindouisme* (Paris: CNRS, 1986).

_____ , "Śaivism and the Tantric Traditions," In *The World's Religions*, ed., Steward Sutherland, Leslie Houlden, Peter Clarke, Friedhelm Hardy (London: Routledge, Kegan, Paul, 1988).

Sharma, L. N., *Kashmir Shaivism*, (Benares: Bharatiya Vidya Prakasana, 1972).

Silburn, Lilian, *Kuṇḍalinī: Energy of the Depths*, trans., Jacques Gontier (Albany: SUNY Press, 1988).

Śiva Sūtras: The Yoga of Supreme Identity, trans., with introduction and notes by Jaideva Singh (Delhi: Motilal Banarsidass, 1979).

Spandakārikās, trans., with introduction and notes by Jaideva Singh (Delhi: Motilal Banarsidass, 1980).

Swami Chetanananda, *The Breath of God*, Cambridge, Massachusetts: Rudra Press, 1988).

_____ , *Songs from the Center of the Well* (Cambridge, Massachusetts: Rudra Press, 1985).

Swami Rudrananda (Rudi), *Behind the Cosmic Curtain: The Further Writings of Swami Rudrananda*, ed., John Mann (Arlington, Massachusetts: Neolog Publishing, 1984).

_____ , *Rudi: In His Own Words*, ed., Jennifer Cross, (Cambridge, Massachusetts: Rudra Press, 1990).

_____ , *Rudi: Spiritual Cannibalism*, 3rd ed., Foreword by Swami Chetanananda (Cambridge, Massachusetts: Rudra Press, 1987).

The Thirteen Principal Upanishads, trans., Robert Ernest Hume (New Delhi: Oxford University Press, 1977).

Utpaladeva, *Shaiva Devotional Songs of Kashmir: A Translation and Study of Utpaladeva's Shivastotravali*, trans., and study by Constantina Rhodes Bailly (Albany: SUNY Press, 1987).

Vijñānabhairava or Divine Consciousness, trans., with notes by Jaideva Singh (Delhi: Motilal Banarsidass, 1979).

Index

Sanskrit words used in the body of text appear in transliterated form without diacritical marks.

The Nityananda Institute

The Nityananda Institute, headquartered in Cambridge, Massachusetts, is dedicated to the active practice of a spiritual life based on the teachings of Swami Chetanananda. The Institute (formerly the Rudrananda Ashram) is named for the Indian saint Bhagavan Nityananda of Ganeshpuri, who is its wellspring and inspiration. However, both Chetanananda and his *guru*, Swami Rudrananda (Rudi) were born Americans, and it is this rich fusion of East and West that gives the Institute its unique character. Even though Chetanananda's teaching is deeply rooted in the non-dualistic Shaiva tradition of Kashmir, his expression is completely Western. He speaks in the language of America; his analogies are more likely to feature basketball's Larry Bird than the gods and goddesses of Indian myth. Like Rudi before him, Chetanananda is the embodied proof that cultural affiliation is no barrier to the highest understanding.

The Institute has many facets: an active community of over three hundred participating members in Cambridge, Massachusetts, taking part in Trika Yoga and Hatha Yoga classes, workshops, and retreats; Centers in Santa Monica, California, and Ann Arbor, Michigan; a thriving publishing enterprise in Rudra Press featuring books and tapes about meditation, health, hatha yoga, and philosophy; and the Abhinavagupta Institute, devoted to furthering translations, study, and commentary in the area of Kashmir Shaivism.